RETHINKING GREEK RELIGION

Who marched in religious processions and why? How were blood sacrifice and communal feasting related to identities in the ancient Greek city? With questions such as these, current scholarship aims to demonstrate the ways in which religion maps on to the socio-political structures of the Greek polis ('polis religion'). In this book Dr Kindt explores a more comprehensive conception of ancient Greek religion beyond this traditional paradigm. Comparative in method and out-look, the book invites its readers to embark on an interdisciplinary journey touching upon such diverse topics as religious belief, personal religion, magic and theology. Specific examples include the transfor-mation of tyrant property into ritual objects, the cultural practice of setting up dedications at Olympia, and a man attempting to make love to Praxiteles' famous statue of Aphrodite. The book will be valu-able for all students and scholars seeking to understand the complex phenomenon of ancient Greek religion.

JULIA KINDT is Senior Lecturer in the Department of Classics and Ancient History at the University of Sydney.

RETHINKING GREEK
RELIGION

JULIA KINDT

CAMBRIDGE
UNIVERSITY PRESS

CAMBRIDGE UNIVERSITY PRESS
Cambridge, New York, Melbourne, Madrid, Cape Town,
Singapore, São Paulo, Delhi, Mexico City

Cambridge University Press
The Edinburgh Building, Cambridge CB2 8RU, UK

Published in the United States of America by Cambridge University Press, New York

www.cambridge.org
Information on this title: www.cambridge.org/9780521127738

First published 2012

Printed and Bound in the United Kingdom by the MPG Books Group

A catalogue record for this publication is available from the British Library

Library of Congress Cataloguing in Publication data
Kindt, Julia, 1975–
Rethinking Greek religion / Julia Kindt.
pages cm
Includes bibliographical references and index.
ISBN 978-0-521-11092-1 (hardback) – ISBN 978-0-521-12773-8 (paperback)
1. Greece – Religion.   I. Title.
BL783.K565   2012
292.08 – dc23   2012013652

ISBN 978-0-521-11092-1 Hardback
ISBN 978-0-521-12773-8 Paperback

For Paul and Daniel

Contents

Figures

Acknowledgements

Robin Osborne, Richard Gordon, and the anonymous reviewers of Cambridge University Press have all made invaluable suggestions with regard to the overall conception and structure of the book.

The following have generously commented on individual chapters or substantial sections of the manuscript: Jan Bremmer, Richard Gordon, Diana Burton, Sarah Iles Johnston, Peter Garnsey and Peter Wilson. A very special thanks goes to Robin Osborne, who not only read through the entire manuscript but has also been an invaluable and extremely generous advisor and mentor ever since my days as his doctoral student at Cambridge.

I would also like to thank my wonderful colleagues at the University of Sydney for their support. In particular I thank Anthony Alexander, Rick Benitez, Alastair Blanshard, Ben Brown, Robert Cowan, Dan Potts, Beatrice McLoughlin, Frances Muecke, Paul Roche, Anne Rogerson, Glenda Sluga, Kathryn Welch and Peter Wilson. Moreover, many ideas put forward in this book were first 'tested' on my students of ANHS2605 ('Ancient Greek Religion') at the University of Sydney. I thank them for the patience and enthusiasm with which they have helped shape my ideas. I also thank my research assistants Liam Ahern, Juliet Flesch, Billy Griffiths, Anthony Hooper, Paul McMullen, Anna Miaczewska and Louise Pryke for their invaluable help, and the Faculty of Arts and Social Sciences at the University of Sydney for supporting my research with two FARSS grants and a research leave.

Beyond Sydney I would like to thank the following colleagues for discussing ancient Greek religion with me: Hugh Bowden, Esther Eidinow, Christopher Faraone, Milette Gaifman, Fritz Graf, Barbara Graziosi, Sarah Iles Johnston, Emily Kearns, Barbara Kowalzig, Bruce Lincoln, Ivana Petrovic, Andrej Petrovic, Verity Platt, Ian Rutherford, Michael Scott and Harold Tarrant.

At Cambridge University Press I have been fortunate to have the expert advice and guidance of Michael Sharp, who never tired of answering my questions.

I am grateful to *Classical Philology, Arethusa* and *Kernos* for granting me permission to include previously published material in this book. A substantial part of Chapter 1 first appeared in *Kernos* 22 (2009). An earlier version of Chapter 2 was published in *Classical Philology* 105 (2010). A version of Chapter 3 appeared originally in *Arethusa* 42 (2009). I also thank the German Archaeological Institute at Athens for the kind permission to reproduce images of items in their collections.

My warm recognition is due to the Bayerische Staatsbibliothek in Munich for supporting my research during my sabbatical stay in 2009, during which substantial sections of this book were written, and during several brief visits in other years.

Several friends in Munich, Cambridge, Chicago, Sydney and elsewhere have provided and continue to provide inspiration: Helen Anderson, Robert Buch, Paul Cheney, Natalie Devlin, Sharon Douglas, Jennifer Esklidsen, Jessica Hobson, Berthold and Eva Hoeckner, Walter Hofstetter, Neil Husband, Ala Khazendar, Cecile King, Kersten Koelsch, Benjamin Lazier, Sjoerd Levelt, Linda McSweeny, Wendy Phillips, Anne Rogerson, Katharina Roth, Stefan Sippell, Luke Slattery, Anik Waldow, Emma and Angus White and Christian Zengerle.

Finally, I would like to thank my parents and my brother for their love. I dedicate this book to my husband Daniel and to my father-in-law Paul Christ, my most unusual and challenging reader.

Abbreviations

Abbreviations of journal titles follow the conventions set out in the *L'année philologique*. Abbreviations of ancient authors and their texts follow Liddell, H. G. and Scott, R. (1940) *A Greek–English Lexicon*, 9th edn, rev. H. Stuart Jones. Oxford.

Agora	*The Athenian Agora: Results of Excavations Conducted by the American School of Classical Studies at Athens.* Princeton
DTAtt.	Wünsch, R. (1897) *Defixionum Tabellae Atticae* (*IG* 3.3, Appendix). Berlin
DTAud.	Audollent, A. (1904) *Defixionum Tabellae.* Paris
FGrHist	Jacoby, F. (ed.) (1936–) *Die Fragmente der griechischen Historiker.* Berlin
IDélos	Dürrbach, F. (ed.) (1923–37) *Inscriptions de Délos.* Paris
IG	*Inscriptiones Graecae*
IvO	Dittenberger, W. and Purgold, K. (eds.) (1896) *Olympia: die Ergebnisse der von dem deutschen Reich veranstalteten Ausgrabung*, vol. v: *Die Inschriften.* Berlin
LIMC	*Lexicon Iconographicum Mythologiae Classicae*
ML	Meiggs, R. and Lewis, D. (eds.) (1988) *A Selection of Greek Historical Inscriptions to the End of the Fifth Century* BC, rev. edn. Oxford
NGCT	Jordan, D. R. (2000) 'New Greek curse tablets (1985–2000)', *GRBS* 41, 5–46
PGM	Preisendanz, K. and Henrichs, A. (eds.) (1973/1974) *Papyri Graecae Magicae: Die griechischen Zauberpapyri*, 2nd edn. (2 vols.). Stuttgart
RE	Wissowa, G., Kroll, W. and Ziegler, K. (eds.) (1894–1980) *Paulys Real-Encyclopädie der classischen Altertumswissenschaft*, new edn. Stuttgart

SEG	*Supplementum Epigraphicum Graecum*
SGD	Jordan, D. R. (1985a) 'A survey of Greek defixiones not included in the special corpora', *GRBS* 26, 151–97
ThesCRA	*Thesaurus Cultus et Rituum Antiquorum*

Introduction

What *is* Greek religion? What is religion *tout court*? Is there such a
thing as '(Greek) religion'?

Richard Buxton[1]

The *polis* anchored, legitimated, and mediated all religious activity . . .

. . . *polis* religion encompassed all religious discourse within it.

Christiane Sourvinou-Inwood[2]

Even a cursory glance at one of the many handbooks and monographs
published in what is now a popular and dynamic area of study (Greek religion) will reveal much information on the intricate links between religion
and society. Who marched in a religious procession (*pompē*) and why?[3]
What can the way in which new cults were introduced to the existing
polytheistic pantheon of Athens reveal about her 'collective religious mentality' during the fifth century BC?[4] And how are blood sacrifice and the
subsequent communal feasting related to the socio-political structures of
the Greek city?[5] These are the kinds of questions that reverberate among
scholars in the field. Indeed, religious practice, control and power have
featured prominently in debates on ancient Greek religion.[6] The main aim
of much productive work done in this area is to demonstrate the various
ways in which religion maps on to the socio-political structures of Greek
society.

There is, of course, nothing wrong with this aim. At the same time,
however, there are also a few obvious omissions in the picture of the
religious dimension of ancient Greece that emerges from this research. For

---

[1] Buxton 2000: 8.   [2] Sourvinou-Inwood 2000a: 15, 24 respectively.
[3] E.g., Motte 1987; van Straten 1995; Neils 1996a; Maurizio 1998.
[4] Garland 1992: viii.   [5] Schmitt Pantel 1992; Evans 2010: 58–62.
[6] See, e.g., Beard and North 1990; Garland 1996; Alroth and Hellström 1996.

example, we find very little on religious beliefs and religious discourse.[7] Neither does individual engagement with the supernatural about private concerns ('personal religion') feature largely.[8] Moreover, there are various religious phenomena and institutions, such as beliefs and practices labelled 'magic' and mystery religions, which are partly or wholly outside the scope of communal and authorised religious practices and which are therefore frequently presented as merely peripheral to our understanding of ancient Greek religion.[9]

What has shaped this picture of ancient Greek religion? One way of answering would be to argue that this representation reflects the realities of life in the ancient Greek city. Another response would be to point to the ancient evidence, which frequently (but not always) supports the polis-centred perspective. Both suggestions would not be entirely misleading, but they would also not tell the whole story. The real answer to the question of what has shaped this picture of the religious in ancient Greece lies in the history of scholarship on ancient Greek religion. The current emphasis on the centrality of Greek religion to Greek politics and society is, in many ways, a response to older scholarship.

Not so long ago, ancient Greek religion was regarded as a marginal topic, far removed from the 'hard surfaces' of Greek life, Greek politics and society.[10] In particular, older scholarship at the beginning of the twentieth century propagated an image of ancient Greek religion that was more concerned with fertility rites and with tracing earlier layers of the Greek religious experience than with the structures and relationships in and of Greek polis society.[11] In the works of Jane Ellen Harrison, for example, there is much on agricultural cycles and their reflection in ancient Greek mythology and ritual, and very little on the place of the religious in politics and society.[12]

Since the days of Harrison, however, we seem to have come full circle. Religion is now generally considered to be absolutely fundamental to our

---

[7] Some scholars even argue that the category of belief was fully absent from the religious dimension of ancient Greece and that ancient Greek religion was all about doing things (ritual). E.g., Burkert 1985: 8; Bruit Zaidman and Schmitt Pantel 1992: 27; Price 1999: 3. For a discussion of the conception of belief and its applicability to the religions of Greece and Rome see Harrison 2000: 20–3; Feeney 1998: 12–46.

[8] For a succinct definition of Greek personal religion see also Instone 2009: 1.

[9] The almost entire absence of magical practices from Burkert's *Greek Religion* is a good example. See Burkert 1985 and my discussion of it in ch. 4. On mystery religions see ch. 1.

[10] See Morris 1993: 32.

[11] E.g., Rohde 1972 (1890/1894) and the works of the so-called 'Cambridge Ritualists': Harrison 1903; 1912; Cornford 1914; Murray 1925.

[12] E.g., Harrison 1912.

understanding of ancient Greek politics and society. What brought about this change in paradigm, however, is first and foremost what scholars have come to refer to as the model of polis religion. Polis religion has moved the study of ancient Greek religion towards the centre of classical studies and turned a once-marginal subject into a central focus of classical scholarship.

Polis religion found its most succinct and prominent formulation in two articles by Christiane Sourvinou-Inwood, dating from 1988 and 1990 but republished together in a more accessible collection of essays in 2000.[13] In its most general conception by Sourvinou-Inwood, the model propagates the primacy of the polis as the dominant worshipping group in ancient Greece.[14] It relies on the notion that the most significant discourse of power relevant for the study of ancient Greek religion is the one 'embraced', 'contained' and 'mediated' by the socio-political institutions of the polis.[15] Numerous studies since then have elaborated the link between Greek politics and society on the one hand and Greek religion on the other, along the lines described above.

In her articles Sourvinou-Inwood synthesised a perspective towards ancient Greek religion that had taken shape much earlier. The idea of polis religion first emerged during the 1960s and 1970s, most notably, perhaps, in the works of Walter Burkert and the so-called Paris School.[16] The simultaneous 'discovery' of ancient Greek blood sacrifice by Burkert and Vernant instigated a much broader 'pragmatic turn' within the study of ancient Greek religion, putting the focus distinctly on religious practices, and on ritual in particular.[17] More importantly, perhaps, both Burkert and the scholars around Jean-Pierre Vernant explained the principles and practices of ancient Greek religion by referring to an internally coherent cultural system, conceived as the archaic and classical Greek polis.[18]

The emergence of polis religion therefore coincided with the adoption of what Kostas Vlassopoulos has referred to as the 'polis approach' to the

---

[13] Sourvinou-Inwood 2000a; 2000b.

[14] The intellectual roots of polis religion reach far back into the history of scholarship on ancient Greek religion, to Emile Durkheim's sociology of religion (as influenced by his teacher Fustel de Coulanges, who had himself a special interest in the ancient Greek city) and the structural anthropology of Claude Lévi-Strauss. See Fustel de Coulanges 1864; Durkheim 1995 (1912). See also ch. 1 for more detail.

[15] See Sourvinou-Inwood 2000a: 20.

[16] For an early formulation of polis religion see Ehrenberg 1960.

[17] Burkert 1983a; Vernant and Vidal-Naquet 1988; Detienne and Vernant 1989. For a more extensive discussion of the history of scholarship on ancient Greek religion, in particular the opposing positions of Burkert and Vernant, see Kindt 2009: 368–71.

[18] E.g., Vernant 1980; Burkert 1985; Vernant and Vidal-Naquet 1988; Bérard and Bron 1989; Bruit Zaidman and Schmitt Pantel 1992.

study of ancient Greek history.[19] The polis approach, as developed during the 1960s and 1970s, posited the existence of the polis as a 'unitary entity and the uniting factor behind Greek history'.[20] Within this perspective, the polis was seen as a quasi-organic entity with a life of its very own: it emerged during the archaic period, saw its climax in fifth-century BC Athens and subsequently declined during the fourth century BC with the loss of Greek independence after the Battle of Chaironeia.[21] The reason for this was that the polis was also seen as 'a solitary entity' with a set of features (an essence) typical to it, one of these being its (striving for) *autonomia*.[22]

It was precisely this conception of *the* Greek polis that allowed Walter Burkert to draw on information from a wide range of sources derived from a wide array of poleis and to present this information in the form of a unified, coherent and authoritative account of archaic and classical Greek religion as such.[23] In Burkert's *Greek Religion*, as in Bruit Zaidman and Schmitt Pantel's *Religion in the Ancient Greek City*, the focus is on the religious structures of the Greek city-state of the archaic and classical periods.[24] The 'polis' of polis religion has a homogeneous body of citizens and a cohesive culture.[25]

However, polis religion did not just borrow the conception of the polis from the polis approach as it came to shape the study of Greek history from the 1960s onwards. In fact, polis religion is central to the polis approach insofar as it underpins the assumption of the Greek city-state as a coherent and stable system maintained and articulated in collective ritual practices.

Since the 1990s, however, classical scholars have started to express their dissatisfaction with this narrow and idealising conception of the Greek polis.[26] It was observed that not all poleis looked the same and that there were significant differences in their social, political and, indeed, religious make-up.[27] The scholars of the Copenhagen Polis Centre in particular have pointed out (rightly I believe) that the history of the Greek poleis continued far into the Hellenistic and Roman periods – an issue that will be discussed in more detail in Chapter 1.[28] The extended temporal focus, however, has made it necessary to accommodate a variety of new social,

---

[19] Here and below see Vlassopoulos 2007: 52–63.   [20] Vlassopoulos 2007: 55.
[21] See ch. 1 in more detail.   [22] Vlassopoulos 2007: 55.   [23] Burkert 1985. See ch. 1 in more detail.
[24] Burkert 1985; Bruit Zaidman and Schmitt Pantel 1992.
[25] A succinct description of the polis approach: Vlassopoulos 2007: 55–63.
[26] The debate is succinctly synthesised in Vlassopoulos 2007: 63–7.
[27] E.g., Gehrke 1986; Hansen and Nielsen 2004.
[28] E.g., Hansen and Nielsen 2004: 16–22; Hansen 2006: 48–50. See also Vlassopoulos 2007: 64–5 for a critical assessment of the significance of the work of the Copenhagen Polis Centre for recent debates about the meaning of the polis as the fundamental structuring principle of ancient Greek history.

political and religious institutions, which coexisted alongside traditional ones. While only a few scholars would go so far as to suggest that we should find another structuring principle for the study of Greek history altogether, there is now growing debate about what we mean by the polis and when we assume it came to an end.[29]

In the field of ancient Greek religion some scholars have responded to such concerns of definition with regard to the underlying model of the Greek city-state, for example, by speaking of Greek religions rather than Greek religion.[30] Moreover, despite the ongoing interpretative appeal of the model, some scholars have also started to pursue an alternative conception of the religious. In particular, those aspects of ancient Greek religion which are not directly bound up in human agency (which is always in one way or the other related to the polis as the primary social, political and cultural unit of Greek life) seem to reveal a dimension which is not, or at least not always, related to the polis. Religious concepts such as death, prayer, sacrifice, *daimones* and *eusebeia* in many ways transcend the polis orientation in current scholarship in the field and offer a more versatile understanding of the religious that is not always and necessarily bound up in the socio-political discourse of the polis.[31] There is also renewed and sustained interest in the personal dimension of ancient Greek religion.[32] Such works have raised the question of whether there might not be more to ancient Greek religion than can (and should) be accounted for in the model of polis religion.

To be fair, not all the questions and problems that emerge from the primacy of the model of polis religion can be laid at the doorstep of those scholars who helped develop it. The impact of the model, the enthusiasm with which it was embraced, and the profound way in which it has shaped current concepts and conceptions of the religious in the ancient world have almost certainly exceeded the expectations of its most fervent advocates. The model, in its original formulation at least, was never meant to be a 'theory of everything', to borrow the physicists' term. In some scholarship, however, it has acquired an all-embracing quality, as in those works that

---

[29] A call to move towards alternative ways to structure ancient Greek history: Vlassopoulos 2007: 221–40. Debates about the meaning and end of the polis: Hansen 2000: 11–34; Hansen and Nielsen 2004: 39–46.

[30] Price 1999, as discussed in ch. 1.

[31] E.g., Jeanmaire 1951; Lloyd-Jones 1971; Gladigow 1979; Pulleyn 1997; Bruit Zaidman 2001.

[32] As for example reflected in recent sourcebooks: Instone 2009; Kearns 2010: 45–141. Greek personal religion is also at the heart of recent studies on oracles and curses: e.g., Eidinow 2007a: 42–55, 125–38, 206–24. Greek personal religion and mystery religions: e.g., Graf and Johnston 2007; Bowden 2010.

focus almost exclusively on the civic and communal dimensions of ancient Greek religion.[33]

This book sets out to explore ancient Greek religion 'beyond the polis'. At the same time it aims to give more than a straightforward account of what is wrong with polis religion. Its individual chapters are much more loosely connected and revolve around two separate but intrinsically related questions. First, the book investigates those dimensions of the Greek religious experience that polis religion cannot explain. Second, it explores in what aspects polis religion renders Greek religion less intelligible than it should be.

While the aim of overcoming problems resulting from an excessively narrow focus on official (polis) religion is the leading investigative focus, I endeavour to illustrate the productivity of a perspective that explores some of the deeper consequences of too narrow a focus on official Greek religion. The goal is to challenge current interpretative models and also to identify those areas of ancient Greek religion that should be preserved and situated within a wider framework of study. For there are some areas which polis religion reveals rather well, and these need to be integrated into a more comprehensive conception of the religious. What we need in particular is a different notion of culture, in which religion is not merely part of a single hegemonic discourse but rather a vibrant symbolic medium for different and competing (power-) discourses, including, though not limited to, the discourse of the official polis institutions. In sum, this book does not intend to replace the conception of polis religion. Instead, individual chapters look at Greek religious beliefs and practices through different lenses, to illuminate those aspects of the religious in ancient Greece that cannot be explained by the model of polis religion.

Rethinking Greek Religion attempts to move current debates forward by highlighting problems in contemporary scholarship, by synthesising existing positions and by identifying promising areas of further debate. The book is meant to serve as a guide to what is interesting about Greek relations with the supernatural beyond the polis paradigm and to what scholars have said about the questions and issues emerging from such a perspective. Its chapters illustrate the exemplary and develop particular areas of Greek religion beyond the polis. This focus is intended to make the whole more accessible and to ground the general, conceptual argument as developed in particular in Chapter 1 in tangible examples and problems. However, the individual chapters also stand in their own right as contributions to

---

[33] See most recently Evans 2010.

the study of particular areas within ancient Greek religion. Chapter 2, for example, contributes to the ongoing discussion about the nature of religious visuality by Elsner and others.[34] Chapter 4 participates in the debate on the relationship between magic and religion, and Chapter 6 raises the question of a theology (or theologies) of ancient Greek religion.

The book gives examples of how methodological perspectives from different, neighbouring disciplines can shed new light on well-known aspects of ancient Greek religion. It invites the reader to embark on an interdisciplinary journey leading from classical scholarship to social anthropology and *Religionswissenschaft* (the comparative study of religions). All chapters combine a rigorous reading of primary sources – be they historiographic, epigraphic, literary, or material in nature – with a discussion of the larger conceptual and methodological issues arising from them. This reflects the fact that the sources available to the student of ancient Greek religion transcend all areas of academic compartmentalisation and expertise. Because ancient Greek religion was not abstract but 'embedded' in all areas of life (see 'embeddedness' in Chapter 1), there is hardly any type of evidence or any genre of Greek literature from which religion is entirely absent. Religious beliefs and practices transcend the literary and the material evidence, including iconography, inscriptions and numismatics. They are also a ubiquitous feature of Greek literature from Homer onwards, via Greek tragedy and historiography (to name just two genres from a much larger group), to the apologetic literature of early Christianity, which, as I show in Chapter 6, relates closely to views expressed in earlier Greek sources and can indeed sometimes help to illuminate them. Moreover, some of our very best evidence for the study of ancient Greek religion is situated on the plane just below high literature. It is not just the works of Homer and Hesiod that are obvious sources for the study of ancient Greek religion – religious beliefs and practices can also be found in the form of a curse tablet buried in a grave, for example, or in Philostratus' account of the wonder-workings of a certain Apollonius.[35] It takes particular diligence to see how these and other sources contribute to the bigger picture we sketch of ancient Greek religion. The sources supporting my arguments illustrate this breadth and versatility. In one sense the individual chapters also demonstrate the interpretative tools available to make these diverse sources speak to each other, to examine them individually and in conversation with each other.

---

[34] Elsner 2007: 1–26.
[35] Philostr. *VA* (see also ch. 6). On the place of curse tablets within the religious culture of Athens see ch. 4.

Although this book aims to move current debates forward by examining the impact of the categories we use on the questions we ask about ancient Greek religion, its overall scope is necessarily selective and incomplete. Not all discussion points of polis religion outlined in Chapter 1 are followed up later. This is not another introduction to ancient Greek religion as such. *Rethinking Greek Religion* offers a critical evaluation of where research in ancient Greek religion stands at present. It should be used in addition to and in conversation with such introductory works as those of Bruit Zaidman and Schmitt Pantel, Bremmer and Price.[36]

Looking into the past raises the question of the future: this book aims to provide some indication of where the study of ancient Greek religion may be headed and makes some recommendations concerning promising areas of future debate. The intention is to spark curiosity about those areas of ancient Greek religion which fall outside the scope of much contemporary scholarship, in the hope that at least some of the questions and conceptual concerns raised here will inspire the reader to take up the thread.

Chapter 1, 'Beyond the polis: rethinking Greek religion' offers a critical appreciation of the model of polis religion. Starting from the central and problematic notion of the 'embeddedness' of Greek religion in the polis, I investigate key problems resulting from the scholarly use of the model and identify how individual works have positioned themselves relative to them. I argue that the strength of the model results from its capacity to direct our attention to a key structuring principle in ancient Greek religion. At the same time, however, we need to look at other discourses of power beyond the polis and explore the ways in which they express themselves within and outside the religious. Overall, the chapter raises a number of themes and questions that are addressed in more detail in subsequent chapters. In many ways, it provides a framework for the investigative threads of the book.

Chapter 2, 'Parmeniscus' journey: tracing religious visuality in word and wood' explores a dimension of ancient Greek religion concerned with personal experience, religious concepts and inquiry into the nature of the divine. These are all aspects of the religious not prominent in works primarily concerned with religious agency, control and power. The chapter revolves around a passage in Athenaeus' *Deipnosophistae* (which itself relies on much earlier material), featuring the experience of a certain Parmeniscus with regard to various divine representations in the form of oracles and a divine statue ('word' and 'wood'). Taking up and expanding Elsner's

---

[36] Bruit Zaidman and Schmitt Pantel 1992; Bremmer 1994; Price 1999.

conception of religious visuality, I show that religious gazing is not limited to ritual-centred visuality, but can also include what I call a 'cognitive dimension': a mode of 'making sense' of divine representations which confronts the viewing subject with his personal expectations of the gods.[37] Overall, the chapter not only promotes a more comprehensive concept of religious visuality than the one suggested by Elsner, it also illustrates, both spatially and conceptually, how productive an approach can be that is not, or at least is not primarily, oriented towards the polis-centred perspective.

Chapter 3, 'On tyrant property turned ritual object: political power and sacred symbols in ancient Greece and in social anthropology', takes issue with the fact that Greek religious beliefs and practices are frequently seen merely as a disguise for socio-political power. This is at least partly due to the prevailing belief of classical scholars in functionalism as the interpretative tool best suited to pursue the larger agenda of many current works in the field: to prove the direct relevance of Greek religious beliefs and practices to Greek society. As a result of this perspective, however, the symbolic dimension of ancient Greek religion is either sidelined altogether, or, if considered at all, frequently put into a different category, separate from socio-political power. The chapter draws on current works in social anthropology in order to suggest that we need a more complicated conception of religious symbols, in which socio-political power is intrinsic to religious signification. The productivity of this approach is exemplified in a fragment from Philochorus attesting to the 'recycling' of symbolic capital after the Thirty, during the restoration of democracy in 403 BC. The case study of the recycling of symbolic capital demonstrates that religious symbols are actively involved in the negotiation of socio-political power and that religion is indeed more than a simple tool for individuals to achieve their political ambitions.

Chapter 4, 'Rethinking boundaries: the place of magic in the religious culture of ancient Greece', draws on the discussion set out in Chapter 3 of the relationship between the world on the one hand and religious symbols on the other. It seeks to expand the boundaries of our conception of the religious. In particular, it investigates the question of what beliefs and practices conventionally referred to as 'magic' add to our overall understanding of the religious culture of ancient Greece. The purpose of this chapter is to anchor questions raised previously, especially with regard to the margins of ancient Greek religion, in a more broadly conceived account of what aspect of the religious dimension of ancient Greece we are trying to rescue.

[37] See ch. 2, n. 20.

More specifically, the focus is on the cultural practice of cursing as a ritual activity, which is both inside and outside polis religion. I argue that it is absolutely essential to bring magical belief and practices into the picture because they reveal a more personal and instrumental side of the religious, supplementing and sometimes even challenging the beliefs and practices of polis religion. Moreover the inclusion of 'magic' uncovers a conversation from within ancient Greek religion about legitimate and illegitimate behaviour and legitimate and illegitimate religious power. I conclude that we need to adopt the conception of a broader religious culture of ancient Greece, which embraces locations of the religious besides those of polis religion.

Chapter 5, 'The "local" and the "universal" reconsidered: Olympia, dedications and the religious culture of ancient Greece', takes up the idea of a broader religious culture and explores its ramifications on the 'panhellenic' level. It investigates the cultural practice of setting up dedications at the sanctuary of Zeus at Olympia and illustrates how multiple identities in the Greek world, including personal, polis and ethnic identities, were represented in the space of the sanctuary, hence mediating between the 'local' and 'universal' dimensions of ancient Greek religion and between polis religion and ancient Greek religion beyond the polis – without, however, assuming a strict duality between the two. On a more general plane this chapter shows how important it is to bring together the literary and material evidence in an integrated approach which does not rely on one illustrating the other but investigates the cultural discourses that have informed both kinds of evidence. Overall, the sanctuary of Zeus at Olympia emerges as a complex space testifying to the existence of an understanding of what it meant to be Greek that is more than the sum of its polis-related parts.

Chapter 6, '"The sex appeal of the inorganic": seeing, touching and knowing the divine during the Second Sophistic', concludes our investigation of ancient Greek religion beyond the polis by bringing together a variety of issues and questions raised in the preceding chapters. Different tellings of the (in)famous story of a young man's desire to make love to Praxiteles' famous Aphrodite of Cnidus as they circulated in the literature of Roman Greece are examined as manifestations of a religious discourse exploring the nature of the divine and its availability to humanity, in particular to human knowledge. By drawing on traditional anthropomorphism represented here in the form of a statue crafted during the classical period, the religion of Roman Greece variously complements our understanding of the religious culture of ancient Greece. Above all, it showcases the existence of a discourse exploring divine ontology and its availability to human knowledge – a discourse which we may want to call theological in nature and which underpins and substantiates our previous investigation of religious beliefs and the symbolic dimension of ancient Greek religion. The focus on the role of divine representations (statues) within this discourse, however, also makes the theological issues flagged in the discussion of magic (Chapter 4) emerge more clearly. It is in this sense, then, that the religion of Roman Greece indeed helps to clarify the picture of the broader religious culture of ancient Greece.

A brief conclusion revisits some of the major points made in the individual chapters of the book and places them into a more general framework. In particular it raises the question of where we go from here and investigates the notion of a theology (or theologies) of ancient Greek religion as flagged in the last chapter.

A final note on conventions of spelling and citations: throughout this book, Greek names are spelt in their Latinised forms except where customarily spelt in their Greek form or where Latinised forms would be odd or misleading. Translations from the Greek and Latin are my own unless otherwise noted.

CHAPTER I

Beyond the polis: rethinking Greek religion

> Because the polis is most cherished and the real religion of the Greeks,
> the battles for her also have the force and terror of religious wars and
> every break with her fundamentally uproots the individual.
>
> Jacob Burckhardt[1]

INTRODUCTION

An inquiry into ancient Greek religion beyond polis religion necessarily
starts from the question of what we mean by polis religion and the impact
of this model on how we conceive of ancient Greek religion as a field of
study. In current scholarship, particularly in the Anglo-American and Fran-
cophone worlds, polis religion has become a powerful interpretative model
for the study of Greek religion. The model is now sufficiently well established that we need to explore its implications as well as the alternatives that
complement or move beyond it. Surprisingly, however, the implications
of the model are rarely discussed in the study of ancient Greek religion.
There is no single account that directly and comprehensively responds to
Sourvinou-Inwood's two methodological articles on polis religion – the
most explicit conceptual formulation of the model.[2]

This chapter offers a critical evaluation of where we stand. It identifies
key problems in the scholarly use of the polis-religion model and examines
how individual scholars have positioned their work in regard to these issues.
Rather than rejecting the model outright, the chapter aims to move the

---

[1] Burckhardt 1943: 62 (my translation).
[2] While many works in the field are implicitly based on a characterisation of Greek religion as polis
religion, the strengths and weaknesses of this model are rarely discussed. Some exceptions: Cole 1995;
Burkert 1995; Jameson 1997; Bremmer 2010. In the field of Roman religion the debate concerning
the implications and the applicability of the civic model is much more advanced: e.g., Woolf 1997;
Bendlin 2000: 115–35; Rüpke 2004; Scheid 2005: 125–8. There is no separate entry on polis religion
in recent reference works, such as Price and Kearns 2003; Jones, L. 2005.

debates forward by exploring its scope and limits. It examines polis religion in its different forms and formulations and discusses the ways in which some scholars have recently sought to overcome the 'polis orientation' implicit in large parts of the work done in this field.

Overall, this chapter argues that the polis model is good at highlighting the significance of the polis as an important structuring principle of the religious in ancient Greece. At the same time I argue that the polis model provides little, if any, help for understanding Greek personal religion and religious phenomena such as magic and mystery religions. I also argue that polis religion is focused more firmly on religious agency and neglects religious ideas and religious discourse. In doing so, the model relies on an implicit conception of religion as simply mapping on to the structures of Greek society – a simplification of the manifold ways in which religious symbols shape and are shaped by society.

WHAT IS POLIS RELIGION?

Christiane Sourvinou-Inwood coined the term 'polis religion' to describe the 'embeddedness' of Greek religion in the polis as the basic unit of Greek social and political life.[3] Significantly, however, her definition of polis religion transcends the level of the individual polis. Polis religion operates on three levels of Greek society: the polis, the 'world-of-the-polis' system and the panhellenic dimension.[4] The definition of Greek religion as polis religion follows this tripartite structure of Greek society and runs along the following lines.

During the archaic and classical periods, Greece was a conglomerate of largely autonomous city-states with no overall political or administrative structure. In the sphere of religion the polis provided the major context for religious beliefs and practices. The reach of Greek religious cults and festivals with their public processions and communal forms of sacrifice and prayer mapped on to the reach of polis institutions, such as the demes, the phratries and the *genē*.

At the same time, the religious inventories of the individual city-states resembled each other because of their shared past and the spread of epic poetry throughout the Greek world.[5] In particular the poems of Homer and Hesiod had unified and structured the Greek pantheon. Religion offered a common set of ideologies and values, such as shared notions of

---

[3] Sourvinou-Inwood 2000a; 2000b.   [4] See Sourvinou-Inwood 2000a: 13.
[5] Sourvinou-Inwood 2000b: 47.

purity and pollution, sacred and profane, human and divine, which were a reference point throughout the Greek world. Herodotus mentioned the religious dimension of a shared feeling of Greekness in book 8, when the Athenians allude to common mythological narratives about the gods and shared forms of prayer and sacrifice (8.144.2). Greek religious beliefs and practices provided a strong link between the individual polis and the rest of the Greek world.

As the polis constituted the basic unit of Greek life, the panhellenic dimension of Greek religion – the religious institutions situated beyond the polis level, such as the large panhellenic sanctuaries or amphictyonies and religious leagues – was accessed through constant reference to the polis. Whenever a delegation visited the oracle of Apollo at Delphi or an athlete participated in the Olympic Games in honour of Zeus, they did so as members of a specific polis. Sourvinou-Inwood concluded that polis religion embodied, negotiated and informed all religious discourse, including religious practices above the level of the individual poleis.[6]

In its general formulation, the model of polis religion reflects Durkheimian efforts to 'make sense' of Greek religion as a symbolic system, a common 'language' (see Chapter 3).[7] In *The Elementary Forms of Religious Life* (first published in French in 1912), the foundational text for the emerging field of the sociology of religion, Durkheim described religion as 'a unified system of beliefs and practices', which brings together and defines those engaged in these beliefs and practices as a 'moral community'.[8]

Durkheim's definition of religion as a set of collective representations proved influential beyond the sociology of religion. In the field of classical studies his conception of the religious had an immediate impact on Jane Ellen Harrison, for example, who drew on Durkheim's conception of religion as a communal enterprise. In *Themis* Harrison variously acknowledged Durkheimian influences in how she conceived of the ways in which Greek myth and ritual reflected and constituted the structures of Greek society.[9]

---

[6] Sourvinou-Inwood 2000a: 20.

[7] Cf. Evans's definition: 'Like spoken languages, cultures also comprise lived frameworks of their own, and they can be analysed as symbolic systems with their own order and organization that work to create meaning within their own context. These lived symbolic and religious systems are in some ways related to spoken languages; and as we do with foreign languages, we can make an effort to learn the symbolic language of religion and ritual in other cultures – even those in the distant past': Evans 2010: 7.

[8] See, e.g., Durkheim 1995 (1912): 44 for a succinct formulation of his definition of religion.

[9] See, e.g., Harrison 1912: xxii, 139, 477, 486. For a more extended discussion of Harrison's contribution to the study of ancient Greek religion see ch. 4.

While Harrison's focus on distinguishing 'primitive' stages in the evolution of religions eventually fell out of favour, inquiry into the social function of religious beliefs and practices (functionalism) provided an increasingly popular interpretative tool in classical scholarship. It was put to prominent use in the work of Walter Burkert, for example, whose position can perhaps best be described as structuralist-functionalist. For Burkert, rituals and the myths related to them provided the key to what was at stake behind religious phenomena as diverse as initiation rites and blood sacrifice, two aspects of the religious, which have the ultimate goal of creating and maintaining group solidarity and communal identity.[10]

Combined with structuralism (the inquiry into the patterns of social and religious organisation within a given culture and society), functionalism remains an important interpretative tool in the study of religious practices to the present day.[11] The model of polis religion is a good case in point, insofar as it draws on ideas first formulated by Durkheim and developed further in subsequent classical scholarship. In particular, the assumption of polis religion as the foundation of a moral community (in the sense of a community sharing a common set of norms and conventions) is Durkheimian in origin. The explicitly structuralist image frequently evoked to describe the symbolic nature of Greek religion is that of religion as a shared 'language' which enabled the Greeks to communicate their experiences of the external world to each other.[12] At the same time, the model of polis religion attempts to overcome the ahistoricity of the strictly structuralist (or even formalist) perspective. It conceptualises the systemic quality of Greek religion as that of a 'meaningful structure' grounded in the specific cultural setting of archaic and classical Greece. The concept of polis religion can hence be understood as an attempt to overcome the weakness inherent in its structuralist roots by grounding religion in the specific cultural setting of the archaic and classical polis as the cultural context of its symbolic meaning.

The model of polis religion has informed current scholarship in a variety of ways. The model itself has assumed different forms and formulations in the works of scholars indebted to a range of intellectual traditions. When discussing the model, therefore, we must distinguish in particular between an Oxford form of polis religion, as described most notably by Sourvinou-Inwood and Robert Parker, and a French version propagated most clearly

---

[10] See, e.g., Burkert 1983a (on blood sacrifice); 1985: 264 (on initiation).
[11] See also ch. 3.
[12] See in detail Gould 2001. See also Burkert 1985: 119; Bowersock 1990: 7; de Polignac 1995a: 152.

in the work of Nicole Loraux and Louise Bruit Zaidman/Pauline Schmitt Pantel.[13]

POLIS RELIGION — A CRITICAL EVALUATION

The 'embeddedness' of Greek religion

Focus on the polis as the basic unit of Greek life gave rise to a crucial assumption underlying many works in the field: that of the 'embeddedness' of Greek religion in the polis. Scholars have made overlapping but not fully congruent claims about this aspect of Greek religion. The idea that Greek religion was embedded in the polis is ultimately derived from Moses Finley's influential conception of the embeddedness of the ancient economy.[14] Finley argued that in the ancient world, single areas of social interaction, such as the economy, are unavailable for conceptualisation. In analogy, Greek religion is also considered to be deeply embedded in the larger network of relationships within the polis. Greek religion was religion-in-practice and Greek religious practices permeated all spheres of life.[15] It follows that it is not possible to reflect upon Greek religion as a category in and of itself.

At the same time, the idea of the embeddedness of ancient Greek religion in the polis also acted as a check on the intrusion of concepts derived from the study of other (monotheistic) religious traditions, in particular from Christianity. Greek religion differed from Christianity in that it had no dogma, no official creed, no Bible, no priesthood in the form of a specially trained and entitled group of people, and no church. In the absence of such powerful organising principles, religion was structured alongside the socio-political structures of the polis.

The notion of the embeddedness of Greek religion in the polis, however, raises the question of exactly how we are supposed to conceive the relationship between the structures of the polis and those of ancient Greek religion. Walter Burkert identified three claims concerning the quality of the link between Greek religion and the polis inherent in the model of polis religion.[16] According to Burkert, the concept encompasses, first of

---

[13] See in particular Schmitt Pantel 1992; Bruit Zaidman and Schmitt Pantel 1992; Loraux 1993; Parker 1996; Sourvinou-Inwood 2000a; 2000b; Parker 2005.

[14] Finley 1973. Cf. 'embeddedness': Bremmer 1994: 2–4; Evans 2010: 48.

[15] The same kind of embeddedness of religion is also discussed in studies of Roman religion: e.g., Rüpke 2004; Scheid 2005: 126.

[16] Burkert 1995: 202.

all, self-representation of the community through religious cults; second, it suggests control of religious practices by the polis through its decision-making organs; and third, polis religion sometimes implies that the polis created and transformed its religious institutions – effectively, the polis 'actually makes religion'.[17]

The qualitative difference between Burkert's second and third claims is that while both stress the aspect of control, the third assigns an even larger degree of agency to the polis by presenting religion as actively shaped by it according to its interests. In contrast to this definition, however, most scholars working with the model of polis religion prefer a more subtle formulation of the link between polis and religion, largely bypassing the question of direct control. In particular the Oxford version of polis religion presents religion as merely mapped on to the institutional landscape of the polis, thus de-emphasising the aspect of agency. In the works of scholars such as Robert Parker and Christiane Sourvinou-Inwood, the distinction between Burkert's first and second claim thus becomes fluid as the socio-political structures of the polis are reformulated and maintained through their representation in religious ritual.

However, can the communal self-representation of social groupings in the polis through religious cults serve as the ultimate proof that the polis and Greek religion were congruent? From the point of view of the polis, it is certainly correct that '[e]ach significant grouping within the polis was articulated and given identity through cult', as Sourvinou-Inwood argued.[18] The important subdivisions of the polis, such as the demes and phratries, were all represented in specific cults. Even politically marginalised groups, such as women, had their own festivals and religious services specifically reserved for them.[19]

The representation of the social groupings of the polis in Greek religion, however, does not allow us to conclude the reverse: that Greek religion was entirely absorbed by the polis. There is plenty of evidence for religious practices unmediated by and with no obvious link to the polis.[20] Take for example the consultation of oracles, such as those at Delphi, Dodona or Didyma or any of the less-known oracular shrines. In support of the polis

---

[17] Burkert 1995: 202. De Polignac 1995a: 78–9 emphasised that this should not be seen as a programmatic policy of the individual poleis.

[18] Sourvinou-Inwood 2000a: 27.

[19] Sourvinou-Inwood 2000a: 27–37; 2000b: 38–44. Cf. Bremmer 1994: 2: 'In ancient Greece . . . religion was totally embedded in society – no sphere of life lacked a religious aspect.' For the religion of the demes and other subunits of the polis, see in detail Jameson 1997.

[20] See now also the sourcebook by Instone 2009, which focused specifically on the personal dimension of ancient Greek religion.

model one could, of course, point out that the fee (*pelanos*) paid before the consultation was negotiated between the officials of the oracle and the polis from which the consultant came.[21] While the economic side of oracle consultations thus fits into the framework of polis religion this is not always true for the questions asked and the responses received there. Our sources tell us, for example, of oracle consultations of a very personal nature, the significance of which was more embedded in personal circumstances than in polis concerns. In particular the corpus of responses from Dodona attests to a variety of personal issues on which divine advice was sought.[22] Questions at Dodona were typically scratched on lead tablets, some brought to light by classical archaeology. Callicrates' question whether he would receive a child from his wife Nike, for instance, hardly reflected a polis concern.[23] Likewise, Thrasyboulos' desire to know to which god he should sacrifice in order to improve his eyesight expressed a personal health issue and hence a private concern.[24] The same was true when Agis consulted Zeus regarding the whereabouts of certain lost blankets and whether or not they were stolen.[25] The polis model is of little help to us in understanding the motivations, intentions and dynamics of these private oracle consultations. Greek religion transcended the polis. Even though his attitude towards religion was not straightforward, Aristotle's perspective seems to support this view: in *Politics*, he imagined a polis from which religion was more or less entirely absent.[26]

Such examples reveal another dimension of the embeddedness of Greek religion, one not included in Burkert's list: the embeddedness of Greek religion in what could be called the 'symbolic order' of the polis. Although private concerns behind oracle consultations and the Greek festive calendars (inasmuch as they reflected the necessities of the agricultural cycle) may have fallen outside the scope of an institutionalised definition of the polis, they remained within the limits of the shared beliefs, ideas and ideals of the polis community.

Christiane Sourvinou-Inwood, in particular, inspired by work in cultural anthropology (notably by Clifford Geertz: see Chapter 3), has focused on

---

[21] See Rosenberger 1999 on the economic side of oracle consultations.

[22] For the oracle of Zeus at Dodona: Parke 1967. It is precisely those oracles that do not fit into the matrix of polis religion that have received relatively little scholarly attention. However, see recently Lhôte 2006.

[23] *SEG* IXX 426. See also Parke 1967: 265, no. 8.

[24] Parke 1967: 267, no. 14.   [25] Parke 1967: 272, no. 27.

[26] This rather strange omission, in light of the importance of religion in and for the polis, is put in context in his *Metaphysics*, which does feature a god, albeit one removed from human interests and concerns.

religion as part of a more general semantics of Greek culture.[27] Several of her works explore religious phenomena as forms of collective representation, which must be studied in the context of the larger cultural system that generated and received them.[28] To 'read' such religious symbols we must place them back in their original culture. 'Reading' as an act of decoding cultural symbols is a concept central to all her monographs. Sourvinou-Inwood's main goal, then, is to reconstruct the ancient perceptual filters which have shaped these symbols and through which they were perceived in their own time.

This is notably different from, and more powerful than, the simple claim that the polis controlled religious practices and institutions. It is also a more all-encompassing concept than the view that Greek religion was projected onto the socio-political landscape of the polis, an idea which Sourvinou-Inwood developed elsewhere.[29] Yet the question arises whether the label of polis religion is still valid. What aspects of this kind of embeddedness are polis-specific? Are the perceptual filters situated first and foremost in the institutions and the ideology of the polis? As soon as we move away from matters of agency and look at larger religious concepts, such as death, pollution and piety, we find that the symbolic order of the polis coincides with the symbolic order of Greek culture and society more generally. Rather than speaking of polis religion, we may therefore prefer to state that Greek religion was embedded in Greek culture with the polis as its paradigmatic worshipping group.

To conclude this line of argument: the relationship between the polis and Greek religion was more complex than has been assumed. As Burkert rightly remarked: 'Polis religion is a characteristic and representative part of Greek religion, but only part of it. There is religion without the polis, even if there is no polis without religion.'[30] In other words, the polis was no less embedded in Greek religion than Greek religion in the polis. The polis provides an essential framework for assessing Greek religion, but it should by no means be the only one.

Inconsistencies

In the previous section we explored the notion of the embeddedness of ancient Greek religion in the polis as implied in the model of polis religion.

---

[27] E.g., Sourvinou-Inwood 1995: 21, n. 27. Geertz's notion of religion is best formulated in Geertz 1973: 87–125.

[28] See Sourvinou-Inwood 1991; 1995; 2003.   [29] Sourvinou-Inwood 2000a; 2000b.

[30] Burkert 1995: 203.

In this section we examine the question of the coherence and consistency of ancient Greek religion following from this notion.

The systemic perspective on Greek religion has been criticised for assuming too much coherence and internal consistency in Greek religious beliefs and practices. In particular, John Gould has pointed to the limits of the assumption of internal coherence within the system of Greek religion: 'Greek religion remains fundamentally improvisatory . . . there is always room for new improvisation, for the introduction of new cults and new observances: Greek religion is not theologically fixed and stable, and it has no tradition of exclusion or finality: it is an open, not a closed system'.[31]

Unfortunately, however, in the historiographic practice of works on Greek religion, such concessions have all too frequently remained mere programmatic statements, made in the introduction to silence potential disagreement before the writer produces yet another account of polis religion which makes perfect sense in all its aspects. According to such views, ideally, all groups present in the polis were perfectly proficient in the 'language' of religion, thus creating a consensual, internally consistent and single-voiced symbolic order. Although scholars working with the model readily admit that the polis consisted of different individuals with different, even diverging, attitudes, there is little space in their works for personal religion, the fault-lines between contradictory religious beliefs and practices, and the internal frictions, inconsistencies and tensions springing from them. Structurally speaking, deviance from the common Greek 'language' of religion is conceivable only as a conscious inversion of the rules set by the polis, thus staying within the same symbolic order.[32]

To clarify: I am not arguing here against the usefulness of structuralism as an interpretative tool as such, which presupposes the existence of a more or less coherent symbolic system.[33] In fact structuralism, as exemplified so skilfully in the works of Jean-Pierre Vernant, for instance, has proved itself superbly capable of illuminating individual strands of Greek thought and literature (such as that of a particular myth in Hesiod, for example). I will myself occasionally draw on this mode of investigation in later

---

[31] Gould 2001: 210. See also Jameson 1997: 184. On Gould's conception of Greek religion see also in detail ch. 3.

[32] Cf. Bendlin 2000: 119, who argues that versatility of religious ritual should be seen not as a symptom of its decline but as a feature of its vigour.

[33] Structuralism inquires into the patterns underlying Greek religious beliefs and practices with the ultimate goal of uncovering the symbolic constructs that constitute much of Greek religious thought. It therefore allows for the constant generation of novel variants, arising against the background of earlier attempts that worked with the same symbolic constructs and structural patterns.

chapters of this book (see Chapters 2 and 6).[34] What I am arguing against is the assumption that there is only a single symbolic discourse in the ancient Greek world – that of polis religion – reaching into all areas of the Greek religious experience and providing a total and uncontested realm of religious meanings. The existence of such a level of coherence is, for example, implied in Burkert's *Greek Religion*, which brings together a vast array of material from different religious contexts in a composite account that aims to explain ancient Greek religion as such, largely to the exclusion of religious divergence and of religious phenomena such as 'magic' (see in more detail the discussion of Burkert's *Greek Religion* in the next section and in Chapter 4).

Against such tendencies, Hendrik S. Versnel dedicated two volumes to the revelation of inconsistencies within the system of Greek religion.[35] A similar point was made by Paul Veyne concerning the coexistence of divergent, even contradictory forms of belief in ancient Greece.[36] Veyne made a strong case for the need to look at beliefs in the context of varying concepts of truth. These concepts of truth, Veyne argued, are inherent in different epistemological discourses (such as mythology and historiography) and much of Veyne's interpretative effort was spent on uncovering their hidden rules. Moreover, Veyne reminded us about variations in religious beliefs over time, which change together with the concepts of truth that underlie them. A good example is perhaps the changing Greek attitude towards mythology and the supernatural. What was for Homer and others a special realm of knowledge authenticated by the Muses, to which the distinction between truth and falsehood did not apply, increasingly became subject to criticism and intellectual scrutiny. In the works of Herodotus, Thucydides and other fifth-century BC thinkers, for example, narratives about the gods were subjected to critical inquiry. The supernatural was no longer on a separate plane but had to 'fit in with the rest of reality' to reassert its place in the cultural and historical memory of Greece.[37] It follows from Veyne's work that Greek religion was not a single-voiced discourse and that its different aspects and their relationship to each other changed over time.

The construction of the polis as an internally and chronologically consistent and monolithic symbolic order is a simplification which does not do justice to the internal dynamics of these states. Recent work in social

---

[34] E.g., Vernant 1981.

[35] Versnel 1990; 1993. Versnel uses such inconsistencies and ambiguities principally as entry points to an alternative reading of religious phenomena, such as henocentrism, and myth and ritual.

[36] Veyne 1988.   [37] Veyne 1988: 32.

anthropology suggests that we replace the concept of culture as a consensual sphere of interaction with a more flexible and fluid understanding of it as open to the internal frictions resulting from change and social transformation.[38] Josiah Ober has borrowed concepts of culture from social anthropology and introduced them into the field of classics.[39] Appropriating Sewell's model of a 'thinly coherent' culture Ober emphasised the need to allow for multiple and even divergent identities within Greek society ('the cultures within Greek culture').[40]

In contrast to a 'thick coherence', the assumption of 'thin coherence' de-emphasises high levels of connectedness among individuals within one culture zone, thus allowing space for cultural contestation and transformation. Accordingly, Ober envisaged a study of Hellenism with a strong focus on the 'dialectical tensions' between various levels and microcosms of Greek culture. Greek, in particular Athenian, society thus appears as a space of internal contestation and debate, with the political (that is, the polis) at its centre but by no means limited to it.[41]

The model of a thinly coherent Greek culture has yet to be applied to the study of Greek religion, but a more flexible concept of culture as contested and changing would certainly be productive. Thin coherence would, for example, allow us to bring in religious movements such as Orphism and the use of magical practices, which have so far been marginalised in the study of polis religion. Discussing the power of the polis model to explain religious beliefs and practices above the polis level, Sourvinou-Inwood stated that 'polis religion embraces, contains, and mediates all religious discourse – with the ambiguous and uncertain exception of some sectarian discourse'.[42] Her cautious ambivalence towards what she referred to as 'sectarian' religious beliefs and practices is symptomatic of the general approach to these cults adopted by scholars working with the polis model.[43] Religious beliefs and practices that do not conform to the polis model (those practices not administered by the polis and not representing the sociopolitical order of the polis) are frequently seen as being by definition not religion proper. The ongoing debate about what separates magic from religion, for example, is frequently supported by a definition of Greek religion

---

[38] E.g., Comaroff and Comaroff 1991 and 1997, as discussed in ch. 3.
[39] Ober 2005: 69–91.   [40] Cf. Dougherty and Kurke 2003.
[41] Ober 2005: 77–82.   [42] Sourvinou-Inwood 2000a: 20.
[43] Bremmer 2010: 22–9 identifies a Christianising distinction between church and sect as the point of reference here and criticises the resulting marginalisation of religious phenomena such as Orphism as 'of a somewhat less respectable or marginal character', a marginalisation which is not supported by the ancient evidence: Bremmer 2010: 2.

as civic religion (see Chapter 4).[44] The much-debated question of the nature and quality of the religious phenomenon referred to as Orphism – in particular whether it constitutes a separate 'religious movement' – may reflect Christianising assumptions about the nature of religion. But this question is also representative of the difficulties we face when we try to position these cults as distinct from mainstream Greek religion.[45] To situate such cults and practices strictly outside Greek religion narrowly defined as polis religion, however, runs the risk of circularity. It marginalises exactly those areas of religious activity that the model cannot sufficiently explain.

The relationship between phenomena such as magic, Orphism and Bacchic cults on the one hand and traditional religious beliefs and practices on the other is much more complicated than a simple separation of the religion of the polis from 'sectarian discourse' might tempt us to assume.

To start with, despite their distinct features, Orphism, Bacchic cults and magical practices responded to and interacted with more widely held beliefs and practices of mainstream Greek religion. The Orphic *Theogony*, for example, is an extension of the Hesiodic genealogy of the gods. It expands Hesiod's theogony by adding two predecessors, Night and Protogonus, to the first king Uranus, and extends its end with the reign of Dionysus.[46] The result is a reorganisation of the Greek pantheon that takes the traditional model as its point of departure.[47] Recent research has stressed that Greek magical practices also overlapped significantly with traditional religion. A look at the *Papyri Graecae Magicae*, for example, reveals the closeness of magical formulae to Greek prayer.[48] Both concepts refer to similar notions of the supernatural. In particular, if we consider religious beliefs as they come together in the minds of those involved in them, a strict distinction

---

[44] The literature on this question is vast. The debate goes all the way back to James Frazer's (now dismissed) distinction between magic and religion as one of coercion and submission. Some of the more productive recent contributions to this debate can be found in Faraone and Obbink 1991; Versnel 1991a; Bremmer 1999. A comprehensive introduction to ancient magic and the debates surrounding it can be found in Graf 1997a.

[45] The old position that sees Orphism as a separate religious movement originated with Rohde 1972 (1890/1894) and was further advocated by Guthrie 1935 and Nilsson 1952 (among others). This position was successfully refuted by Linforth 1941; Zuntz 1971; Burkert 2006 (1977). West 1983: 1 refers to it as the 'pseudo-problem of the supposed Orphic religion'. The debate is nicely summarised by Parker, who advocates the cautious middle position prevailing in scholarship at the time, and who concludes that 'the question about the unity of Orphism must be left unanswered': Parker 1995: 487.

[46] Parker 1995: 487–96.

[47] On the relationship between Orphic and Hesiodic theogony see Guthrie 1935: 83–4. Cf. Edmonds 2004: 75–80.

[48] On the overlap between prayer and magic see Graf 1991.

between mystery religions and magic on the one hand and traditional religion on the other becomes problematic.

Strict distinction between both types of religious activity becomes even more untenable if we consider that those involved in magic, Orphism and other 'unlicensed' (Parker) or 'elective' (Price) cults were not recruited from socially or politically marginal groups. As Stephen Halliwell recently pointed out, 'membership in some kinds of separate religious groups could coexist with involvement in more "mainstream" forms of Greek religion, and still more with full participation in communal life'.[49] To equate religious marginality with social marginality is 'a simplification of the nature of (Greek) religion itself'.[50] Some of the Orphic gold tablets were found in the tombs of relatively affluent and hence socially accepted members of society.[51] Likewise, those engaged in polis religion were the same people who would in specific circumstances resort to magic.[52] Religious phenomena such as magic, Orphism and Bacchic cults remained deeply embedded in the cities' socio-political and normative structures.

Some of the most productive current work therefore focuses on the relationship between the city and 'unauthorised' religious beliefs and practices without simplifying either entity as closed and monolithic.[53] For example, in an article exploring the relationship between representations of maenadism in Greek tragedy and art, particularly on vases, Robin Osborne has argued convincingly that during the fifth century BC ecstatic female worship of Dionysus was an accepted part of Athenian religious experience and not a unique or unusual feature.[54] From this point of view, the *Bacchae* of Euripides 'is not helping Athenians to come to terms with the alien but helping them to see just how shocking were the rituals to which they were so accustomed'.[55]

The notion of 'thin coherence' might provide an invaluable framework for this and other areas of study investigating the unity and diversity of Greek religious discourse. It was the diversity of Greek religious beliefs and practices in particular that composed the fabric of Greek polytheism. Thin coherence might therefore offer conceptual guidance in further developing a framework for researching religious identities that both are, and are not, like polis religion without overemphasising similarities or differences between religious phenomena. To explain away existing inconsistencies is more dogmatic than the religion we seek to explain.

---

[49] Halliwell 2005.　　[50] Halliwell 2005.
[51] See Parker 1995: 496. On these tablets see also Graf and Johnston 2007; Bowden 2010: 148–55.
[52] See Graf 1999: 1–2.　　[53] E.g., Edmonds 2004.
[54] Osborne 2010.　　[55] Osborne 2010: 402.

At this stage, however, we must include a caveat: the study of inconsistencies is fruitful only when it is itself 'embedded' (along the lines suggested by Ober, for example) in a wider framework of perspectives exploring the nature of different – even divergent – belief systems within the wider, general culture. The simple presentation of inconsistencies cannot be heuristically satisfying, as we cannot be sure that what we are dealing with is more than just our failure to see coherence. The only way to distinguish, to some extent at least, our own failure to understand from true plurality of belief is to place such dissonances within a larger framework of cultural contestation.

The 'local' and the 'universal'

Classical scholars have extended the notion of the polis as a closed hermeneutic system from the individual polis to the 'world of the polis' system and, beyond this, to the panhellenic dimension of Greek religion. As a result, most general introductions to ancient Greek religion show an intrinsic and ultimately unresolvable tension between 'local' religious beliefs and practices and Greek religion more broadly. In such works the 'local' is always implied as the conceptual antipode to a more general, more typical, less idiosyncratic layer of Greek religion and vice versa (see Chapter 5 for a correction of this view). Unfortunately, however, despite the heavy weight they are made to carry, both concepts (the 'local' and the 'universal' or 'panhellenic') remain largely undefined in current scholarship.[56]

Take for example Walter Burkert's description of the Greek gods in *Greek Religion*. His account of Aphrodite is a description of her typical representations and areas of competence as the goddess of love and sexuality.[57] Local variations are mostly used to illuminate such general features. The appearance of pictorial representations of Aphrodite dressed in 'long sumptuous robes' and wearing the *polos* in the first half of the seventh century BC is welcomed by Burkert as the 'normal representation of the goddess' that superseded the orientalising nude figure.[58] What motivated this change? In what pictorial and religious local contexts do these 'normal representations' of the goddess appear, hence assigning them a special meaning? Likewise, the depiction of the nude Aphrodite about to take a bath, crafted by Praxiteles around 340 BC for the sanctuary at Cnidus, is mentioned only in passing to introduce the general popularity of this theme in later times: 'for centuries this figure remained the most renowned representation

---

[56] E.g., Sourvinou-Inwood 1978.   [57] Burkert 1985: 152–6.   [58] Burkert 1985: 155.

of the goddess of love, the embodiment of all womanly charms'.[59] The circumstances which explain this change in representation as well as the contexts in which this statue featured at Cnidus remain unexplored. Burkert's account is driven by the overall aim of bringing single local aspects of the Greek pantheon together into one more or less coherent narrative of ancient Greek religion.[60] Similar observations could be made concerning the way in which Burkert and other scholars deal with forms of *epiklēseis* ('invocations'), divinatory rituals and initiation procedures that are specific to a given polis. The rituals that do not conform to a standard model of Greek religion are sidelined in such accounts. The consistency of Greek religion seems to be merely an observation of the similarity evident once sufficient local variations are stripped away. Until we find a more complex conceptualisation of the fabric of Greek religious beliefs and practices, Greek religion, at least in our general accounts of it, will appear to be less than the sum of its parts.

It is in this area of scholarly activity that the model of polis religion has proven most productive: the polis model can provide a viable way around such problems. If fully embraced, it can furnish a framework with sufficient flexibility to do justice to the diverse and particularistic nature of the Greek world. In particular, the focus on the specificity of individual poleis, a central tenet of the model of polis religion, can help correct simplifying assumptions concerning the unity of ancient Greek religion. It is therefore one of the model's strengths that it embraces the plurality of Greek religious beliefs and practices in a manner that moves significantly beyond the impasse between local and general layers of ancient Greek religion.

Robert Parker's comprehensive account of the religious life of just one individual polis is a good example of a productive use of the polis model in this way.[61] Two of his works are entirely devoted to Athens and offer a thorough investigation of religious practices of different social groups such as the demes and phratries by themselves and in their interaction with each other. In Parker's work the local is not conceptualised as the

---

[59] Burkert 1985: 155. On Praxiteles' Aphrodite see also ch. 6.
[60] This approach is justified in Burkert 1985: 8: 'Would it not be more correct to speak in the plural of Greek religions? Against this must be set the bond of common language and, from the eighth century onward, the common Homeric literary culture . . . in spite of an emphasis on local or sectarian peculiarities, the Greeks themselves regarded the various manifestations of their religious life as essentially compatible, as a diversity of practice in devotion to the same gods, within the framework of a single world.'
[61] See Parker 1996; 2005. See also Faraone 1985.

(implicit) antipode of Greek religion as such, but functions rather as its own self-contained unit of investigation.

While Parker's work has shown a way around this problem for the study of 'local' religion as it manifested itself in individual poleis such as Athens, the question emerges of how we are to extend this focus to the study of religious institutions usually associated with the other, 'panhellenic', side of the spectrum (the sanctuaries of Delphi and Olympia immediately come to mind, but also the religion of Homer, etc.). Here, too, we need to find ways to move beyond the simple dualities of the 'local' and the 'universal' and, as it were, between polis religion and Greek religion beyond the polis, for example by placing them into a more pluralistic religious landscape (see Chapter 5).[62]

Developments beyond the Classical period

The assumption of a relatively stable and coherent religious system implied in the model of polis religion has also influenced the temporal focus of many studies of ancient Greek polis religion, which, in turn, has been supported by the traditional definition of the polis. Traditionally, classical scholarship has worked with a conception of the polis as an independent form of social and political organisation that was considered to have come to a more or less sudden end during the second half of the fourth century BC. When Philip II defeated the Thebans and Athenians at the Battle of Chaironeia in 338 BC he subjected them to Macedonian supremacy, hence putting an end to the Greek city-state as defined by independence (*autonomia*). The model of polis religion implicitly relies on such a definition of the polis: most studies exploring polis religion focus on the religious system of the archaic and classical periods only as a time of relative religious coherence.[63]

Despite the fundamental changes in the religious landscape between the eighth and fourth centuries BC, these periods are frequently constructed as a uniform epoch in which time can be ignored in favour of a 'mutually sustaining universe of unchanging meaning'.[64] But the model of polis religion has become so powerful that even works covering later periods frequently rely implicitly or explicitly on the definition of Greek religion as polis religion. The result is either an overemphasis of continuities in religious beliefs and practices or the acknowledgement of differences – without, however,

[62] See Scott 2010: 270–2.

[63] E.g., Burkert 1985; Bruit Zaidman and Schmitt Pantel 1992; Bremmer 1994.

[64] Cf. Sewell's brilliant definition of synchronic analysis, which, rather than offering a series of snapshots, constructs its referent as a 'uniform moment or epoch' in which 'different times are present in a continuous moment': Sewell 1997: 40.

attempting to ground these differences in a more comprehensive account of Greek religion during the Hellenistic and Roman periods.[65] We still lack, for example, a comprehensive work on Hellenistic religion, which strikes a subtle balance between continuity and change.[66]

In this respect Parker's two-volume work on Athenian religion can serve as an example of the difficulty of navigating around the anti-historicist tendencies that are so widespread in studies based on the model of polis religion. In contrast to the work of Bruit Zaidman and Schmitt Pantel, which is structured entirely thematically, Parker recognises the need to include both perspectives.[67] His first volume is explicitly entitled *Athenian Religion: A History*.[68] This chronological study of the polis religion of Athens is supplemented by a second volume, which is thematically organised.[69] However, Parker's decision to split his account into separate volumes reflects and ultimately embodies the difficulty of the model in combining synchronic and diachronic perspectives and structure with agency. Just as the synchronic perspective is at the heart of cultural analysis, it needs to be in direct communication with the diachronic perspective, since it reveals the very processes that shape and are shaped by it.[70] For a diachronic account to go beyond providing only a 'thin' narration of the particulars of change over time it must be grounded simultaneously in 'thick' synchronic analysis.[71]

---

[65] See, e.g., Griffiths 2005, who describes the elements of Hellenistic religion but does not ground them in a more comprehensive account of Greek religion of the Hellenistic period. An outline of the guiding principles of such an account can be found in Gordon 1972. Gordon introduces the term 'selective continuity' as a programmatic term for his nuanced discussion of Hellenistic religious beliefs and practices between continuity and change. See also the dualistic categories of 'locative' vs. 'utopian' cultures that Jonathan Z. Smith developed in order to differentiate Hellenistic from earlier styles of religion: Smith 1978a: 88–103, 129–47.

[66] Despite its strong chronological focus, Mikalson 1998 provides a worthwhile case study for Hellenistic Athens, paying particular attention to the balancing of the needs of the individual and society. A comprehensive study of Hellenistic religion, however, should integrate the evidence for Athens with that for other areas of the Hellenistic world, as the religious outlook of the time varied significantly and depended on factors such as geographical location and social class: see Gordon 1972. Pakkanen 1996 offers a re-evaluation of four key concepts of Hellenistic religion (syncretism, the trend towards monotheism, individualism and cosmopolitanism) by investigating the mysteries of Demeter and the cult of Isis in early Hellenistic Athens. Some aspects of Hellenistic religion are also discussed by Corrington 1986; Sørensen 1989; Mendels 1998.

[67] Bruit Zaidman and Schmitt Pantel 1992; Parker 1996.

[68] Parker 1996.   [69] Parker 2005.   [70] See n. 64.

[71] A good example of how diachronic change could fit into the religious landscape of Greece is characteristic of the work of another eminent scholar of Greek religion – Michael Jameson. He sketches a subtle and multifaceted framework of religious innovation, thus giving a balanced account of continuity and change in Athenian religious practice during the transition from the archaic to the classical period: e.g., Jameson 1997. I would like to thank Jan Bremmer for pointing this out to me.

There is, however, a larger question looming in the background of the discussion of the problem of historicity and issues of continuity and change, a problem which is fundamental to the study of ancient Greek religion beyond the polis: that of what we take the polis to be. This question is important because the way in which we answer it will have serious ramifications for what can and cannot be understood by polis religion.

The conception of the sudden end of the polis in the fourth century BC has recently been challenged. In particular, the scholars of the Copenhagen Polis Centre have made a strong case for adopting a much broader conception of the polis, as existing beyond the classical period.[72] Morgens Herman Hansen, for example, has argued that *autonomia* (in the sense of full independence) was never really 'an irreducible characteristic' of the polis.[73] Even before the Battle of Chaironeia some poleis were dependent upon others. The poleis inhabited by the Lakedaimonian *perioikoi*, for example, were dependent upon Sparta.[74] Moreover, several cities had already lost their independence when they joined the Delian or Peloponnesian Leagues.

Scholars like Hansen have therefore suggested that it is more productive to refer to a conception of *autonomia* as encompassing self-governance rather than full independence.[75] Hansen and Nielsen work with a definition of the polis as 'a small, highly institutionalised and self-governing community of citizens . . . living with their wives and children in an urban centre . . . and its hinterland . . . and slaves'.[76] This conception of the polis, however, continued to exist far into the Hellenistic and Roman periods. The end of the Greek polis as a self-governing entity, then, occurred during late antiquity and in a gradual process that started with the centralised bureaucracy set up by Diocletian in the third century AD and was accelerated by a variety of factors, including the early medieval migrations (in the western part of the Empire) and the spread of Christianity (in the East).[77]

For the study of ancient Greek religion several important implications follow from this broader definition of the polis. It flags the need to bring the religion of Hellenistic and Roman Greece more firmly into the picture we sketch of ancient Greek religion – a need which will be variously addressed throughout this book, notably in Chapter 6. Moreover, the inclusion of post-classical Greek religion makes it all the more necessary to allow for inconsistencies and to move away from an overly narrow focus on those aspects of Greek religious culture rooted in official (civic) discourse.

---

[72] See Introduction, n. 28.   [73] Hansen 2006: 48.   [74] See Shipley 1997.
[75] Hansen 2006: 49.   [76] Hansen and Nielsen 2004: 31.
[77] Hansen and Nielsen 2004: 20; Hansen 2006: 50.

The Hellenistic and Roman periods witnessed not only an increase in Greek personal religion and a turn towards a more spiritual experience of the divine but also saw the rise of new religious institutions and the introduction of new beliefs and practices (for example, emperor worship, the emergence of exotic cults, such as the ones of Isis and Serapis, and the rise of holy men) which took their legitimacy and their binding force from contexts of social and political life beyond the polis. The adoption of a broader definition of the polis, it follows, necessitates the adoption of a broader conception of the religious culture of ancient Greece, in order to accommodate such features of the religious.

Religious ideas versus religious practice

The temporal focus on the religion of the archaic and classical periods is not the only limitation of the model of polis religion: the preference of religious practice is another. Scholars working with the model of polis religion focus strongly on religious agency while largely excluding religious beliefs from their accounts of Greek religion.[78] Although Sourvinou-Inwood hoped to have 'proposed certain reconstructions of ancient religious perceptions pertaining especially to the articulation of polis religion', religious beliefs do not feature in her definition of polis religion.[79] It may be tempting to point out that the category of belief is a typical twenty-first-century interest, which does not help to describe the realities of ancient Greek religion. But the very fact that Greek culture had no word to say *credo* ('I believe') and no creed (no prescribed, organised system of belief) does not mean that the category of belief itself – in the sense of certain shared assumptions about the nature of the divine – was absent from ancient Greek religion. Ancient Greek culture was rich in narratives which relied on Greek notions about the nature of the gods and their availability to human knowledge in order to make sense (see the examples discussed in Chapters 2 and 6). Magical practices, too, relied on shared religious conceptions about the nature and power of certain gods inherent in Greek religion, for example by inverting the way in which they feature in official Greek religion (see Chapter 4). The relative absence of religious beliefs and of religious discourse more generally from some works in the field therefore warrants an explanation.

The model of polis religion was successful in helping us analyse religious practice, owing to its embeddedness in the polis, since human agency

---

[78] E.g., Jameson 1997 focuses mainly on ritual and leaves out religious beliefs almost entirely. Thanks again to Jan Bremmer for bringing this to my attention.

[79] Sourvinou-Inwood 2000a: 37.

(at least during archaic and classical times) always refers in one way or another to the polis. Pauline Schmitt Pantel's *La cité au banquet* may serve as an example of the kind of questions asked within the framework of polis religion: her book is a comprehensive investigation of the role of conviviality as a religious, social and political institution in the formulation of identities within the archaic and classical Greek poleis.[80] Other works demonstrate the close link between religion and power in pagan priesthood, or depict the introduction of new gods as a powerful tool to achieve social and political change.[81]

The neglect of religious beliefs came at a high price, however. In an attempt to distinguish one's own work as much as possible from the earlier associative studies of Greek religious beliefs, it became desirable to draw a somewhat artificial line between religious beliefs on the one hand and polis-oriented religious practice on the other. Walter Burkert, for example, concluded his argument about the existence of a Greek religion beyond the polis by pointing out that 'there were no attempts of a polis to influence "belief", a concept which hardly exists in practical Greek religion. It was Wilamowitz who wrote *Der Glaube der Hellenen.*'[82]

It was Burkert, however, who wrote *Homo Necans*, a work that assigns a central role to the deep-seated meaning of blood sacrifice.[83] Against this background it is curious that he made so strict a distinction between religious beliefs and practices. In the statement quoted above, religious belief is divorced from religious practice and becomes a product of modern rather than ancient imagination. While this might have been true for the earlier unreflected theology of older scholarship (the works of Harrison, Cornford or Murray, for instance), it is certainly less correct for the reconstruction of Greek religious beliefs and practices that carefully reflects on its own premises.[84] In addition, to note that the polis did not try to influence belief and that belief was absent from 'practical Greek religion' is to state that to believe and to act are two fundamentally separate activities.[85] Belief and practice may in theory be separate, but they may also be causally related. Belief informs practice just as much as practice informs belief. To return to Burkert's example, the practice of Greek blood sacrifice cannot properly be understood without taking into account a variety of beliefs that fed into this practice. These included, but were not limited to, Greek notions about the gods and their reciprocal relationship with humanity and Greek ideas

---

[80] Schmitt Pantel 1992.　　[81] Beard and North 1990; Garland 1992.　　[82] Burkert 1995: 205.
[83] Burkert 1983a.　　[84] Harrison 1903; 1912; Murray 1912; Cornford 1914.
[85] Cf. Evans 2010: 7: 'Ancient Greek religion had little to do with belief, and a great deal to do with practice and observance of common ancestral customs.'

about sacrificial purity and the special status of blood. The real challenge would have been to find a way of reconciling Greek religious beliefs and practices as they came together in the minds of those involved in them.

'Beyond the polis' from the polis level upwards

Finally, in discussing the potential and the limits of the polis model, it is important not only to 'look down' from the level of the polis and to focus on the reluctance of the model to address issues of personal belief and so on, as I have done in the sections above, but it is equally pressing and valid to 'look up' from the level of the polis to religious practices not contained by or articulated within the context of the polis.

When it was first published in 1984, François de Polignac's influential study *Naissance de la cité grecque* (published in English as *Cults, Territory and the Origin of the Greek City State*) triggered a widespread debate concerning the links between religious identity and polis identity. De Polignac's claim that the city came to define itself first and foremost as a religious community inspired various case studies further exploring the religious landscape of Greece as a bipolar geometrical plane, in which the city was shaped in a dynamic tension between centre and periphery. In the larger picture of studies on ancient Greek religion, de Polignac's pointed formulation represented a broader trend that tended to overemphasise the role of the polis as the main organising principle of Greek cultural practices including, but not limited to, religion. Other socio-political units besides the polis, such as the *ethnē*, were seen as remnants in a larger evolutionary scheme that culminated in the polis.[86] As a result, the existence of alternative worshipping communities and individual religious practices outside the framework of the polis has been neglected by the model of polis religion just as much as personal issues of belief during the classical and Hellenistic periods.

In response to de Polignac's generalising claim, classical scholars sought to draw a more complicated picture of religious transformation. The critical discussion of his work induced de Polignac himself to give up strictly bipolar synchronicity in favour of a more chronologically and geographically nuanced picture.[87] The larger significance of this debate for scholarship on Greek religion certainly lies in its re-evaluation of the role of the polis in

---

[86] E.g., McInerney 1999: 1–7 argued that the focus on the polis led to the scholarly neglect of ethnic identity.

[87] E.g., the changes de Polignac made in the English edition of his work and, in particular, in de Polignac 1995b.

relation to other units of collective identity (see the discussion of Olympia in Chapter 5). The prevailing view now seems to be that the polis did not so much replace older identities as offer an alternative model, which continued to coexist with other forms of identity and organisation. Accordingly, recent works in the field stress that the coming of the polis (in itself by no means a chronologically identifiable 'event') is just one episode in a much longer history of religious transformation. This change of focus enables a more differentiated perspective, which takes into account alternative worshipping communities that continued to exist besides the polis during the Iron Age, the archaic and later periods.

Catherine Morgan, for example, suggested that we complicate our picture of Early Iron Age and archaic cult practice in various ways.[88] She advocated a more nuanced chronological investigation of how the development of the polis did and did not affect early Greek cult activity. Drawing in particular on material remains from the margins of the emerging polis world (Thessaly, Phokis, East Locris, Achaea and Arcadia), Morgan revised widespread notions in scholarship that were based primarily on the cases of large and central poleis, such as Athens, Sparta and Argos, which were atypical in many ways.[89] For the region of Thessaly, for instance, Morgan traced the process in which a local Early Iron Age cult of Enodia gradually turned into a pan-Thessalian deity identified with the Olympic divinity of Zeus Thaulius.[90] Pointing in particular to the existence of *ethnos* sanctuaries in this and other territories, she concluded that 'the priority accorded to the polis . . . as the most dynamic, creative and influential form of political organisation is no longer sustainable'.[91] In several archaeological case studies Alexandros Mazarakis Ainian reached a similar conclusion.[92] Most notably, perhaps, in his rich and comprehensive investigation of the genesis of the Greek temple between the eleventh and the eighth centuries BC, he pointed to the existence of other worshipping communities above the polis level.[93]

The picture that emerges from such research suggests that from about 700 BC onwards the polis provided an important organising principle of Greek religious beliefs and practices. At the same time, Greek religion remained a vehicle for the communication of other, larger identities, most notably that of ethnic identity.[94] For the late archaic, classical and Hellenistic periods, there is plenty of evidence of ritual activity administered by the *ethnē*, not the poleis. An inscription, for example, dating probably

---

[88] E.g., Morgan, C. 1994; Morgan, K. A. 2003.   [89] See Morgan 2003.   [90] Morgan 2003: 135–55.
[91] Morgan 2003: 6.   [92] E.g., Mazarakis Ainian 1985; 1988.   [93] E.g., Mazarakis Ainian 1997: 393.
[94] E.g., Hall 1997; Morgan 2003; Freitag et al. 2006.

from 216 BC, testifies to the existence of a sanctuary of the Acarnanian League.[95] The sanctuary was that of Apollo of Actium, which housed an important festival.[96] During the Hellenistic period this sanctuary served as a symbolic centre of the league distinct from its political centre, which remained on Leucas.[97] A treaty dating from around 300 BC likewise attests to religious practices administered by the *ethnē*: the sanctuary of Athena Itonia served as the centre of the Boeotian *ethnos*; the Pamboeotia, a Boeotian festival featuring games held in honour of Athena Itonia, were held in Coronea even before that time.[98] As well as *ethnos* cults, there were several religious institutions, in particular large and important sanctuaries, that were administered by amphictionies. These leagues of several poleis, such as the pan-Ionian amphictiony, which looked after a common Poseidon sanctuary located on the semi-island of Mycale, provide another example of Greek religious structures situated beyond the polis.[99]

CONCLUSION

To sum up, there is no single approach that either can or should supersede the polis model. The model's strength lies in its capacity to explain an important structuring principle of ancient Greek religion. For a religion that lacked the organisational structures characteristic of most modern religions, such as a structured community of believers (such as a church) and a systematic and authoritative statement of belief (such as a creed), it offers an alternative concept of religious administration and signification. Most notably, perhaps, if fully embraced, the model of polis religion helps us to move away from generalising assumptions about the nature of 'Greek religion as such' and encourages us to pay closer attention to the fabric of Greek religion as an agglomeration of 'local' variants.

The weaknesses of the model, however, spring from its narrow and problematic promotion of the polis as the primary discourse of power relevant for the study of ancient Greek religion. The model of polis religion in some forms and formulations renders Greek religion less comprehensible than it ought to be. There is, for example, a certain conceptual vagueness in works based on the polis model concerning the nature of the embeddedness of Greek religion in the polis. The exact quality of the relationship

---

[95] *IG* IX² 1, 583.   [96] See Habicht 1957.
[97] See Parker 1998a: 27. Parker includes a special appendix, listing evidence for various religious practices among the *ethnē*.
[98] See Buck 1979: 88–90; Schachter 1981: 117–27. Parker 1998a: 30.
[99] On this and other amphictionies see Tausend 1992: 55–7.

between religious structures and socio-political structures remains under-theorised in many works based on the model. Diverging claims range from the symbolic (or ideological) embeddedness to a more practice-oriented embeddedness of Greek religion in the polis. One result of this is that scholarly accounts oscillate between the depiction of religion as a mainly passive force within society (mapping on to the reach of polis institutions) and the depiction of a more active role of religion at the other. Both per-spectives, however, assume that the structured (systematic) character of Greek religion ran parallel to the political and social structures of the polis. This assumption often results in a focus on synchronic coherence and con-sistency. Under such a paradigm local differences and diachronic change are conceived merely as an inversion of existing structures – or, worse, as deviation and decline from 'proper' Greek religion.

Further, the model does not ask all the questions one might wish to ask about Greek religion. While the polis model is able to explain the official response to religious activity it does not necessarily provide a key to understanding the appeal of this activity from the point of view of those involved in it.[100] Nor does the focus on the mediation of the polis help us to appreciate the religion of alternative socio-political units above and below the polis level.[101] In particular, the strong focus on religious practices combined with the relative neglect of religious beliefs is a serious limitation of current scholarship in the field.

---

[100] To use an example from Roman religion: scholars working with the polis model would point out that the Bacchanalia scandal of 186 BC demonstrates the power of the polis (of Rome) to suppress religious activity that it perceived to be against its interests. This offers an explanation of the political dimension of this scandal. It does not, however, explain the appeal of this mystery religion to the individual believer, both male and female.

[101] See Woolf 1997: 77–82.

CHAPTER 2

Parmeniscus' journey: tracing religious visuality in word and wood

But what is 'social energy'? . . . We identify *energia* only indirectly, by its effects: it is manifested in the capacity of certain verbal, aural, and visual trances to produce, shape, and organize collective physical and mental experiences.

Stephen Greenblatt[1]

There is no innocent eye, seeing is an active and not a passive process.

Hans Gerhard Kippenberg[2]

INTRODUCTION

Chapter 1 identified the focus on the polis and its socio-political institutions as a paradigm in current scholarship on ancient Greek religion and offered a critical appreciation of this approach. I argued that the neglect of religion as a personal experience and as a matter of thought is one of the unfortunate side effects of the polis-religion model on scholarship in the field, which frequently favours religious agency. This chapter explores a dimension of ancient Greek religion that takes the individual believer – and the student of ancient Greek religion – well beyond the boundaries of the polis and its socio-political institutions, both physically and intellectually. The goal is to demonstrate the benefit of a perspective that is not focused primarily on religious agency, control and power as mediated and overseen by the polis. Instead, I investigate the modes of thinking that informed ancient Greek religion as well as some of the concepts that underlay it: what we might want to call the 'cognitive dimension' of ancient Greek religion.

How can we access what and how the Greeks thought about their gods? In the absence of a prescriptive creed and other explicit reflections about the modes and modalities of human/divine interaction, the cognitive dimension of ancient Greek religion inevitably seems lost to us. Can an

---

[1] Greenblatt 1988: 6. [2] Kippenberg 1985/1986: vii.

interdisciplinary perspective, perhaps, help us recover how the Greeks conceived of the divine and its availability to human knowledge? A look beyond classical studies reveals a rich literature investigating how the human mind conceives of and processes certain kinds of information (cognitive theory).[3] However, cognitive theory is frequently quite abstract, and it is not always easy to see how it can help us to illuminate the ancient evidence.[4] It may therefore be more useful to take as our point of departure a scholar working in a neighbouring discipline who has successfully studied the thoughts of a past culture. I will return to the discussion of cognitive literature later in this chapter.

In *The Great Cat Massacre* Robert Darnton promoted a way of writing French cultural history that focused explicitly on past ways of thinking and on the strategies we need to employ in order to recover them.[5] He started from a seemingly eccentric source, the notes of a worker recounting his time as an apprentice in a printing shop in pre-revolutionary Paris.[6] These notes describe a strange ritual: the mass killing of cats after mock trials, which some residents of eighteenth-century Paris found hilariously funny. Starting from this dark and macabre episode, the funny side of which largely escapes us today, Darnton gradually recovered the cultural associations and ways of thinking which made the ritualised killing of cats meaningful. Contextualised in various symbolic systems and contemporary discourses 'the great cat massacre' turns out to be an elaborate social commentary in which cats served as placeholders in a 'metonymic insult' targeting equally the bourgeois lifestyle, differences of class and female sexuality.[7]

In Darnton's account, then, the strange and unfamiliar does not merely highlight the difference between the past and the present. That which seems obscure and peculiar to us today becomes a pathway into *l'histoire des mentalités* – the ways of thinking, the cosmologies and the mythologies of a past culture. Darnton spoke of the need 'to be shaken out of a false sense of familiarity with the past, to be administered doses of culture shock'.[8] Our failure to understand signifies the gap between past and present and points to the need to dig much deeper into the past: 'When we cannot get a proverb, or a joke, or a ritual, or a poem, we know we are on to something. By picking at the document where it is most opaque, we may

---

[3] The literature on cognitive theory is vast. For some accessible general works/introductions see, e.g., Goldman 1986; Branquinho 2001. For the application of cognitive theory in the interdisciplinary study of religions see Lawson and McCauley 1990; Andresen 2001; Tremlin 2006; Whitehouse and Laidlaw 2007; Geertz and Jensen 2010.
[4] For the use of cognitive theory in classical studies see, e.g., Minchin 2001; Beck 2006.
[5] Darnton 1984.   [6] Darnton 1984: 75–104.   [7] Darnton 1984: 99.   [8] Darnton 1984: 4.

be able to unravel an alien system of meaning. The thread might even lead
into a strange and wonderful world view.'[9]

This chapter also starts from a somewhat eccentric source: an excerpt
from Semus' lost *History of Delos* (Δηλιάς), dating perhaps from the late
third century BC. It is preserved in Athenaeus' *Deipnosophistae*, a loosely
conceived collection of learned tales and fragments of earlier authors dating
from the third century AD.[10] Even though the story of laughter – first lost
and then regained – as told by Athenaeus/Semus is certainly less disturbing
than the killing of cats in pre-revolutionary France, we may share Darnton's
experience of wonder in not getting the joke. After all, the story features a
scene in which the human protagonist laughs at a divine image, and what
is at stake in this peculiar account is by no means immediately obvious.
By relating the series of incidents featured in the story to the 'surrounding
world of significance', and by drawing various interpretative lines between
the text and its cultural, historical and, indeed, cognitive context, Greek
ways of thinking about the gods become intelligible. So, let us start at the
beginning: with the story itself.

PARMENISCUS' JOURNEY

Παρμενίσκος δὲ ὁ Μεταποντῖνος, ὥς φησιν Σῆμος ἐν ε΄ Δηλιάδος, καὶ γένει
καὶ πλούτῳ πρωτεύων εἰς Τροφωνίου καταβὰς καὶ ἀνελθὼν οὐκ ἔτι γελᾶν
ἐδύνατο. καὶ χρηστηριαζομένῳ περὶ τούτου ἡ Πυθία ἔφη· εἴρῃ μ᾽ ἀμφὶ γέλω-
τος, ἀμείλιχε, μειλιχίοιο· δώσει σοι μήτηρ οἴκοι· τὴν ἔξοχα τῖε. ἐλπίζων δ᾽ ἂν
ἐπανέλθῃ εἰς τὴν πατρίδα γελάσειν, ὡς οὐδὲν ἦν πλέον, οἰόμενος ἐξηπατῆσθαι
ἔρχεταί ποτε κατὰ τύχην εἰς Δῆλον· καὶ πάντα τὰ κατὰ τὴν νῆσον θαυμάζων
ἦλθεν καὶ εἰς τὸ Λητῷον, νομίζων τῆς Ἀπόλλωνος μητρὸς ἄγαλμά τι θεωρήσειν ἀξιόλογον· ἰδὼν δ᾽ αὐτὸ ξύλον ὂν ἄμορφον παραδόξως ἐγέλασεν. καὶ τὸν
τοῦ θεοῦ χρησμὸν συμβάλλων καὶ τῆς ἀρρωστίας ἀπαλλαγεὶς μεγαλωστὶ
τὴν θεὸν ἐτίμησεν.

But Parmeniscus of Metapontum, as Semus states in Book 5 of his *History of
Delos*, a distinguished man by birth and wealth, was unable to laugh after he
had descended into and returned from the oracle of Trophonius. And when he
inquired at Delphi about this matter the Pythia replied: 'You, implacable one, ask
me about soothing laughter; the mother will give it to you at home; honour her
greatly.' He expected that if he returned back home he would be able to laugh
again. When events did not turn out according to plan, he believed that he had
been deceived. By chance he once went to Delos. He marvelled at all the things the
island had to offer and also entered the temple of Leto, assuming that the statue
of Apollo's mother would be something noteworthy to gaze at. But when he saw

---

[9] Darnton 1984: 5.   [10] *FGrHist* 396 F10 = Ath. 14.614a–b.

that it was just a misshapen piece of wood he unexpectedly burst into laughter. He understood the meaning of the oracle and, cured from his inability, he honoured the goddess extensively.

A critically inclined mind might, of course, observe that the story, as told by Athenaeus/Semus, shows suspicious signs of literary fashioning. Above all, Parmeniscus' adventure follows the set pattern of human misinterpretation of divine language well known from oracle stories in Greek literature.[11] It also features the revelation of the meaning of oracular ambiguity in a not entirely unexpected twist, a topos that features prominently within the oracular genre.[12] Is this perhaps just another aetiological story that explains a particular dedication, as Felix Jacoby and others have suggested?[13] The inventory of the Letoon of the year 156/5 BC mentions a bronze plaque dedicated by a certain Parmiscus, generally believed to be identical with the Parmeniscus of our story.[14] Moreover, the historicity of Parmeniscus is also attested by Diogenes Laertius, who describes him in passing as a Pythagorean philosopher.[15]

As I will illustrate in this chapter, the account relating Parmeniscus' multiple encounters with the divine has something interesting to say about Greek perceptions of the divine because of – not despite – its narrative shaping. As Darnton pointed out, historical storytelling, like all storytelling, 'sets the action in a frame of reference; it assumes a certain repertory of associations and responses on the part of its audience; and it provides meaningful shape to the raw stuff of experience'.[16] I will argue that the way in which Parmeniscus' experience of the divine is framed and presented in the account of Athenaeus/Semus grants us an invaluable glimpse into Greek representations of divinity – in both word and wood – and into the modes of thinking associated with them.

THEORIA AND THE GREEK RELIGIOUS GAZE

To begin our inquiry into the meaning of the story, let us start at the end when Parmeniscus gazes at the statue of the goddess Leto and, rather unexpectedly (παραδόξως), bursts into laughter. One way in which classical scholars have started to explore the mental conceptions and modes of

---

[11] See, e.g., Kindt 2006; 2007; 2008.
[12] See Fontenrose 1978: 58–87; Maurizio 1993; Bowden 2005: 49–51.
[13] Jacoby in *RE* II.2 (1923): 1358. Fontenrose 1978: 328 classified this oracle story as not genuine. On these kinds of aetiological stories see also Steiner 2001: 82.
[14] See *IDélos* 1417 A col. I, 109–11. Bruneau 1970: 211, n. 3 and Romano 1980: 203 identify the Parmiscus of the bronze dedication with the Parmeniscus of our story.
[15] D. L. 9.20.   [16] Darnton 1984: 78.

thought of the ancient world is through the paradigm of vision. As Hans Gerhard Kippenberg has stated in another context, seeing is always an act of information processing and as such is partial, partisan and biased.[17] Ekphrasis, 'an extended and detailed literary description of any object, real or imaginary', in particular provides a direct way into ancient ways of looking and into the patterns of thought associated with them.[18] But subtler, less detailed and openly descriptive references to how the world takes shape in the eyes of the beholder have also been instructive for classical scholars in establishing different ways of looking in the ancient world: the aesthetic gaze (focused on the aesthetic qualities of artistic objects, such as statues), the erotic gaze (focused on the gendered features of the human body) and the religious gaze, to name just a few examples.[19]

What is the religious gaze? Jas Elsner and other scholars of ancient art history have established the existence of a specifically religious way of looking in the ancient world ('religious visuality').[20] The religious gaze, according to Elsner, is oriented towards the ritual function of material artefacts, such as cult statues. The ritual-centred way of 'looking on' is different from other, competing forms of visuality, most notably, perhaps, from the traditional subject of Greek art history, the naturalism of classical *mimēsis*. Religious visuality is not primarily concerned with the aesthetic quality of objects and artefacts; its main focus is their function in religious ritual. Religious gazing applies whenever a viewer finds himself face to face with a material object (a sanctuary, a temple, a statue) that lends itself as an entry point to religious and/or mythological reflection. It features prominently in Pausanias' *Description of Greece*, an account driven by the desire to ground the Greece of Pausanias' present (the second century AD) in a mythical and divine landscape of past glory through a focus on material objects.[21]

Religious visuality also features in a more institutionalised form, however, as a central aspect of what Andrea Nightingale has referred to as the 'cultural practice' of *theōria*.[22] In his survey of *theōria* Ian Rutherford

---

[17] Kippenberg 1985/1986: vii (see the epigraph above).
[18] The definition is by Ruston from the *Oxford Classical Dictionary* (p. 515). On *ekphrasis* see also Heffernan 1993; Goldhill 1994; Webb 2009 and the contributions to the special issue on *ekphrasis* in *CPh* 102 (2007), in particular the programmatic articles by Bartsch and Elsner 2007 and Goldhill 2007.
[19] The different kinds of gaze, including the aesthetic and erotic, are described in Elsner 2007: xi–xvii. On the erotic gaze see also Goldhill 2001c and Vout 2007 (in the context of Imperial Rome).
[20] Elsner 1995: 88–124, 125–58; 2007: 29–66. See also Platt 2002.
[21] See Rutherford 2001; Hutton 2005b; Elsner 2007: 29–48.
[22] Nightingale 2004: 40–71. On *theōria* see also Rutherford 1995; 2000; 2001. On the larger topic of religious pilgrimage (including *theōria*) in the Greco-Roman world, see the excellent collection of Elsner and Rutherford 2005. On pilgrimage see also Dillon 1997; Rutherford 2000.

sketched the semantic spectrum of this complex concept.[23] *Theōria* and related words or idioms (such as θεωρός and κατὰ θεωρίαν) could be used in different contexts to refer to 'a type of festival or show', 'being a spectator at a festival', 'a sacred delegation', 'a consultant at an oracle', 'an official sent out to announce festivals' and 'a state official'. More general uses include 'sightseeing' and 'exploration'. The core meaning of the concept, however, seems to revolve around a key set of elements: *theōria* typically involved travel (the theoric journey), a sacralised mode of looking at a specific object or of watching a theoric event, such as religious games, and, possibly, the return home and re-entry into society with a report of the things perceived and learned.[24] There were three typical purposes of *theōria*: to visit a religious festival, to consult an oracle and to undertake a journey for one's own instruction. While the first two forms can be carried out by an individual or a public delegation, the last form existed only as a purely personal experience, of which Solon's travels after his reforms at Athens are an obvious example.[25]

Our story does not explicitly refer to Parmeniscus' adventures as *theōria*. In fact, the concept of *theōria* is not mentioned at all, and the verb *theōrein* (to look at, to behold) is used only in regard to Parmeniscus' activity at Delos prior to entering the temple of Leto. However, the story features – even highlights – key elements of *theōria*: travel to special religious sites, such as oracles and temples, and gazing on a religious object (the statue). We do not hear whether Parmeniscus originally travels to Trophonius on state business or whether his trip concerns religious or other matters, but it is certainly a deeply private concern that drives him to visit Delphi and later Delos. The incidents related in the story can therefore be read as a sequence of multiple acts of personal *theōria*.[26]

Parmeniscus' first trip to the oracular institution of Trophonius initiates, even necessitates, further contact with the divine insofar as his continued inability to laugh poses a problem that is put to the Delphic oracle.[27] The response he receives at Delphi seems at first to send him back home, but it

---

[23] Rutherford 2000: 134–8. Rutherford's account effectively supersedes various older attempts to outline the meaning of *theōros* and *theōria*, e.g. Bill 1901; Buck 1953; Koller 1957. Cf. 'changing cultures of viewing': Goldhill 1996.

[24] Nightingale 2004: 40–4.

[25] Hdt. 1.30. On Solon's *theōria* see Rutherford 2000: 135, 142; 2001: 48; Nightingale 2004: 63–4.

[26] Rutherford 2000: 138–9 refers to Athenaeus' text in passing as an example of a story that reports the viewing subject's response to sacred objects.

[27] The temporary loss of the ability to laugh was a well-attested effect of the oracular procedure at the oracle of Trophonius in Lebadeia (Boeotia). A detailed eyewitness account of the mantic procedure of the oracle during the second century AD can be found in Paus. 9.39.5–40.2. For a discussion of Pausanias' Trophonius see Pirenne-Delforge 2008: 325–31. On Trophonius see Bonnechere 2003. See also Dietrich 1965: 348–51; Clark 1968; Rosenberger 2001a: 35–40.

is not until he has travelled a third time, to the sacred island of Delos, that he reaches full insight and closure. Parmeniscus' three acts of *theōria* are linked to each other in a complex triangular relationship of cross reference and causation. The first two encounters with the gods share the formal identity of oracle consultations, but it is only when he faces the statue of Leto that his ability to laugh, a form of expression that he has lost as a result of his first encounter with the divine at Trophonius, is restored. In an explosive act of parallel causation, his newly regained ability to laugh brings with it insight into the meaning of the Delphic oracle.

There are also differences between Parmeniscus' three encounters with the gods. The first two journeys are intentional acts of *theōria*, carried out to gain specific information from the gods. The third, the one that brings final insight, happens 'by chance' (κατὰ τύχην) and without a definite question in mind.[28] The way in which this third encounter with the gods features in the story contributes specifically to the scholarly debate surrounding the problems involved in distinguishing between sacred and secular *theōria*.[29] Parmeniscus' final trip to Delos starts off as a case of secular *theōria*, directed towards the pure enjoyment of the island's tourist sites. Rather unexpectedly, it turns into a form of religious *theōria* when he gains insight into the poetics of divine representation (in the form of oracles and statues) and, in doing so, into the inscrutable ways of divinity. The story shows that what defines religious *theōria* is not necessarily where it unfolds, nor on what kind of objects it is focused, as Rutherford and others have argued.[30] It is defined by a certain form of (religious) visuality, which is distinguished from other (worldly) ways of looking on.[31]

STATUES AND THE INQUIRY INTO DIVINITY

In order to understand what is at stake behind Parmeniscus' continued focus on divine representations, it may be worth bringing cognitive theory into the picture at this point and considering what it has to offer with regard to human perceptions of the divine. Cognitive approaches towards religion variously stress the fact that anthropomorphism is a strategy of the human mind to come to terms with a profoundly complex, over-determined and potentially dangerous world.[32] In order to survive in this

---

[28] Ath. 14.614b.
[29] E.g., Rutherford 2000; Elsner and Rutherford 2005: 21–2; Scullion 2005.
[30] See Rutherford 2000: 139; 2001: 43–4. See also Cohen 1992.
[31] At the same time religious *theōria* is also enacted and embodied in the most worldly and visceral of activities, namely laughter (see below).
[32] Guthrie 2007 (with further literature).

world, the human mind is fundamentally hard-wired to detect the presence of other agents (i.e., gods) which may potentially affect our lives.[33] One way of doing this is to look for the physical manifestations of such beings – hence the human inclination to see faces in random cloud formations in the sky. Another is to deduce the presence of such agents from the physical traces they allegedly leave – hence the inclination to wonder whether the manifestation of a highly unlikely occurrence is due to chance or whether it reflects supernatural agency. From the cognitive point of view religion is a 'system of thought and action for interpreting and influencing the world, built on anthropomorphic and animistic premises'.[34] Religion, in this perspective, appears to be a fundamentally human way of 'making sense' of the world – a conception of the link between religion and the world we inhabit that is in itself problematic and that I will examine in more detail in the next two chapters.[35]

The production of statues representing divinities is part of this more general human inclination to conceive of the world as inspired and meaningful. It grounds fairly abstract assumptions about the existence of supernatural agents firmly within the human sphere by giving them a physical presence. To give the gods a body – any body – allows humanity to seek to influence, perhaps even control, the world by interacting with these agents in a variety of tangible ways. Statues of gods and goddesses were focal points of Greek religious discourse.[36] Often (though not always) they were housed in the temple of their respective divinity and represented this divinity in various ritual contexts associated with it.[37]

Once they were ceremonially installed in their *naos*, they could become the focus of intense prayer and worship. Some statues enjoyed offerings of food and drink in their temples and on the altars outside.[38] Others even received specially fabricated garments.[39] Every now and then some statues also left their homes and were carried through their host community in a sacred procession.[40] In these different rituals, statues served as focal points

---

[33] See, e.g., Boyer 2001: 137–68; Andresen 2001; Guthrie 2001; Tremlin 2006: 107–42.

[34] Guthrie 2007: 37.

[35] Cf. religion as an 'attempt to reduce chaos to order': Guthrie 2007: 44.

[36] See Gladigow 1985/1986; Burkert 1985: 88–92; Vernant 1991: 158–9; Gaifman 2006. See Mylonopoulos 2010: 1–19 on the difficult distinction between cult statue and votive statues.

[37] Temples were not a necessary precondition for the erection of a divine statue; statues could exist without temples. E.g., *ThesCRA* II. 5: 417–507: 418 (with further evidence). See Scheer 2000: 54–66 for rituals involving divine images.

[38] Burkert 1985: 89; Graf 2001: 230; Steiner 2001: 106–13.

[39] The most prominent example is arguably the new *peplos* which is handed over to Athena Polias at the festival of the greater Panathenaia. See, e.g., Barber 1992; Steiner 2001: 103. See also Graf 2001: 229, n. 10.

[40] Burkert 1985: 100–1.

in human attempts to obtain divine favours, for example by offering the gods dedications, prayer and sacrifice. Cognitively speaking and put in more abstract terms, by visualising the existence of agents more powerful than us, by giving them a physical body and by incorporating them into a variety of rituals, humanity seeks to mediate between the vastness of the universe (those aspects which are beyond human grasp) and the necessities of everyday life.

One problem with cognitive approaches to religion is that while they may explain the neurological foundations of all religions rather well, what they can contribute to our understanding of a particular religious culture, such as that of the ancient Greeks, is much more difficult to assess. In order to move beyond general and generalising statements about the cognitive function of anthropomorphism and divine representations as such we must therefore subject the cognitive perspective itself to cultural analysis. We must ask what is specifically Greek about how the divine body was imagined and represented – a line of inquiry which will eventually bring us back to Parmeniscus and his puzzling response to Leto's image.

A striking feature of ancient Greek representations of divinity in statuary form is the fact that there are surprising differences in the extent to which they did or did not resemble the human body.[41] Starting from fairly simple representations of the gods made out of wood or metal during the archaic period (later sometimes referred to as *xoana*), Greek statuary representation gradually moved towards more complex anthropomorphic sculptures crafted in marble, bronze and ivory.[42] In the fifth century BC, this form of religious imagination and artistic workmanship saw its culmination in the famous chryselephantine statues, with golden robes draping ivory bodies of the divine that were fabricated around a wooden core.[43] Statues like Phidias' acclaimed Zeus at Olympia (ca. 430 BC) and his Athena Parthenos of the Acropolis (ca. 447–438 BC) did not just aspire to imitate the human bodily form, they frequently exceeded it both in size and by turning the divine statue into something more perfect and gleaming than the human body. The *agalma* of the god or goddess was both a dedication to divinity

---

[41] See Vernant 1991: 35–6 for the point that Greek anthropomorphism did not imitate the human body, but that in Greek thought 'the human body reflects the divine model as the inexhaustible source of a vital energy'. On the problematic anthropomorphism of the Greek gods see also Henrichs 2010: 32–5.

[42] As Donohue 1988: 121–50 has shown, *xoanon* came to adopt the meaning of archaic, wooden cult statue only relatively late, in the context of the iconoclastic polemic of the first century BC. Until then the meaning of *xoanon* was much broader and much less clearly defined. It referred to different kinds of statues as well as to other carved objects. See Donohue 1988: 9–53.

[43] Burkert 1985: 91. For the chryselephantine statues see in particular Lapatin 2001.

and a representation and an evocation of it, 'glorious gifts in which the gods must also delight'.[44]

When considering these developments it may be tempting to assume, as older scholarship has done, a gradual evolutionary progression from relatively simple, aniconic wooden statues to complex and fully anthropomorphic representations of divinity.[45] But even though the Greeks were eventually able to craft fully anthropomorphic statues, aniconic representations never went completely out of fashion. Indeed, iconic modes of divine representation coexisted with simpler, semi-iconic or aniconic ways of indicating the presence of the Greek gods.[46] The Argive Heraion, for example, accommodated two cult images when Pausanias visited it: a gold and ivory statue of the goddess (by Polycleitus) as well as a much older and simpler representation of the same goddess.[47] Another example is the Athenian Acropolis, which came to house several representations of Athena, including Phidias' colossal chryselephantine statue of Athena Parthenos and a much older and simpler representation of Athena Polias, which, according to Pausanias, had once fallen from the sky.[48]

Because of the continued presence of the older, aniconic statues in Greek sanctuaries and because of their continuous involvement in Greek religious ritual, classical scholars have come to see different types of sculptural representations of the Greek gods as complementary and competing statements of Greek religious discourse concerning the nature of divinity.[49] All divine images have to mediate between two diverging thoughts: the general otherworldliness of the supernatural on the one hand, and the need to make the supernatural tangible and available to human interaction/knowledge on the other. Fritz Graf speaks of two divergent necessities that motivate and quite literally shape divine representations: the necessity to make the absent (and ultimately unknowable) present and the necessity of maintaining the insurmountable ontological gap separating humanity from divinity.[50] The result is a fundamental 'ambivalence' (Graf) of all divine images between human productions and divine representations.[51]

---

[44] Burkert 1985: 91. This gleaming quality is sometimes also captured in white paint in depictions of statues on vases, see Schefold 1937: 66.

[45] See, e.g., Homolle 1879. See Donohue 1988; 2005: 38–56; Spivey 1996: 29; Gaifman 2010 for a criticism of this perspective.

[46] Donohue 1988: 5 defines the worship of aniconic sculptures as 'the veneration of objects that represent but do not purport to show the appearance of deities'.

[47] Paus. 2.17.4–5. See Romano 1980: 3 with further examples.

[48] Paus. 1.24.5–26.7. See also Herington 1955; Graf 2001: 236.

[49] See, e.g., Gordon 1979; Steiner 2001: 103; Graf 2001: 237–43; Gaifman 2010: 67; Platt 2011: 77–123.

[50] Graf 2001: 234–5.   [51] Graf 2001: 229.

The cruder and less naturalistic form of the semi- and aniconic statues highlights the discrepancy between divinity and its material representation in a much more immediate way than iconic representations of divinity. They virtually compel the viewer to acknowledge the very fact that humanity can engage with divinity only mediated. As Steiner put it, '[c]oncealment and containment . . . form two dimensions of the single enterprise: in assuming a form or body not his or her own, the god simultaneously masks and contains an untenable force'.[52] The aniconic statue demarcates the presence of divinity, but not by imitating the human body; its crude form captures and stresses the unbridgeable gap separating the human from the divine sphere.

By contrast, iconic sculptural representations of divinity externalise the divine essence that aniconic representations of divine presence seek to conceal. They communicate the otherworldliness of the divine through a surplus of splendour and bodily perfection.[53] The literary sources describing iconic sculpture abound in words expressing the shining radiance of artistic workmanship. Gold, silver, bronze and marble were used to bring out the otherworldly quality of the gods in the very material of their cult images.[54]

What does Parmeniscus see when he enters the temple of Leto? We cannot know. Although the Letoon at Delos has been excavated by the French, the wooden statue of the goddess had perished long before. Nonetheless, we can at least get an idea if we look more carefully at what remains of the temple. Cult statues, like the one of the goddess Leto at Delos, were not just stashed away in some dark corner but were typically placed on a pedestal in the middle of the *naos*. Excavations at Delos have revealed the foundations of the base on which Leto's statue was placed, and from these foundations, which measured 2.20 by 2.90 metres, we can infer that the statue was probably considerably larger than life.[55] Moreover, the very temple inventory of the Letoon that mentions Parmiscus' dedication also provides a variety of information on the cult statue.[56] From the inscription we learn that Leto was indeed made of wood, that she was clothed in a linen *chitōn* and mantle, and that she was wearing sandals. We also read

---

[52] Steiner 2001: 81. See also Vernant 1991: 153–5.   [53] Steiner 2001: 104.

[54] See Gordon 1979: 13; Vernant 1991: 36–45.

[55] Gallet de Santerre 1959: 44 with pls. IV, XXXV (6). It is, of course, also a possibility that a second pedestal with a much smaller statue was placed upon the foundations, but there is no archaeological evidence suggesting this.

[56] *IDélos* 1417 AI, 100–117.

that she was seated on a wooden throne featuring tortoiseshell and ivory inlay.[57]

EXPERIENCE AND EXPECTATION

When Parmeniscus crosses the threshold of the temple of Leto and looks at the statue of the goddess, he enters a distinctly religious space.[58] But according to the story he does not seem to find what he expected. The shape and quality of the larger-than-life statue appear to direct Parmeniscus' gaze to its own crude materiality, rather than to its role as a representation of divinity. The aesthetic dimension of the statue (or rather, the lack of it), at least at first sight, seems to deny it any role as the focal point of religious discourse. Through the eyes of the viewing subject, Leto's 'looks' are presented as quite literally disappointing.

It may indeed be tempting to point out that in highlighting Parmeniscus' disappointment the story reflects typically Hellenistic or later expectations of how divinity should be represented, but this would be to misunderstand the principles and practices of divine representation in ancient Greek religion more generally. From the epic tradition onwards there was a clear expectation that the gods looked like men.[59] Representations of men, however, gradually became naturalistic from the seventh century onwards, and so did representations of divinity.[60] Parmeniscus' encounter with Leto, it follows, flags the representation of divinity in the human sphere as a problem intrinsic to ancient Greek religion as early as its representation in epic poetry.

However, the clash between aniconic and iconic representations of divinity changed over time. By the fifth century BC the fully anthropomorphic images of the Greek gods and goddesses had become default objects of religious veneration.[61] In particular the statues produced by famous artists (such as Phidias' Zeus or Praxiteles' Aphrodite of Cnidus) were sometimes

---

[57] More information on Leto's possessions comes to us from the epigraphic evidence: for example, that her *himation* was adorned with purple dye in the third century BC. See *IG* XI 154 A, 21–22. See also Romano 1980: 203.

[58] Of course Parmeniscus had already entered religious space when he entered the sanctuary. The temple, however, provides a much more immediate framing for the viewing of the cult statue it housed. It therefore makes sense that the story refers to the temple (and not the sanctuary) to highlight the transition (and transformation) of the viewing subject. On the temple as a frame for the viewing of a divine statue see also Graf 2001: 234.

[59] See, e.g., Vernant 1980: 36–9. On epiphany see Platt 2011.

[60] See Osborne 1998: 75–85, 159–63. See also ch. 6 (with specific examples).

[61] Vernant 1980: 152; Graf 2001: 236–8.

visited for the purpose of sightseeing and appreciation of their aesthetic qualities. To be sure, the older, aniconic statues were still present, but they had come to fill the role of an altogether different category of divine representation. Graf spoke of a 'dichotomy of function' between the two types of image. On the one hand there were the fully anthropomorphic cult statues which provided a focal point of human/divine encounter and which signified the principal (if never complete) availability of the divine to human interaction and knowledge.[62] On the other hand, the older, semi- or aniconic divine statues crafted out of wood assumed a more subversive role. They always had a peculiar air about them, but, as in our story, they featured increasingly in contexts highlighting a reversal of the ordinary and the expected and, in doing so, confronted onlookers with their very own expectations of the divine.[63]

Parmeniscus clearly expects to find a glorious and dazzling representation of Apollo's mother: νομίζων τῆς Ἀπόλλωνος μητρὸς ἄγαλμά τι θεωρήσειν ἀξιόλογον ('assuming that the statue of Apollo's mother would be something noteworthy to gaze at').[64] What he finds instead is an unsightly statue that alludes to the human bodily form, the wooden origins of which are still all too visible: ἰδὼν δ' αὐτὸ ξύλον ὂν ἄμορφον παραδόξως ἐγέλασεν ('But when he saw that it was just a misshapen piece of wood he unexpectedly burst into laughter').[65] In depicting the clash between Parmeniscus' expectation of the divine and his experience of it, the story reflects the tension between aniconic and iconic representations of divinity.

Elsner has pointed out that '[v]iewing the sacred is a process of divesting the spectator of all the social and discursive elements which distinguish his or her subjectivity from that of the gods into whose space the viewer will come'.[66] Religious visuality unfolds in and defines a distinctly religious space in which the experiences and expectations of everyday life are temporarily set aside to enable a more immediate encounter with the divine, an encounter that follows its own (religious) rules and regulations. '[R]itual-centred visuality denies the appropriateness of . . . interpreting images through the rules and desires of everyday life.'[67]

Parmeniscus' experience at Delos, as told by Athenaeus/Semus, highlights the very moment of 'divesting' as a precondition of experiencing

---

[62] Graf 2001: 237.

[63] The post-classical period witnessed the emergence of various narratives, which featured semi- or aniconic divine statues in a way that raised human attention to the manifold ways in which divinity might reveal itself. See, e.g., Paus 10.19.3. For further examples see, e.g., Donohue 1988: 237–476; Steiner 2001: 82–5.

[64] Ath. 14.614b.   [65] Ath. 14.614b.   [66] Elsner 2007: 23.   [67] Elsner 2007: 25.

the true nature of the divine. The whole account hinges on Parmeniscus' sudden, almost explosive transition from a state of ignorance to a state of insight and learning. Parmeniscus first appreciates the island's attractions from a purely aesthetic point of view. The word used to describe his gaze prior to entering the temple of Leto is *thaumazein*, to wonder, to marvel at. When he finally enters the temple, he extends this aesthetic visuality to the statue of the goddess. But the statue of Leto does not provide a trajectory for the aesthetic gaze. It redirects this gaze back to the viewing subject. The surprise caused by the apparent drastic mismatch between his expectation of the divine statue and its actual manifestation triggers Parmeniscus' laughter. In doing so it prepares him for the transition from an externalised gaze, focused on the surface of things and on the ornamental, to a much deeper religious vision, based on an aesthetics that appreciates the specific mode of representation of the aniconic statue. The purely external appreciation of aesthetic qualities turns into a deeper, more penetrating and complex vision focused on the quality of divinity, in particular of divine representation. This form of *thaumazein* does not precede the form of understanding reached through *theōria*, but is part of the theoric gaze.[68] Parmeniscus' laughter, we may assume, changes in quality as it becomes self-reflective.[69] It starts off as a naïve and unreflected response to the apparent crudeness of divine form and turns into an astonished appreciation of the complexities of divine representation as Parmeniscus grasps the meaning of the oracle.

The series of incidents related in the story draw direct and multiple links between representations of divinity in the form of speech (oracles) and statues. The story juxtaposes the ambiguous oracle Parmeniscus receives at Delphi with the statue of Leto and its way of signification: the temporary breakdown of divine representation (the fact that the statue does not conform to Parmeniscus' expectation) brings about the revelation of divine meaning (the oracle). The story highlights the visual aspect of *theōria* as a cultural institution while at the same time drawing our attention to the very fact that religious visuality extends far beyond the physical act of gazing. Oracles, too, draw on elements of pictorial signification. In the metaphors and other tropes they use as carriers of their meaning, oracles make use of images in much the same way as divine statues.

[68] On *thaumazein* as part of *theōria* see Nightingale 2004: 261.
[69] Halliwell 2008: 5 spoke of the 'double-sided character' of laughter in Greek thought and literature 'at the interface . . . between body and mind, between instinct and intention'. In our story laughter appears likewise as a double-sided gesture that accompanies, even instigates, the transition from a state of ignorance to a state of insight.

The link between the semantics of both types of imagery is reflected through the perception of the viewing subject. Parmeniscus responds to both representations of divinity – oracles and statues – in exactly the same way. His encounters with the divine are driven by his expectations concerning the nature of divinity, in particular of divine representation in the human sphere. Parmeniscus expects oracles to speak in human language. Human language is characterised by the attempt to minimise ambiguity in order to maximise success in the transmission of information. Except perhaps in poetic language, which draws explicitly on polysemy, in the human sphere ambiguity is nothing but a semantic possibility prior to its realisation in actual speech.[70] The fact that Parmeniscus is not yet ready to engage in this other type of visuality, which is, at least to some extent, disengaged from personal circumstance, is nicely expressed by the very fact that he can conceive of the 'mother' featuring in the oracular response as referring only to his own.[71] Religious visuality involves a much broader and more detached way of 'reading' images.

Just as Parmeniscus expects the oracle to speak in plain human language, he assumes that divine statues represent divinity in human form. Both expectations are frustrated in the end. Parmeniscus' first response is to suspect deception: οἰόμενος ἐξηπατῆσθαι ('he believed that he had been deceived').[72] This suspicion is typical of those mortals in Greek thought and literature who cannot (yet) read the poetics of divine representation.[73] Jean-Pierre Vernant spoke of the 'inevitable tension' that all forms of divine representations must introduce: 'The idea is to establish real contact with the world beyond, to actualise it, to make it present, and thereby to participate intimately in the divine; yet by the same move, it (the divine idol) must also emphasise what is inaccessible and mysterious in divinity, its alien quality, its otherness.'[74] Parmeniscus does not yet understand the subtle balance between identity and alterity that every divine representation must strike if it is to remain a meaningful mediator between the human and divine spheres.[75] He eventually learns to adopt a much deeper gaze that penetrates the surface of verbal and material images in order to capture what lies beneath.

---

[70] See Kindt 2007: 7.

[71] A similar mistake is made by the sons of the Roman king Tarquinius Superbus: Livy 1.56.10–11.

[72] Ath. 14.614a.

[73] I.e., the complaint of Croesus at the Delphic oracle in Hdt. 1.90–91 and the chorus's suspicions about the Delphic response in E. *Ion* 685.

[74] Vernant 1991: 153; see also 1991: 314–17.

[75] On oracular ambiguity as a mediation triple see Kindt 2008.

In visualising Parmeniscus' change of perspective the story draws attention to larger questions concerning the identity of divinity and its representation in the human sphere. It is significant that Parmeniscus learns that the gods both are and are not like mortals by gazing at two images – one evoked in oracular language, one material – both of which challenge and support the anthropomorphism of the Greek gods. The oracular reference to Leto as Apollo's mother confirms the idea that the pantheon is indeed structured in parallel to the human sphere, with its family and other relations. Parmeniscus' subsequent encounter with the wooden statue of Apollo's mother, in contrast, seems to question the notion of anthropomorphic gods by drawing attention to the image's (wooden) materiality and the divine otherness it represents.

In making the connection between imagery crafted in word and in wood, the account of Parmeniscus' multiple encounters with the divine encourages us to compare both forms of divine representation.[76] Plain oracular language and iconic sculptures of gods and goddesses provide a way of representing divinity that emphasises the likeness between the human and divine spheres. Both forms of divine representation are oriented towards humanity as the ultimate point of reference for the visualisation and imagination of the divine. Ambiguous divine language and the semi-iconic representation of divinity, in contrast, direct attention to the fact that divinity both is and is not like humanity. According to the same logic, unintelligible sounds and utterances and the aniconic representation of divinity ultimately emphasise alterity and the insurmountable gap that exists between gods and mortals.[77]

It is significant that a breakdown in the iconic sculptural representation of the statue brings about the insight into the ambiguous meaning of the oracle. In juxtaposing both forms of divine representation, the story turns on much more than the simple point that images represent divinity in a way that may look surprisingly different from the way they do at first. Parmeniscus' encounter with the gods defines religious visuality as a complex way of engaging with the divine, which interacts with humanity in different and changing representations.

---

[76] Vernant 1991: 154 argued that archaic idols are not images *stricto sensu*.

[77] Unintelligible speech emphasising the gap between the human and divine spheres features prominently in a passage in Plutarch, in which he describes an oracle consultation going wrong: Plu. *Moralia* 438b. A non-Greek delegation to Delphi tried to consult the Pythia despite an omen indicating that she was not ready to deliver oracles. The divine response to the human attempt to force the Pythia to deliver oracles was expressed via the Pythia's language, which was rough and unintelligible.

Through its narrative appropriation of the religious gaze, the story reflects on the very semantics of religion as a discourse of 'making sense'. The subject's gaze on the divine statue becomes itself a trope for reflection on the nature of divinity and its relationship to humanity.[78] Parmeniscus' encounter with the divine turns into a commentary on the modalities of religious visuality.[79] By referring to generally recognised religious authorities such as the Delphic oracle, the story also gives a certain kind of authority to the religious statements it makes in this respect.

RELIGIOUS VISUALITY AS 'RITUAL-CENTRED VISUALITY' AND 'COGNITIVE VISUALITY'

As I stated above, Elsner understands religious viewing as ritual-centred viewing.[80] Religious gazing conceives of sacred objects, such as altars and cult statues, by appreciating, even insisting on, the role these objects play in religious ritual. In other words, the religious gaze captures predominantly those qualities of altars and cult statues that are significant for the part they play in religious ritual; other information pertaining to these objects, such as aesthetic qualities, not relevant to the way in which they feature in ritual, is left out. Elsner has further explored the ways in which religious gazing features in Greek literature. He has shown that the narrative structure of a text itself can follow (and hence describe) the physical act of gazing. A prime example is Pausanias' description of sixty-nine altars at Olympia, which closely follows the liturgical order of the Elean sacrificial procession and highlights those features of the altars relevant to their role in ritual.[81]

The story, however, suggests that religious visuality should not be limited to ritual-centred visuality. Ritual is, in fact, conspicuously absent from Parmeniscus' multiple encounters with the divine. We hear nothing about the ritual procedure at Trophonius that ultimately causes the inability to laugh or at Delphi that generates oracular responses. Nor do we learn anything about the kind of purifications, sacrifices and prayers involved in the worship of the goddess Leto at Delos. Instead, the story focuses on the statue's impact on the viewing subject, in particular on the gap that Parmeniscus needs to bridge between its form and its content. The structure

---

[78] It is fitting that this story is built around Parmeniscus, a philosopher, since *theōria* (albeit more frequently in its civic form) was widely appropriated in philosophical discourse as a trope for understanding and learning. See Nightingale 2004.

[79] On the debate concerning the problematic distinction between sacred and secular in Greek culture see below n. 82.

[80] Here and below see Elsner 2007: 1–26.   [81] Paus. 5.13.8–15.9 discussed by Elsner 2007: 13–19.

of the narrative turns entirely on Parmeniscus' change of perspective as he learns to appreciate the nature of divinity: his original expectation of divine representations that remains unfulfilled, his interpretative disengagement from his own personal circumstances, and his insight into the versatility of divinity and divine representation. In the story, at least, religious visuality is represented as a mental (cognitive) activity, as an insight gained into the nature of divinity, not as a mere extension of ritual. Religious gazing, we can conclude, should encompass both 'cognitive visuality' and 'ritual-centred visuality' – without, of course, assuming a strict duality between the two.

In tracing Parmeniscus' change of perspective, the story makes an interesting point about the problematic relationship between the sacred and the secular dimensions.[82] One area in which this distinction is under scholarly discussion is with regard to *theōria* and Greek pilgrimage more generally.[83] Is it possible to distinguish sacred from secular (purely recreational) sightseeing? Rutherford suggested that whenever the places visited were religious centres, we should speak of 'sacred sightseeing'.[84] He further argued that the kinds of object viewed may also help to differentiate 'sacred sightseeing' from the secular variant. Religious objects were prime foci of religious travel. For Rutherford their presence can thus serve as a marker of *theōria* as 'sacred sightseeing': 'because the viewing of them took place against the background of a network of religious assumptions it can be described as a religious activity'.[85]

The story told by Athenaeus/Semus, however, complicates the picture. It shows that neither the presence of religious space nor that of religious objects is a sufficient indicator for religious viewing. Parmeniscus employs both types of visuality, religious visuality and another, more worldly (one might say secular) kind of viewing, spatially within the strictly religious context of the Delphic oracle and the temple of Leto. Moreover, he extends both types of visuality to distinctly religious representations: just as he misreads the Delphic oracle, he initially looks at the divine statue in the temple with an aesthetic gaze. Parmeniscus' first way of looking is shaped less by religious than by worldly assumptions. What finally enables him to make

---

[82] The *communis opinio* now seems to be that Greek culture knew no absolute distinction between the two. Connor has shown the sacred and the secular to be two separate yet interrelated realms: Connor 1988. Disagreement, however, erupts concerning the way in which this relationship features in specific contexts, e.g., Scullion 2005.

[83] See above n. 22. As Rutherford 2000: 138, n. 26 has rightly observed, the visual is strangely absent from Dillon's account of Greek pilgrimage: Dillon 1997.

[84] Rutherford 2000: 135. See also the contribution by Cohen 1992, who argued that pilgrims travel to the centre of their world and tourists to the periphery.

[85] Rutherford 2000: 139.

the transition from one type of visuality to the other is his capacity to separate his interpretation from his own personal circumstances. In the story, at least, the distinction between the sacred and the secular (here expressed in the form of different, yet related, types of visuality) is neither solely spatially configured nor solely object-related, but cognitive. The frame of mind with which one enters a given space and looks at a specific object determines whether religious visuality (and hence information processing) applies – or not. In short, it matters less what one looks at, or where one looks, but how.

CONCLUSION

If all this seems a rather large structure to build on a single story, then it may be worth pointing out that the sustained focus on one particular account has revealed not just the religious images and modes of thought contained within it, but also the broader religious concepts and discourses to which this story relates and from which it derives its meaning. Following Darnton's method of using an obscure and seemingly eccentric passage as an entry point to a recovery of past ways of thinking, we have drawn multiple interpretative lines between the text and its cultural and intellectual contexts, gradually revealing the religious concepts, modes of thought, symbolic systems and religious discourses that informed Parmeniscus' various encounters with the divine. The peculiar story about laughter lost and later found as told by Athenaeus/Semus turns out to be a story about human knowledge of the divine, in particular through divine representations as perceived through the eyes of the viewing subject. It illustrates the existence of a cognitive dimension of ancient Greek religion, which, in its focus on the individual believer and his approach to divinity, lies fully outside the principles and practices of polis religion. Starting from Parmeniscus' point of view, however, further research is needed to explore the multiple ways in which divine representations (in both oracles and statues, as our story suggests) reveal Greek modes of thinking about the gods, as well as the subtle changes in these modes over time.

CHAPTER 3

On tyrant property turned ritual object: political power and sacred symbols in ancient Greece and in social anthropology

For it is only by repetition that signs and practices cease to be perceived or remarked; that they are so habituated, so deeply inscribed in every-day routine, that they may no longer be seen as forms of control – or seen at all. It is only then that they come to be (un)spoken of as custom, (dis)regarded as convention – and only disinterred, if at all, on ceremonial occasions, when they are symbolically invoked as eternal verities.

Jean Comaroff and John Comaroff[1]

INTRODUCTION

In the first two chapters of this book I referred variously to ancient Greek religion as a 'symbolic system', a 'language' which allows those fluent in it to 'make sense' of the world they inhabit. The model of polis religion draws on such a conception of ancient Greek religion insofar as it posits the existence of religion as a more or less coherent symbolic order, which maps onto the structures of Greek society. I turn next to an investigation of this notion.

In the interdisciplinary study of religions, the investigation of religion as a symbolic system is most closely associated with the American anthropologist Clifford Geertz. Geertz variously promoted symbolic analysis, both as a theoretical position, for example in his account of religion as a cultural system, and as an interpretative practice, best exemplified, perhaps, in 'Deep play: notes on the Balinese cockfight'.[2] Symbolic analysis focuses on the study of the kind of symbols a particular religious tradition generates, both in terms of symbolic practices (cockfighting in Bali) and conceptions (sin and evil in Christianity). It studies the way in which these symbols correlate with each other and the way in which they relate to the world. Javanese

---

[1] Comaroff and Comaroff 1991: 25.

[2] Cf. 'Religion as a cultural system': Geertz 1973: 87–125. 'Deep play: notes on the Balinese cockfight': Geertz 1973: 412–53.

religion, for example, draws on the conception of evil as resulting from uncontrolled passion. This conception of evil allows the Javanese to distinguish desirable from undesirable behaviour, to identify such behaviour and to control it.[3]

Geertz's account of religion as a cultural (symbolic) system has been immensely influential. It inspired Robert Darnton's account of the ritual killing of cats in pre-revolutionary France (what he referred to as 'the great cat massacre'), for example, which I discussed in the beginning of the last chapter.[4] It was also in many ways implied in our discussion of religious visuality in the previous chapter, insofar as I traced the way in which Parmeniscus' gaze focused on the symbolic nature of divine representations. Within the interdisciplinary study of religions, the analysis of religion as a symbolic language (symbolic analysis) has become a key interpretative tool. Geertz's approach has inspired accounts as divergent as that of Dale Eickelman on the role of religious intellectuals in Muslim societies and of José Casanova on the role of religion in the modern world.[5]

The study of the symbolic dimension of ancient Greek religion is much less popular within classical studies. This is due, at least in part, to a continuing attachment to functionalism as the interpretative tool most appropriate to the pursuit of the larger agenda of current works in the field (see Chapter 1). Functionalism inquires into the significance (function) of a particular religious institution or practice for society. This line of inquiry is best suited to proving the direct relevance of Greek religious beliefs and practices to the polis. As a result of this perspective, however, the symbolic dimension of ancient Greek religion is frequently sidelined or treated as merely an extension of functionalist analysis. It is used to support the notion of a primary, polis-oriented discourse of power as relevant for the study of ancient Greek religion as polis religion.

Ancient Greek religion, however, has also been described as a symbolic language, most notably by John Gould.[6] In his influential article 'On making sense of Greek religion' Gould draws on the work of Clifford Geertz and other eminent social anthropologists in order to give an account of what ancient Greek religion is fundamentally like. This chapter takes as its starting point an investigation of Gould's indebtedness to Geertz and moves to a more general discussion of the conceptualisation of religious symbols in both classical scholarship and social anthropology as indicative of where the two disciplines currently stand relative to each other. I argue

---

[3] Geertz 1973: 131.   [4] Darnton 1984.   [5] Eickelman 1985; Casanova 1994.
[6] Gould 2001. See also Evans 2010: 7.

that ultimately Gould, like Geertz, separated religious symbols from the domain of power. This separation helps us to explain why it is relatively easy to sideline the symbolic dimension altogether in accounts of ancient Greek religion and society. It also illuminates why those scholars interested in the symbolic frequently depict religious symbols as aesthetic phenomena that can (once again) be separated from the 'hard surfaces' of Greek life (that is, from politics and society).[7]

Current ethnographic studies reveal a more productive conceptualisation of religious symbols as intrinsic to socio-political power. The explanatory potential of this approach for the study of ancient Greek religion will be exemplified with regard to the cultural practice of the 'recycling' of symbolic capital after democracy was restored at Athens in 403 BC as testified in a fragment from Philochorus.[8] In promoting a conception of religious symbols as intrinsic to socio-political power and vice versa, this chapter also sets up the discussion of the place of 'magical' practices in a more broadly conceived religious culture of ancient Greece in Chapter 4.

CLIFFORD GEERTZ: SOCIAL ANTHROPOLOGY AS AN INTERPRETATIVE SCIENCE

Culture as a symbolic system

Classical studies and anthropological scholarship have a long history of mutual borrowing and interdisciplinary exchange, but as a way into the relationship between the two disciplines I shall start with a discussion of Geertz, his intellectual context and the responses his work triggered within social anthropology.[9] Geertz's work has become foundational within social anthropology itself and in all other disciplines concerned with the study of culture. Even though social anthropology has now moved decisively beyond Geertz, students of religion as a symbolic system in particular must still respond to his work, and the way in which they have done so reveals important aspects of the dynamics of interdisciplinary debate.[10]

Geertz belonged to a small group of scholars whose individual contributions to the advancement of knowledge formed a coherent agenda adding

---

[7] Morris 1993: 32.   [8] *FGrHist* 328 F181.

[9] See Cartledge 1994 for an outline of the history of the relationship between both disciplines. See also Humphreys 1978: 15–30; Redfield 1991. For two early – now outdated – studies exploring the relationship between anthropology and the classics see Evans 1908; Kluckhohn 1961.

[10] Throughout this chapter I refer to symbols and the 'symbolic dimension' of religion in the Geertzian sense of 'any object, act, event, quality, or relation which serves as a vehicle for a conception – the conception is the symbol's "meaning"': Geertz 1973: 91.

up to a large edifice of ideas. His standing as the most significant champion of the so-called 'interpretative turn' in social anthropology was grounded in the fact that it was developed on two mutually reinforcing planes. His ethnographic agenda evolved in constant oscillation and mutual exchange with more general programmatic reflections on the scope and nature of the concepts used in social anthropology. In this regard, Geertz took his place within a strong trend of social anthropology in the United States at the turn of the twentieth century (Franz Boas, Alfred Kroeber, Robert Lowie) that anticipated the methods of E. E. Evans-Pritchard and Bronislaw Malinowski.[11] That Geertz's framework for the study of religion was developed both in theory and in practice gives those who are keen to learn from him the unique opportunity of exploring the extent to which his conceptual contribution informed and was informed by his ethnographic practice.

In the early 1960s Geertz began to develop the ethnographic agenda that would change social anthropology, the repercussions of which would be felt in neighbouring disciplines.[12] At the time, there was a larger trend in the American social sciences away from behaviourism and the methods of the natural sciences towards interpretation, in particular the interpretation of symbols.[13] Geertz both embraced and advanced this move. He explicitly formulated his position in response to the then prevailing paradigms of positivism and functionalism, which he regarded as reductionist and merely scratching the surface of the kind of analysis social anthropology could offer. He suggested that social anthropology should focus on the study of culture, rather than the narrower concept of society, because culture encompasses a much wider array of ideas, customs, values, motivations and institutions than 'society' is able to include.[14] This was essentially a move away from the Parsonian sociology that had influenced him in his early professional years towards an understanding of anthropology as an interpretative science.[15]

The focus on culture as the key unit of ethnographic inquiry and the radical redefinition of this concept is at the heart of Geertz's contribution to social anthropology and of his ongoing appeal to other areas of scholarly discourse. Following Max Weber's notion of man as 'an animal suspended in webs of significance he himself has spun',[16] Geertz's concept of culture encompasses precisely those webs of significance: 'The culture concept to

---

[11] On this trend as well as on the intellectual influences on Geertz more generally, see Pals 1996: 237.
[12] Early works by Geertz already demonstrate his interest in cultural analysis, see, e.g., Geertz 1960; 1963a; 1963b.
[13] Kuper 1999: 80–2.   [14] See Geertz 1973: 3–30.   [15] See Kuper 1999: 75–121.
[16] Geertz 1973: 5.

which I adhere . . . denotes an historically transmitted pattern of meanings embodied in symbols, a system of inherited conceptions expressed in symbolic forms by means of which men communicate, perpetuate, and develop their knowledge about attitudes toward life.'[17]

Despite such succinct formulations, however, Geertz did not pursue a monolithic concept of culture. In fact, it is in his understanding of it and the way in which it should be researched that one can best trace his intellectual development over time. Richard Parker pointed to a series of subtle shifts in Geertz's concept of culture.[18] Throughout his career, Geertz developed his notion of culture to allow for an ever higher degree of flexibility in the relationship between the symbolic and the non-symbolic. What began as a simple programme for human behaviour was soon extended into a 'model for' and 'model of' reality, and finally turned into a flexible medium of symbolic commentary on society.

The second step is most succinctly formulated in his definition of religion as a cultural system, in which Geertz suggested that religion (like all systems of symbols) serves as both a 'model for' and a 'model of' reality: 'Culture patterns . . . give meaning . . . to social and psychological reality both by shaping themselves to it and by shaping it to themselves.'[19] His work on the Balinese cockfight, in which he showed how the cultural practice of the cockfight reflects the modalities of Balinese society, presents culture as a symbolic medium for social commentary.[20]

Such subtle shifts, however, should not obscure the fact that Geertz's concept of culture in its different forms and formulations is essentially semiotic. It focuses on meaning as encoded in and made possible by socially constructed symbols. To use an example from Geertz himself: whether a contraction of the eyelid is a sympathetic gesture of companionship (winking) or merely a more or less meaningless mannerism (twitching) depends on the situational symbolic value of the movement – a distinction which cannot be captured by a purely formal description.[21] Culture, according to Geertz, is thus the symbolic context that makes meaningful human interaction possible. This context is public, communal and tangible and is, at least in principle, separate and separable from the psychological and social dimensions of society. As Daniel Pals has nicely put it: 'I cannot wink privately at you unless there is something public – a context of meanings – shared by both of us – that enables you to take from the wink the same meaning I give to it.'[22]

---

[17] Geertz 1973: 89.　　[18] Here and in the following see Parker, Richard 1985.
[19] Geertz 1973: 93.　　[20] Geertz 1973: 412–53.　　[21] See Geertz 1973: 6–7.　　[22] Pals 1996: 241.

Although Geertz's concept of culture is essentially semiotic, it is not only semiotic. In his ethnographic studies Geertz at times moved significantly beyond the 'reading' of culture as a symbolic system. His account of Islam in Morocco and Indonesia, for example, includes much information on the historical background of these societies and on their social structure.[23] Here and elsewhere, Geertz managed to investigate culture in its social and historical contexts without, however, reducing it to behavioural and social structures.[24] David Gellner pointed us to a (perhaps not) surprising side effect of this: Geertz had 'more detail on trade, irrigation, land-holding and village-level organisation' than, for example, the Marxist anthropologist Maurice Bloch.[25]

At the same time, Geertz is sometimes accused of neglecting the historical circumstances involved in the production of cultural 'texts'. As William Roseberry asserted, Geertz, in his discussion of the Balinese cockfight, mentioned issues of gender, colonialism and politics as affecting the cockfight, but did not engage in a deeper discussion of their significance in the production and dissemination of cultural symbols.[26] This effectively excluded an historical dimension that would capture the processes in which symbols were shaped.[27]

According to Geertz, the anthropologist's task is to explore cultural patterns of meaning, the symbolic dimension included in social interaction. Adapting a term from the English philosopher Gilbert Ryle, he referred to the practice of ethnography as 'thick description', a term which has since become programmatic of his entire agenda.[28] To give a 'thick description' means to go significantly beyond the narrow, formalistic, 'thin' description of social practices. 'Thick description' explores the deeper symbolic dimension that precedes and is included in social action, a task which Geertz himself exemplified in many of his own ethnographic studies, most notably perhaps on the Balinese cockfight.[29]

Taken together, Geertz's theoretical reflections on the nature of social anthropology and the ethnographic practice of 'thick description' which it informed, inaugurated a profound reorientation of social anthropology 'not as an experimental science in search of law but an interpretative one in search of meaning'.[30] The scope and methods of social anthropology now resembled those of other hermeneutical sciences, which explains

---

[23] Geertz 1968.
[24] See Munson 1986: 23 on how this applies to religion as a cultural system.
[25] Gellner 1999: 141.   [26] Roseberry 1989. See also Sewell 1997: 36.
[27] Cf. ch. 1 on the need to combine synchronic and diachronic analysis.
[28] Ethnography as 'thick description': Geertz 1973: 3–30.   [29] Geertz 1973: 1–37.
[30] Geertz 1973: 5. See also Geertz 1980.

the influence of Geertz on different interpretative traditions such as the new historicism of Stephen Greenblatt and the cultural history of Natalie Zemon Davis and Robert Darnton.[31]

As a result, the ethnographic agenda also changed. Ethnographic research now progressed in a more piecemeal and cumulative manner. Ethnography no longer sought to 'generalize across cases but to generalize within them'.[32] The search for grand syntheses was replaced by a search for an ever more elaborate picture of cultural meanings. Subsequently, various scholars have discussed the preference of the particular over the general as one of the most serious shortcomings of cultural anthropology as an interpretative science.[33] Can there be a true advancement of knowledge generated by interpretative anthropology beyond an ever more detailed (but ultimately unverifiable) description of cultural phenomena – a mode of analysis which has largely lost its capacity to generalise across different cases? Despite such challenging questions, however, Geertz's agenda has had a profound impact on the discipline of social anthropology. With the 'symbolic turn' he inaugurated, social anthropology established itself as the leading strand in the interdisciplinary study of cultures.

Religion as a cultural system

Geertz's views on religion are central to his overall efforts to propagate a semiotic model of culture and the practice of ethnography as 'thick description'. His conceptual piece 'Religion as a cultural system', later republished in his seminal *The Interpretation of Cultures*, is among the most succinct and fully realised formulations of a cultural (symbolic) system.[34] It firmly reflects the second stage in his intellectual development, in which he conceptualised culture as an extremely flexible symbolic medium of 'making sense'.[35] Geertz described the individual elements of religion and their relationship to each other and explored the difference between religion and other symbolic forms of expression, such as art or science. Several

---

[31] These scholars have pioneered methodological approaches for the study of culture. All three explicitly acknowledge the influence of Geertz: Darnton 1984; Greenblatt 1997; Davis 2005.

[32] Geertz 1973: 26.

[33] E.g., Gellner 1999: 136–7; Shankman 1984. Geertz's repositioning of the scope and methods of social anthropology has been widely criticised by scholars from a variety of backgrounds and positions, see, e.g., Ortner 1997. Positivists dislike his move away from the general laws of the social sciences towards lofty symbols. Functionalists have criticised him for neglecting questions of the use and abuse of religious beliefs and practices in society. Finally, postmodernists and those with a general interest in semiotics have taken offence at his concept of signification.

[34] Geertz 1973: 87–125.   [35] See above and Parker, Richard 1985: 63.

aspects of his general definition of culture were developed in detail using religion as an example. In addition, several of his ethnographic studies focused explicitly on the dimension of religion.[36]

Geertz formulated his definition of religion as a series of necessary propositions which he further 'unpacked' throughout his article. He argued that religion is

1) a system of symbols which acts to 2) establish powerful, pervasive, and long-lasting moods and motivations in men by 3) formulating conceptions of a general order of existence and 4) clothing these conceptions with such an aura of factuality that 5) the moods and motivations seem uniquely realistic.[37]

Proposition 1 stresses the symbolic and systematic aspects of religion, thus revealing Geertz's indebtedness to structuralism. A symbol is everything that serves as a vehicle for a conception (the symbol's meaning).[38] Geertz himself mentioned objects, acts, events, qualities and relations as examples. At the heart of his definition of religion, however, is the interplay between ethos and world view, included in propositions 2 and 3. Religious symbols evoke emotions of different intensity; motivations, in contrast, have a 'directional cast' – that is, they make people inclined to act in a certain way.[39] This powerful ethos of religion is grounded in its metaphysical dimension: religion relates these moods and motivations to a general order of existence – this is what makes them powerful, pervasive and long lasting.

The appeal of Geertz's definition of religion lies partly in the balance it strikes between being general and specific, precise and vague. Unlike many other universal definitions of religion that tend to focus on a single essence of the religious, his definition includes a series of essential propositions.[40] These propositions not only include the symbolic dimension, they also explain the appeal of religious symbols to the emotional ('moods and motivations'), the world view that religion constructs ('conceptions of a general order of existence') and, finally, the authoritative and persuasive power of religion, which 'clothes' general conceptions of order in an aura of factuality. The result is an extremely flexible definition encompassing different ways of looking at religion.

---

[36] Geertz explored various religious traditions. His major studies in this area are Geertz 1960; 1968.
[37] Geertz 1973: 90.   [38] See Geertz 1973: 91–4.   [39] See Geertz 1973: 94–8.
[40] 'Essentialist' definitions of religion: Tylor 1871/1873 ('the belief in Spiritual Beings'); Tillich 1963: 4 ('religion is the state of being grasped by an ultimate concern'); Spiro 1966: 96 ('an institution consisting of culturally patterned interaction with culturally postulated superhuman beings'). A universalist (or essentialist) definition of religion is one that seeks to capture the essence of all religions. A historical definition, in contrast, looks at one specific religion in its historical and cultural context. See Saler 1993: 87–157.

At the same time, Geertz intentionally left certain areas of his definition of religion under-theorised. For example, he never spelled out the conceptions of a general order of existence that religion formulates, or whether they are grounded in truth.[41] The reason for this is that although, according to Geertz, all religions necessarily include a metaphysical dimension, they can do this in very different ways. The omission of an explicit evaluation of the truth claims inherent in the metaphysical dimension of religion had the startling result that Geertz's definition was embraced by both theology and the comparative study of religions.[42]

Geertz's universalist definition of religion is in line with his larger concept of culture. He distinguished between the cultural, social and psychological dimensions in order to avoid the reductionism he criticised in functionalist or positivist accounts of religion. He looked at religion first and foremost as a cultural fact in its own right and not, as the functionalists would have it, as a mere expression of social needs and/or economic tensions.[43] At the same time, as Frankenberry and Penner rightly pointed out, although Geertz focused on giving a substantive account of religion as a symbolic system, one should not overlook the fact that a functionalist dimension is included in his definition of religion itself.[44] For Geertz, religion addressed the fundamental human need to create meaning. The definition of religion along these lines thus opens up the study of religion as the 'thick description' of those systems of meanings that religions convey while locating their function in the very nature of *homo semioticus*.

THE SYMBOLIC IN CURRENT SCHOLARSHIP ON ANCIENT GREEK RELIGION

Geertz's definition of religion as a cultural (symbolic) system has been influential in the field of social anthropology and beyond. The analysis of symbols has become an integral asset in the toolbox of social anthropology and the interdisciplinary study of religions alike.[45] In classical scholarship,

---

[41] See Frankenberry and Penner 1999: 634.
[42] Some examples: Lindbeck 1984: 19–29, 30–45; Asad 1993: 43–54; Eickelman 2005. The vagueness in Geertz's definition concerning the nature of this authority and, as a result, the truth value of religion makes his definition appealing for the believer and non-believer alike and prepares the ground for communication between social anthropology and theology: Morgan 1977. Frankenberry and Penner 1999: 621 regarded Geertz's lack of engagement with the truth conditions inherent in his definition of religion as a major flaw.
[43] See Pals 1996: 243.
[44] Frankenberry and Penner 1999: 626. A substantive definition of religion is one that says what religion *is* in contrast to a functionalist one that says what religion *does*.
[45] See, e.g., nn. 2, 5.

however, symbolic analysis plays a much more contested and limited role. Geertz's approach does not translate easily into the study of ancient Greek religion. His model of religion as a symbolic system is too abstract and philosophical to reveal its immediate value for classical scholarship.

If we look at how and where symbolic analysis features in research in the field, it seems to be surprisingly absent. By and large, symbolic analysis has never really taken off in classical scholarship on ancient Greek religion. This relative lack of symbols is due, at least in part, to the fact that classical scholars are still under the spell of functionalism as the interpretative tool best suited to pursue the larger agenda of current works in the field: to prove the direct relevance of Greek religious beliefs and practices for Greek society.[46] If the symbolic dimension features at all, it is mostly as a possible extension of structuralist or functionalist analysis.[47]

It is, of course, impossible to give a comprehensive overview here of the state of the study of religious symbols in classical scholarship. Instead I focus on two specific areas of research – research on the deposition of votive offerings (dedications) at Greek sanctuaries and the study of ritual processions – and investigate how religious symbols feature in current scholarship. How these areas have been approached serves as a background against which I will develop an alternative model of religious signification.

Votives

Classical archaeology has revealed numerous dedications at Greek sanctuaries. Some items, such as *kouroi* and *korai* (statues or statuettes of boys and girls which were popular during the archaic period), representations of body parts (particularly at healing sanctuaries) and statues of gods and goddesses, were specifically produced to serve as votives. Sanctuaries have also yielded a large variety of other items that originally served another purpose, including coins, jewellery, the spoils of warfare and tripods.[48]

Over time the dedication of particular items went in and out of fashion, reflecting changing tastes as well as historical circumstance. Weapons and armour were routinely put up on so-called *tropaia*, posts made of wood,

---

[46] The strong emphasis on the manifold links between the religious and the socio-political (neither, of course, distinctly defined in the ancient world) is itself a response to an earlier tradition in classical scholarship (i.e., the works of the Cambridge School), which depicted religion as a somewhat obscure aspect of Greek culture, separate and separable from Greek politics and society.

[47] E.g., in the works of the Paris School, see Buxton 1981.

[48] For Olympia see, e.g., Willemsen 1957; Herrmann 1979 (tripods); Philipp 1981 (jewellery); Bol 1989; Kunze 1991 (armoury).

bronze or stone, and displayed to commemorate victories on the battlefield, mostly of one Greek city over another.[49] The dedication of *tropaia* at Olympia, for example, peaked around 450 BC and declined sharply during the second half of the fifth century BC.[50] Classical scholars have attributed this to new legislation banning the erection of *tropaia* in the sanctuary and the need to mask internal Greek conflicts.[51]

Some dedications reveal the names of those who made the dedication as well as their purpose.[52] From an inscription dating from about 400 BC found in Phalerum, for example, we learn that a certain Xenocrateia founded a sanctuary of Cephisus (a river-god and protector of youth) and dedicated a votive relief to him and the other gods who shared his altar 'for the upbringing' of her son Xeniades.[53] The relief shows the woman and her son surrounded by a number of gods and goddesses.[54]

From such inscriptions it emerges that votives were dedicated either by individuals or by people representing the entire community. They therefore represent personal religion as much as the communal religion of the polis.[55] Sometimes, as in the case of amulets, the religious practice of dedicating items to a divinity came close to, or even overlapped with, what classical scholars have referred to as magic (see Chapter 4).[56] Dedications sometimes feature in the literary evidence, most prominently in Aristotle's discussion of *megaloprepeia* ('magnificence'), which includes extensive commentary on dedications.[57] They also feature in the account by Herodotus of the generous dedications put on display at Delphi by King Croesus of Lydia and in Pausanias' *Description of Greece*.[58] They appear, too, in various temple inventories.[59] This rich array of evidence makes the cultural practice of dedicating items at a temple one of the best-attested aspects of ancient Greek religion.

Traditionally, a distinction is made between dedications of elaborate craftsmanship like the famous Aphrodite of Cnidus by Praxiteles or the

---

[49] See, e.g., Olympia, Archaeological Museum, inv. no. B 3042 (part of a Corinthian helmet); inv. no. B 51 (helmet); inv. no. B 5538 (greaves).
[50] Scott 2010: 191–6. See also ch. 5 in more detail.
[51] See most recently Scott 2010: 193 (with further literature).   [52] E.g., Lazzarini 1976.
[53] *IG* I³ 987, Athens, National Archaeological Museum, inv. no. 2756.
[54] For a picture of the relief see van Straten 1981, fig. 23.
[55] On votives as representative of personal religion see, e.g., Parker in *ThesCRA* I. 2.d.: 279 and, in particular, van Straten 1981.
[56] On amulets see Bonner 1950; Kotansky 1991; 1994; 1995.   [57] Arist. *EN* 4.2.1–19.
[58] Hdt. 1.50–51; Paus. 5.21.1–27.12; 6.1.1–19.15 (dedications at Olympia); 10.9.1ff. (dedications at Delphi).
[59] See, e.g., Harris 1995 with extensive evidence from Athens.

Peplos Kore and more mundane items without much aesthetic value. While
the former frequently play a key role in the reconstruction of Greek art
history, the latter receive much less scholarly attention.[60] Votive deposits
fall mainly within the area of expertise of classical archaeologists, who con-
centrated first on their collection, systematisation and description. Because
Greek sanctuaries frequently yield a considerable amount of evidence, some
order and overview of the excavated material is needed before anything else.
Building on such preliminary work, ancient historians and classical archaeologists have sought to investigate the significance of dedications of both
types by placing them within their socio-cultural and religious contexts.
This has opened up a variety of productive avenues to pursue, including
the link between the form and function of a dedication.[61] Votive offerings
appear to have fulfilled a variety of roles, including warding off danger,
bringing about the long-awaited advent of offspring or finding a cure for a
disease.[62]

Symbolic analysis can help to establish the significance of votives within
an even broader context. As Walter Burkert argued, at the very core of
the dedication of items at sanctuaries lay an act of symbolic exchange.[63]
Mortals invested 'symbolic capital' in a specific god, who would reciprocate
the value in his or her area of competence.[64] Besides prayer and sacrifice,
the dedication of votives was therefore a third means by which human
beings established symbolic 'traffic' between their own mortal sphere and
that of divinity. The forms of this 'traffic' and its volume provide insights
into the relationship between the two spheres. However, there is more to
seeing dedications as symbolic capital: the public display of votive offerings within a sanctuary long after their original dedication added another
layer of symbolic 'investment', ultimately also directed at the members of
the worshipping community itself. Temple inventories displayed on *stēlai*,
in particular, provided an additional medium for the dissemination of
symbolic capital. Because dedications reflected a variety of key moments
(warfare, etc.) within the communal life of a city, it is certainly correct

---

[60] See Whitley 2001: 3–16 for a criticism of this separation.
[61] See van Straten 1981; Alroth 1989. See also the survey by Osborne 2004.
[62] E.g., Alyattes' dedication of a silver bowl at Delphi for recovery from a disease: Hdt. 1.25; Pericles'
    dedication of a statue to Athena Hygieia as a thank-offering for saving the life of a workman who
    had had an accident in the temple: Plu. *Per.* 13.8; a representation of a woman in labour from Cyprus
    dating from the sixth century BC: Nicosia, Cyprus Museum, inv. no. 1935/B. 56 (for an image and
    further literature see van Straten 1981: 99 with fig. 44). On the function of votive offerings: Rouse
    1902: 189; van Straten 1981: 80–104 (with further examples); Parker in *ThesCRA* I. 2.d.: 278–280.
[63] Burkert 1987: 43–4.   [64] *Locus classicus* for 'symbolic capital': Bourdieu 1977: 171–83.

to point out that 'the temple treasure . . . embodied . . . the whole city, its organisation, its public life and its achievements'.[65]

Further questions follow. What were the cultural conventions guiding and regulating the investment of dedications as 'symbolic capital'? Who could invest a sanctuary with such capital and remove it? And why were some items removed from display relatively soon after their dedication while others remained in place for a long period of time? Despite the obvious merits of such an approach, however, this avenue is rarely pursued.[66] In this area of study, functionalism still takes the form of the investigation of dedications as a direct means to achieve one's ends, without, however, devoting much consideration to the symbolic dimension of this transaction. A comprehensive study interrogating the symbolic dimension of dedications at Greek sanctuaries to replace the conceptually outdated work by Rouse is long overdue.[67]

Processions

While the symbolic 'value' of votives has not been fully appreciated in classical scholarship, processions regularly feature in the scholarly literature as a primary symbolic medium of ancient Greek religion. Because of the rich literary, iconographic and epigraphic evidence available for the study of processions, it is possible for classical scholars to appreciate the symbolic value of the different elements and features of individual processions. It is no exaggeration to say that practically every aspect of a procession is considered as symbolic: who participated (and who did not), what route was chosen and, in particular, the kinds of object displayed during the procession.[68] Greek religion saw 'the development of a class of ritual equipment which, whatever its original or notional function in ritual performed at the sanctuary, came to be thought of as primarily conspicuous wealth to be displayed in the procession, the *pompē*, and was referred to as *pompeia* . . . The procession had become an end in itself.'[69]

Almost every festival featured one or several processions – and we know that there were many festivals throughout the year at Athens and elsewhere in the Greek world.[70] Processions, however, were more than a simple

[65] Linders 1987: 120.
[66] On the symbolic dimension of dedications see, e.g., Linders 1987: 118–22; Langdon 1987; Osborne 1994; Morris 2000: 277.
[67] Rouse 1902.
[68] Cf. 'centrifugal vs. centripetal processions': Graf 1996b. See also Graf 1995b.
[69] Jameson 1999: 325.
[70] See Parker 2005: 155–217, 486–7 on Athenian festivals and the festival year.

transfer of ritual objects from one place to another before a communal sacrifice.[71] They were a public spectacle and, as such, about performance and spectatorship.[72] As Jenifer Neils succinctly put it, 'ostentation and display play a prominent role in procession, whether they come in the form of musical accompaniment, elaborate dress, or aristocratic conveyances, like horse-drawn chariots'.[73] The literary description of specific processions and the iconography of processions as depicted on various Greek vases and, most prominently perhaps, on the Parthenon frieze at Athens, testify to the rich and many-layered texture of this religious spectacle.[74] Rather than a realistic representation of a specific procession, pictorial representations of processions depict an idealised version, highlighting those aspects considered to be particularly endowed with cultural meaning.[75]

In current scholarship processions are frequently characterised as a prime platform for communal self-representation and public display and are therefore taken as reflecting the socio-political structures of Greek society.[76] In particular, the procession of the Panathenaia, among the most prominent of Athenian festivals, with its parading of different socio-political groups, has been taken as representative of the democratic structures of Athens.[77] Processions thus ultimately support a picture in which religious structures map on to the socio-political structure of society. As Graf put it with regard to the *pompē* of the Panathenaia: 'the procession manifests what Athens is, not only to foreign by-standers but to the citizens and the participants'.[78]

Some festivals, however, in particular those associated with Dionysus (such as the Anthesteria and the Lenaia festivals at Athens), included processions featuring the display of *phalloi*, for example, or the singing of obscene songs, and challenged the norms and conventions of everyday

---

[71] On different types of processions see Nilsson 1951. Connor 1987: 50 depicts processions as a means for political leaders (such as Cleisthenes, Pisistratus and Solon) 'to articulate community values and emerging consensuses about state policy'. See also Motte 1987.

[72] E.g., Kavoulaki 1999.   [73] Neils 1996a: 178.

[74] See Neils 1996a. For the description of processions in literary sources see, e.g., Hdt. 1.60; Ath. 196a–203b. A procession in honour of Athena is depicted on a black-figure *oinochoe* (London, British Museum 1905.7–11.1) dating from the early fifth century BC (see van Straten 1995 figure 8 for an image). See also the procession in honour of Dionysus depicted on a black-figure *skyphos* (Bologna, Museo Civico, inv. no. 130; image: van Straten 1995, fig. 9).

[75] Maurizio 1998.

[76] See (among others) Bremmer 1994: 39–43; de Polignac 1995a: 40–2, 84–6; Graf 1995b; 1996b; Kavoulaki 1999; Jameson 1999. See Maurizio 1998 on the relationship between the Panathenaic procession and Athenian democracy. She argued that the procession did not just reflect politics but provided a platform for the expression of different, even diverging, modes of identity and belonging.

[77] E.g., Neils 1992: 27 discussed and challenged by Maurizio 1998: 297. Cf. the Panathenaia as 'a site of political contestation': Maurizio 1998: 415, n. 3.

[78] Graf 1996b: 58.

life.[79] Rather than a simple representation of social structures, such processions (and the festivals to which they belonged) are seen as reformulating social structures through the temporary inversion of the ordinary. Because of these manifold links between processions and social order, however, individuals occasionally used processions as a means of achieving their own ends. A good example is the procession (featuring a tall woman dressed up as Athena) staged by Pisistratus when he first returned from exile in the 550s BC with the ultimate goal of re-establishing himself as a tyrant at Athens.[80]

An examination of current research on votives and processions reveals that the potential of symbolic analysis in classical scholarship has not yet been fully realised. For the dedication of votive offerings as a cultural practice, especially, many questions concerning their role as 'symbolic capital' remain unaddressed. Geertz's definition of religion remains 'good to think with' for the classical scholar because it reminds us of the symbolic dimension of ancient Greek religion, which should no longer be neglected by scholars. A more thorough embrace of Geertz, and of symbolic analysis more generally, promises to open up a variety of avenues for the classical scholar.

The picture looks better for the study of processions, but a review of how processions feature in current works in the field has revealed a tendency for classical scholars to see symbolic analysis as a mere extension of structuralist or functionalist analysis. Processions are seen to represent existing socio-political structures and, at times, to maintain these structures through the temporary inversion of the ordinary. As such, processions (and the religious more generally) serve as an extension of the study of society and social structure but, with the exception of Connor's interpretation of Pisistratus' return, they are rarely seen as intrinsic to the power discourses driving that society.[81]

Because of the reluctance of classical scholars to embrace Geertz and symbolic analysis, it is all the more significant that Geertz has inspired one of the most authoritative accounts of ancient Greek religion: John Gould's

---

[79] On *phalloi* displayed during processions see for example Ar. *Ach.* 243; Semus in Ath. 622b–c. Besides such scattered literary references there is also a substantial iconography of phallic display, see Keuls 1985: 78–9.

[80] See Hdt. 1.60.2–5 with Connor 1987: 42–7. For a less instrumental link between processions and the individual see Graf's interpretation of the procession of the Eleusinian Mysteries as leading both physically and symbolically out of the polis in order to allow a personal encounter with the divine: Graf 1996b: 61–5.

[81] Connor 1987: 46 interprets the incident related in Hdt. 1.60.2–5 as an example of the theatricality of Athenian society, as a 'ritual drama' involving both Pisistratus and the Athenian onlookers and 'affirming the establishment of a new civic order'.

influential essay 'On making sense of Greek religion'. It is to a discussion of this essay that I shall now turn. What can we learn from considering Gould's translation of Geertz's definition of religion into classical scholarship as an attempt to reveal its intrinsic explanatory power for the study of ancient Greek religion?

JOHN GOULD: 'ON MAKING SENSE OF GREEK RELIGION'

Greek religion between the primitive and the sublime

'On making sense of Greek religion', published first in a collection of articles in 1985 and republished in another in 2001, stands out in its use of ethnographic material. It does much more than draw on ethnographic data to explain certain aspects of Greek religious beliefs and practices. Gould relies on studies by Clifford Geertz, Godfrey Lienhardt and other eminent anthropologists in order to explain the nature of ancient Greek religion as such. In many ways his article is an ambitious attempt to define, with the help of comparative data, the very core of ancient Greek religion. What can it teach us about the representation of anthropological models in classical scholarship?

In his article Gould aimed to bring out equally both the eternal, sublime and the primitive, archaic aspects of ancient Greek religion. He started from the premise that we should not make a judgemental distinction between mystical, magical and superstitious ways of thinking on the one hand, and scientific or common-sense ones on the other.[82] He saw all as equally valid ways of explaining the world. Religion, he argued, is not a pseudo-science. He then set out to 'make sense' of religion as a way of dealing with the realities of ancient Greek life. In Gould's account, the archaic, primitive aspects of ancient Greek religion reflect the primitive realities of life in ancient Greece.

The Greeks, like other ancients, Gould argued, were subject to disease and natural disasters in a much more immediate fashion than modern societies.[83] Moreover, they lacked the technical and scientific means of mitigating the instant and pressing impact of these natural forces. The ancient world was a world of crop failures, famines and plagues, a world in which 'chaos . . . is never far away' and which was 'far closer to present-day India than to anything in our own immediate experience'.[84] Gould went on to explain the darker aspects of ancient Greek religion as a way of

---

[82] Gould 2001: 2–3.   [83] Gould 2001: 6.   [84] Gould 2001: 6.

responding to these uncertainties and challenges. The slaughter of daughters in Greek mythology and the belief in divine anger and retribution, as well as the occurrence of disturbing revelatory dreams and of divine possession, mirrored these uncertainties of Greek life. They addressed the uncanny and threatening aspects of human existence and reflected the resulting doubts and anxieties.[85]

But Gould also highlighted the presence of the sublime. In particular he saw in Homeric divinity a manifestation of a layer of Greek religion that was both elevated and cognitively sophisticated. The Homeric gods, he stated, 'are imagined as comprising an extended family of anthropomorphic beings, with Zeus . . . as head and master of the company. Conceived as a metaphor of human experience, this is a brilliant stroke; the model of the family provides a framework within which we can intuitively understand both unity and conflict as the working out of a complex web of loyalties, interests, and obligations'.[86] For Gould, the particular explanatory power of the Homeric pantheon resides in its capacity to embrace both unity and diversity: 'The Homeric image of divinity is an image of marvellous and compelling adequacy; it underwrites and explains the human sense of contradiction and conflict in experience, and yet contains contradiction within a more fundamental order.'[87]

But even behind the brilliance of the Olympian gods as exemplified by Homer, Gould detected a darker side to Greek religion, in the Fates, Furies, Gorgons and other 'older, more primitive powers' of Hesiodic myth and the prominent role they played in Greek tragedy.[88] He saw the coexistence of both the archaic/primitive and the elevated/sublime dimensions as being at the very core of ancient Greek religion – indeed, all religions. 'The essence of divinity lies in the paradoxical coexistence of incompatible truths about human experience. In this there is much that is universal in the creation of religious imagery, and much that is illuminatingly Greek.'[89]

The distinction between the primitive and the sublime is odd. It places Gould's account somewhat uneasily between the traditional and more recent self-fashioning of classical studies and of social anthropology. Traditionally, social anthropology and classical studies stood at divergent, even opposing, ends of the spectrum of disciplines concerned with the study of culture. While the former specialised in allegedly 'primitive' societies, the latter constructed the teaching of Greco-Roman language and culture as the vehicle of an education that ultimately served a western-oriented type

---

[85] Gould 2001: 211.   [86] Gould 2001: 226.   [87] Gould 2001: 226.
[88] Gould 2001: 227.   [89] Gould 2001: 233.

of elitism. This image of the ancient world was still heavily indebted to the Victorian view of 'the Glory that was Greece' as the exemplar of a rational and enlightened society.[90]

In his provocative study *The Greeks and the Irrational* E. R. Dodds fundamentally challenged this image. By showing the presence of the 'irrational' (in the form of shamanism, maenadism, magic) in the rational (Greek philosophical reasoning) and vice versa, Dodds effectively revealed these categories as a false dichotomy. He also challenged the elevated picture of Greece and aligned the study of the Greco-Roman world with that of other contemporary cultures. Since then the rational, the irrational and the non-rational have largely vanished from scholarly discourse.[91] Moreover, classical studies largely stepped back from their supremacist claims, contemporaneously, perhaps, with the decline of Greek and Latin in secondary education, and anthropologists these days would surely frown upon reference to any culture, at home or abroad, as 'primitive'. Gould's account followed in Dodds's footsteps in attempting to present a complex picture of ancient Greek religion that included both rational and irrational aspects. Yet with its evocation of the dark and the light, the primitive and the sublime as fundamental categories, it appears to be heavily laden with anthropological notions that were already outdated by the time his article was first published.

The most worrying aspect of Gould's use of ethnographic material, however, is his failure to differentiate between religion as represented in Greek literature, on the one hand, and the ethnographic data of the anthropologist, on the other. While his point that we should not reduce Homeric religion to mere literary fiction is well taken, it is disturbing to see him move so easily between ancient Greece and modern societies.[92]

As Paul Cartledge pointed out, data derived from social anthropology is used in classical scholarship mainly in two ways. First, it may be used to compare and to fill the gaps in the ancient evidence with the much more abundant material available from ethnographic research (Cartledge calls scholars pursuing this approach the 'lumpers'); second, it is used as a contrasting background against which the specific features of the ancient data are brought to light (the 'splitters').[93] Gould generally belonged to the

---

[90] See Cartledge 1994: 4.
[91] The rational still features variously in Oswyn Murray's works, most notably, perhaps, in Murray 1997. See also Harrison 2006 for a critique.
[92] Gould 2001: 25.
[93] Cartledge 1994. The anthropological method of the 'splitters' has shaped the writing of history, in particular of cultural history in the style of Darnton, who uses 'the strange' (that which is not directly intelligible) as an entry point to recover another reality, different to the one of the historian: Darnton 1984: 3–7 as discussed in ch. 2.

first category of 'lumpers'. What he in effect offered was the application of a universal definition of religion (religions are 'languages' that formulate responses to the world) tailored to conceptualise the historically specific religion of the ancient Greeks. In fact, Gould's definition oscillates between the two poles of a universal (or anthropological) and a culturally specific (or historical) definition of religion. Gould thus did not use data derived from social anthropology primarily to find an essentialist definition of religion that would include the Greeks. Instead, in his claim that religion *is* a response to the world, he presupposed such an essence. This presupposition of essence then served as a common denominator enabling him to compare Greek religion with that of other cultures.

Gould repeatedly referred to Godfrey Lienhardt's seminal study on the religion of the Dinka, 'because it offers a wealth of recorded detail that is hardly ever available in the Greek evidence'.[94] However, the way in which he compared Dinka and ancient Greek religion entirely disregarded the form in which information on ancient Greek religion is available to us. The unusual and emotionally detached behaviour of a young Dinka boy who showed uncontrolled movement reminded Gould of the Cassandra scene in Aeschylus' *Agamemnon*. Gould compared its interpretation by the Dinka as a sign of divine possession to the response of the chorus to the behaviour of Phaedra in Euripides' *Hippolytus*. The Dinka example, Gould argued, 'could be rendered without distortion into Greek terms'.[95] He even went so far as to reverse the narrative sequence of an incident related by Herodotus to make the ancient example fit his explanation. For Gould, the story of the Spartan Glaucus, whose family died out during the lifetime of Herodotus, served as an example of an uncanny event that was explained as a result of various religious offences (the breach of an oath, the dishonest consultation of an oracle).

However, this explanation is valid only, as Gould readily admitted, if we reverse the sequence of events as outlined by Herodotus in 6.86.[96] If we follow the story as told in the *Histories*, the episode involving Glaucus seems to be exploring questions of justice and injustice in the context of the divine.[97] Significantly, perhaps, in this reading, the destruction of Glaucus' family appears to be the ultimate consequence of his immoral behaviour and a representation of the gravity of that behaviour, rather than a trigger for religious sense-making by Herodotus and others.

As David Gellner pointedly remarked: 'Anthropologists are specialists in other people's meanings.'[98] It is in this sense, perhaps, that the classicist is also essentially an anthropologist, despite the tendency, still sometimes

---

[94] Gould 2001: 9.   [95] Gould 2001: 10–11.   [96] Gould 2001: 13.
[97] See the interpretation of Harrison 2000: 117–20.   [98] Gellner 1999: 136.

found in classical scholarship, to convert the ancients – in the words of Moses Finley – 'into good chaps practically like us'.[99] Classics and anthropology share many thematic interests and face common methodological problems which challenge all who strive to understand a culture different from their own.

Despite the obvious synergies between the two disciplines, however, there are profound differences that are frequently glossed over by classical scholars drawing on ethnographic material. To state the obvious: anthropologists work with the living, while classicists explore a culture that has long ceased to exist. Classical scholars are therefore unable to engage in that most cherished of anthropological methods – participant observation. Their 'informants' are illustrious figures such as poets, historians and philosophers. These are, in the anthropological sense, at least one step removed from the cultural practice itself and can be accessed only through the medium of literature.

These differences, however, make it necessary to modify and test those models derived from social anthropology in terms of their applicability to classical scholarship. For our investigation, this means that we must first consider the symbolic dimension of Greek religion within its literary contexts. How is the representation of its symbols shaped and determined by the generic conventions of a given work? How do religious symbols fit into the overall outlook of a work? Only when we have answered such questions can we move on to establish the role of such symbols with regard to cultural practice.

Despite its undeniable merits, Gould's account shows less care in the handling of comparative data than one would wish. In addition, it is over-burdened with outdated anthropological concepts. A close look at another example of Gould's use of the Greek literary evidence identifies his reception of Geertz as central to his use of ethnographic data. As we shall see in the next section, his discussion of the horrific suicide of the Spartan king Cleomenes demonstrates that Gould, like Geertz, constructed religious symbols as separate from the domain of power.[100]

Geertz, Gould and the symbolic dimension of ancient Greek religion

In Book 6 of the *Histories*, Herodotus reported that after Cleomenes returned from Arcadia, he behaved so erratically that his relatives decided

---

[99] Finley 1985: xiii.

[100] Hdt. 6.75–84; Gould 2001: 12–13. For a reading of the different interpretative layers that can be drawn from Herodotus' account of Cleomenes more generally see also Robert Parker's inaugural lecture: Parker 1998a.

to restrain him. Cleomenes, however, managed to get possession of a knife and sliced up his own body until he died. Herodotus stated that the majority of the Greeks believed that this was some form of divine punishment – and disagreement erupted only about the nature of Cleomenes' offence. The Athenians, for example, believed that his invasion of the sacred land of Demeter and Persephone in Eleusis triggered divine punishment. The Argives, in turn, attributed his death to the disrespect he showed towards Argive fugitives and the holy ground of Argos, while the rest of the Greeks maintained that it was a result of his bribery of the Delphic oracle. The Spartans themselves, however, found a much more worldly and ultimately un-Spartan explanation for the shocking death of their king: his adoption of Scythian drinking habits.

Gould read the diverging Greek interpretations of Cleomenes' suicide as different responses to an 'uncanny' incident: 'Problems of interpretation, where conflict of interest may be reflected in conflict of interpretation, are bound to occur. The horrific self-mutilation and suicide of the Spartan king Cleomenes is uncanny enough to be a sign of divine activity.'[101]

The claim that religion is a response to chaos – chaos understood as a 'tumult of events which lack not just interpretations but interpretability' – is perhaps Gould's most significant conceptual borrowing from Geertz.[102] This claim involves sophisticated conceptual borrowing and adaptation, and goes beyond a simple takeover of Geertz's major premises. In contrast to Geertz's compact list of necessary propositions, which he introduced at the beginning of his essay, Gould's definition of religion evolved throughout his article. Both scholars' definitions took the form of a series of essentialist claims about the nature and quality of religion.

Gould adopted from Geertz the notion of religion as a cultural system. He set out to define Greek religion as 'a complex and quite subtle statement about what the world is like and a set of responses for dealing with that world'.[103] The intellectual debt to Geertz is immediately apparent if we take into account Gould's further addition to his definition:

---

[101] Gould 2001: 214.
[102] Gould 2001: 207. It might be a trivial point to make, but this is a reductionist view of 'world' and ultimately also of religion as a response to it. For to reduce 'world' (as relevant for the study of religion) to 'chaos' means to assign to religion a place in society that deals only with those aspects of life that cannot be explained otherwise (aspects which are thus perceived as 'chaos'). On religion as a response to chaos see also Geertz 1973: 99–108. Geertz, of course, did not 'invent' the religion-as-response-to-chaos hypothesis; it has a much longer history in scholarly discourse. It was developed in the sociology of religion (see, e.g., Berger 1969, esp. 71–2). Nor was Gould the first scholar to use this hypothesis in classical scholarship. An early example of this line of reasoning: Grote 1862: 296–8. On religion and chaos see also Smith 1978a: 129–46.
[103] Gould 2001: 204.

If we want an analogy to help us understand religion, one that will direct our attention positively to what is important in religious systems, we should turn . . . to language. Like language, religion is a cultural phenomenon, a phenomenon of the group (there are no 'private' religions, any more than there are 'private' languages, except by some metaphorical devaluation of the two terms), and like language, any religion is a system of signs enabling communication both between members of the group in interpreting and responding to experience of the external world and in the individual's inner discourse with himself as to his own behaviour, emotional and private.[104]

While the symbolic aspect is included in the analogy between religion and language (and his reading of language as a 'system of signs'), the second part of Gould's article explicitly stresses the systematic character of the 'language' of Greek religion as defined in the first.[105] For Gould, as for Geertz, religion was a cultural phenomenon in the sense that it transcended the individual ('there are no "private" religions, any more than there are "private" languages'). Both definitions link a substantive account of religion as a system of signs to a functionalist one that describes what religion does in society. It formulates a general order of existence (Geertz); it provides a set of responses for dealing with the world (Geertz/Gould).[106]

However, despite the centrality of this claim to Gould's argument, his account leaves under-theorised exactly how the two key elements of his definition, 'world perceived as chaos' and 'response', are related to each other. It seems to suggest that the two are separate categories, that 'world' exists, if not necessarily prior to, at least independently of 'response'. The same sense of conceptual separation between 'world' and 'response' is implied in his suggestion that to 'make sense' of Greek religion involves a two-stage process, that both layers of 'world' and 'response' can (at least in theory) be considered separately:

[T]o make sense of it, to see what religion is a response to and what kind of response it is, we need . . . to take account of differences of two kinds: firstly, differences of the 'world', that is between our experience of the external world and that of the ancient Greeks, and secondly, institutional differences, in the response, differences between two traditions and conventions in the organization of religious thought and behaviour.[107]

---

[104] Gould 2001: 206–7.
[105] See Gould 2001: 216–34 for his account of the systematic quality of Greek religion.
[106] On substantive and functional theories of essence in the comparative study of religion see Saler 1993: 24.
[107] Gould 2001: 208.

This suggestion directly echoes Geertz's recommendation to separate the interpretation of symbols from investigation of their relationship to the socio-political sphere.

The anthropological study of religion is therefore a two-stage operation: first, an analysis of the system of meanings embodied in the symbols which make up the religion proper, and, second, the relating of these systems to social-structural and psychological processes.[108]

Like Gould, Geertz also conceptualised the interpretation of religion in two steps. Gould, however, seems to have applied the strict division between the two interpretative steps much more strongly and schematically than Geertz. He set out to identify the differences between ancient and modern experiences of the world, differences he saw as ultimately grounded in the larger degree of contingency of Greek life. It is in this context that Gould's observations concerning the archaism and primitivism of ancient Greek life belong. The Greeks, like other ancients, he argued, were less protected from natural forces such as famine and disease than modern societies.[109] Moreover, they lacked the technical and scientific means that could have eased the instant and pressing impact of these natural forces. The ancient world was one of crop failures, famines and plagues – a world that, as we have noted, Gould found comparable to present-day India.

Gould concluded his account of the high degree of contingency in Greek culture and society by pointing out that 'in such a world, the threat of chaos . . . is never far away. Yet the religious institutions and systems of belief of ancient Greeks were equally different, less structured, less "worked out" than those we tend to take for granted.'[110] Was he implying a connection between the ubiquity of chaos and the relative lack of religious structure? Was he suggesting that the flexibility of religious structure somehow participates in, follows from, mirrors or represents the lack of structure in a 'world' perceived as chaos?

Gould seems to have been implying a structural analogy between 'world' and 'religion': 'The improvisatory character of Greek myth is not just a literary fact, not only the source of its perennial vitality in literature, but also the guarantee of its centrality in Greek religion. It is not bound to forms hardened and stiffened by canonical authority, but mobile, fluent and free to respond to a changing experience of the world.'[111] It was the flexibility of Greek myth and ritual that enabled the 'language' of Greek religion to represent and respond to chaos perceived as a lack of meaning. But Gould

---

[108] Geertz 1973: 125.   [109] Gould 2001: 208–9.   [110] Gould 2001: 209.   [111] Gould 2001: 211.

never addressed the question of how this structural analogy comes about. He did not explain to what extent the versatile structure of Greek religion was related to the lack of structure in the world as experienced by the Greeks. This question, however, is of paradigmatic importance because it sets up the way in which religion is studied in relation to other aspects of Greek culture and society.

This semiotic vagueness in Gould's religion-as-language analogy, however, leads to a more fundamental problem, which he shared with Geertz. Talal Asad, a social anthropologist with a particular interest in the concepts involved in the comparative study of religions, extended his criticism of Geertz to the claim that his conceptualisation of religion resulted, in effect, in the separation of religion from the domain of power.[112] Asad saw this as a problem intrinsic to universal definitions of religion – that is, to definitions of religion that identify the essence of all religions. Like all universal definitions of religion, Asad argued, the account Geertz gave of religion as a cultural system allows the separation of the religious symbol from the social practice that establishes its meaning. The same point applies yet more forcefully to Gould, who shared Geertz's conception of religious signification. By conceptualising the two layers separately, both scholars set religious symbols apart from the social actions and processes from which they derived their meaning, in effect assigning religious symbols a *sui generis* quality.[113]

To return to the example of Cleomenes' suicide and the responses this surely 'uncanny' incident triggered in Greek religious discourse: there is much more to the competing explanations that the Greeks offer than Gould is ready to include. The various interpretations reflect the ways in which Greek religion as an explanatory discourse was used to negotiate different or even diverging interests. While the Athenians suggested that Cleomenes' behaviour resulted from his prior violation of sacred land, the Argives blamed it on his prior violation of war dead. Both explanations relied on religious conceptions common to all Greeks of what constituted acceptable and unacceptable behaviour. Both explanations also referred to

---

[112] Asad 1993: 27–54; see also Asad 1983. Asad is perhaps the most serious representative of the materialist line of criticism with regard to Geertz's conceptualisation of the religious. He is part of a relatively recent trend in social anthropology that not only acknowledges the significance of the historical dimension in understanding foreign cultures, but also historicises the methods and concepts used in their investigation.

[113] Compare Asad's point on religious symbols being *sui generis* in Geertz's concept of religion: Asad 1983: 250. On Geertz's tendency to turn culture into an aesthetic object see Ortner 1997: 10.

the widespread notion that the gods would punish unacceptable behaviour. Athens and Argos hence used the common Greek 'language' of religion in order to pursue their own interests and to discredit Sparta and Cleomenes. The Spartan interpretation, in contrast, which explained Cleomenes' erratic behaviour by referring to his prior exposure to Scythian drinking habits, was an attempt to challenge and ultimately refute this use of religious discourse as an authoritative one: the horrific self-mutilation was presented as having no religious relevance whatsoever.

The competing Greek interpretations of Cleomenes' death used religion as an authoritative discourse to validate a model of historical causation that supported local interests and maintained the status quo. Gould's interpretation, however, does not move beyond the description of the different Greek responses to the death of Cleomenes. In his account, the hidden power discourses and political ideologies driving the diverging representations of royal suicide as a divine sign (or merely as a result of a much more worldly over-enthusiastic consumption of alcohol) are not unpacked. Arguably, however, it is exactly these competing power discourses and hidden ideologies that Herodotus found intriguing and that compelled him to preserve the different voices within his own account.[114] Gould, however, was as indifferent to their existence as he was to the narrative framing of the evidence. For him, the example of Cleomenes' death served simply to demonstrate how religion 'makes sense' of the world as a response to chaos.

Paradoxically, perhaps, Gould's account seeks to place Greek religion in Greek society but depicts too schematic a relationship between the two. This harbours the real risk of seeing culture (and religion as part of it) as an aesthetic object that can be distinguished from the 'hard surfaces' of Greek life.[115] Gould, like Geertz, 'moves away from a notion of symbols that are intrinsic to signifying and organising practices, and back to a notion of symbols as meaning-carrying objects external to social conditions and states of the self'.[116] Because of his somewhat limited conceptualisation of the religious symbol, Gould has done little to help translate Geertz and symbolic analysis more generally into classical scholarship on ancient Greek religion. In 'making sense' of Greek religion he followed the prevailing line

---

[114] See, e.g., the different accounts for the origins of the Greco-barbarian conflict in the beginning of the *Histories* (Hdt. 1.1–5). See also the competing versions of the genealogy of the Spartan kings in Hdt. 6.51–54, which blend questions of genealogy, ethnicity and the legitimacy of power.
[115] See Ortner 1997: 10.   [116] Asad 1993: 31.

too closely to challenge prevailing scholarly conceptualisations of what ancient Greek religion was.

THE SYMBOLIC AS ORNAMENTAL IN CLASSICAL SCHOLARSHIP ON ANCIENT GREEK RELIGION

The extent to which the conceptualisation of religious symbols as separate and separable from the domain of power is embedded in current scholarship in the field is best demonstrated by the fact that even those scholars who focus on the study of religious representation frequently sketch religious symbols as aesthetic objects that can once again be separated from the 'hard surfaces' of Greek politics and society. A good example is Robin Osborne's otherwise excellent article on Greek notions of death.[117] Writing against the widespread trend of using the material record as a mere illustration of assumptions derived from the literary evidence, Osborne corrected the idea of a single, uniform construal of death in archaic and classical Greece. The innovative nature of Osborne's account is particularly noticeable if we compare his study with those of other students of ancient Greek religion. Scholars such as Donna Kurtz and John Boardman, Robert Garland and Ian Morris focused extensively on the ritualistic aspects of death and, in doing so, depicted a largely monovocal statement of what Osborne showed to be a polyvalent discourse.[118]

Juxtaposing several representations related to death and the dead, Osborne sketched an intriguing image of a whole spectrum of alternative notions of what it meant to die. In his account, the visual representation of death draws the spectator into a sophisticated negotiation of belief and practice, of subject and object, 'of seeing and being seen'.[119] Through the careful unpacking of imagery, he was able to uncover deeper layers of meaning. The pictorial representation of several mythological scenes on a pot used to bury a young boy in Eleusis, for instance, was interpreted as 'a construal of death, a discussion of the nature of death as sensory deprivation. Death comes when the visual world closes in on you, when you yourself are to be seen in a pot.'[120]

Osborne's account went a long way in demonstrating how productive symbolic analysis can be for the study of ancient Greek religion. The strength of his contribution lay in its revelation of different levels of symbolic meaning in the imagery presented and in the links he established

---

[117] Osborne 1988.   [118] Kurtz and Boardman 1971; Garland 1985; Morris 1992.
[119] Osborne 1988: 4.   [120] Osborne 1988: 4.

between visual/artistic context and the situational context of the individual burial. His account revealed that Greek construals of death and the dead were vehicles for much larger conceptions of life, community and the individual. Ultimately, Osborne's approach revealed a picture of ancient Greek religion as a central mediator between the individual and community and between life and death. To borrow a metaphor from Geertz/Gould: his account showed that Greek religion indeed served as a 'language', not so much for the formulation of final answers, but as an instrument of reflection 'upon the fragility of human life and upon the delicately balanced relationship between man and the natural world, between man's ability and inability to control his environment'.[121]

It was, however, no coincidence that Osborne chose to publish his article in *Art History*. His account failed to establish a link between the symbolic dimension of funerary ritual and the socio-political domain of power. As Ian Morris has rightly remarked:

Osborne offers an intriguing poetics of archaic ritual and overcomes the separation between sociology and psychology that plagued earlier approaches; but in doing so he succumbs to the 'ever-present' danger that Geertz noted and loses contact with the hard surfaces of life. The approach ends up being every bit as reductionist as earlier all-embracing theories. The hard surfaces of seventh-century Attic society were excessively hard, and social conflict, whether along class or regional lines . . . should be at the heart of any history of the period.[122]

While Morris was certainly right in pointing out the absence of the 'hard surfaces' of Greek culture and society from Osborne's account, I do not believe this is, as he suggested, representative of the generic limitations of symbolic or culturalist analyses.[123] Surely Osborne's type of analysis is in principle compatible with an interest in the politics of gender, class distinctions and the poetics of socio-political power. Osborne himself at times showed possible points of departure for such a different investigative focus, for example when he pointed to the privileged background of the deceased or to the gendered representation of death in a tombstone in the Kerameikos cemetery.[124] To have addressed such aspects more squarely would have further complicated Osborne's account and helped avoid accusations of aestheticism.

If the reluctance to include these aspects more prominently is representative of anything, it is of a certain tendency in classical scholarship to follow

---

[121] Osborne 1988: 13.   [122] Morris 1993: 32.   [123] See Morris 1993: 28–32.

[124] See Osborne's discussion of the Athenian Croesus: Osborne 1988: 8–11 and of the grave relief that depicts Hegeso with a woman servant and 'female adornment': 1988: 18.

Geertz and Gould in conceiving of the symbolic dimension as separate and separable from the domain of power. Examination of current works in social anthropology reveals a much more complicated conceptualisation of religious signification than the one we find in classical scholarship. Scholars such as Victor Turner, James Fernandez and Marshal Sahlins, to mention just a few from a much larger cluster, have shown that power is intrinsic to signifying practices.[125] In their two-volume work on the colonial frontier in South Africa, Jean and John Comaroff, in particular, have demonstrated how productive it is to see the symbolic as actively involved in and hence inseparable from the negotiation of socio-political power.[126] What makes their accounts conceptually relevant here is their focus on symbols, including religious symbols, as a prime medium of conflicting power discourses: the colonial frontier as a space of contestation and negotiation between the Nonconformist Christian missionaries and the indigenous people of Southern Tswana. In this two-way encounter, socio-political power structures are involved in the production and shaping of symbols just as they are themselves shaped by them. Symbolic analysis, it can be concluded from the works of Comaroff and Comaroff, should be seen as a central interpretative tool on a par with structuralism and functionalism.

A more dynamic approach is needed in classical scholarship that does not depict religious beliefs and practices merely as a disguise for ambitions in the political sphere. The socio-political power of Greek religion must be seen as grounded to a significant extent in the persuasive and authoritative power of its symbols.

THE SYMBOLIC VALUE OF TYRANT PROPERTY TURNED RITUAL OBJECT

One brief example will suffice to illustrate how productive a more flexible and complicated conceptualisation of the symbolic dimension is for the study of ancient Greek religion. Osborne has made a convincing case for the way in which symbolic analysis can reveal the plurality of voices and points of view that shaped Greek religious discourse, but he has left open the question of how compatible this type of analysis is with questions of socio-political power. Our example below explores the symbolic value of 'tyrant-property-turned-ritual-equipment' and demonstrates that the

---

[125] See, e.g., Turner 1967; Fernandez 1982; Kirch and Sahlins 1992.
[126] Comaroff and Comaroff 1991; 1997. For an appreciation of the significance and impact of their work in social anthropology and beyond, see the review essays in *AHR* 108: Elbourne 2003; Engle Merry 2003; Dening 2003.

symbolic dimension of Greek religion was indeed an important medium for the negotiation of socio-political power.

It is, in particular, against the background of the symbolic value of processions as discussed towards the beginning of this chapter that we can appreciate the special symbolic spectacle that the Athenians enjoyed in 403 BC, after the overthrow of the Thirty. A fragment from Philochorus attests that after the restoration of democracy, the Athenians used equipment that was specifically fashioned for processional use (*pompeia*), equipment that had been crafted (*kataskeuazein*) out of the property of the Thirty Tyrants.[127]

Harpocration s.v. πομπείας καὶ πομπεύειν· ... πομπεῖα δὲ λέγεται τὰ εἰς τὰς πομπὰς κατασκευαζόμενα σκεύη, ὡς ὁ αὐτὸς ῥήτωρ <ἐν τῷ> Κατ᾽ Ἀνδροτίωνος ὑποσημαίνει. 'πομπείοις δέ' φησι Φιλόχορος 'πρότερον ἐχρῶντο οἱ Ἀθηναῖοι τοῖς ἐκ τῆς οὐσίας τῶν λ΄ κατασκευασθεῖσιν. ὀψὲ δέ' [φησί] 'καὶ Ἀνδροτίων ἄλλα κατεσκεύασεν.'[128]

Processions and parading: ... equipment made for the processions is called πομπεῖα, as the same orator [Demosthenes] mentions in his *Against Androtion*. 'Earlier,' Philochorus says, 'the Athenians used as processional equipment that which had been fashioned out of the property of the Thirty. Later, Androtion also fashioned others.'

This casually reported incident, as Charles Fornara and David Yates have pointed out, has so far received little scholarly attention.[129] As a document for the symbolic dimension of ancient Greek religion, however, this fragment is remarkable, for it testifies how, after the oligarchic revolution and the restoration of democracy, religion was used in Athens as a symbolic medium to negotiate the frictions and internal divisions that accompany any kind of socio-political change.

The riches of tyrants, their wealth and possessions were themselves symbols well before this episode. During the reign of the Thirty Tyrants between 404 and 403 BC, the great affluence of the Tyrants was seen as one of the most ruthless representations of oligarchic power. Xenophon stressed the fact that the Tyrants did not hesitate to silence dissenters in order to seize their property and enhance their own personal wealth. In 404 BC, for

---

[127] *FGrHist* 328 F181. See also Wilson 2011.

[128] The text given here is from Fornara and Yates, who have adapted *FGrHist* 328 F181 according to recent research on Harpocration by John Keaney: Fornara and Yates 2007: 31. See also Keaney 1991: 217, π80. The translation is also from Fornara and Yates with changes.

[129] Fornara and Yates 2007. Fornara and Yates suggest that the fragment was not an atthidographic entry but probably originated from one of Philochorus' other works.

example, the Thirty proclaimed that all those who were not on their roll would lose their estates (to the Tyrants and their friends, of course).[130]

Julia Shear has recently offered a detailed assessment of Athenian responses to the Thirty.[131] She has shown that one of the challenges the Athenian populace mastered after the restoration of democracy and the far-reaching amnesties was that of unifying the internally divided citizen body. As at other transitory points in history, most notably, perhaps, after the oligarchy of 411 BC, there was a special need for the fashioning and refashioning of (democratic) power, increased, possibly, at this time by the brutal regime of the Thirty and the widespread abolition of democratic institutions during their short tenure. The Athenian populace overcame this challenge by implementing a variety of measures, including (but not limited to) a complex spatial politics directed towards reclaiming the Acropolis and the Agora as civic spaces and the inscribing and displaying of new laws and decrees aimed at 'remaking Athens as the democratic city'.[132]

Religion, in particular the celebration of common festivals and the swearing of oaths, was an important aspect of propagating a unified, democratic Athens.[133] This was an area in which the populace could claim the moral high ground, since the Tyrants were considered oblivious to the norms and conventions of ancient Greek religion.[134] They did not, for example, shy away from violating the Greek religious institution of *hiketeia* (supplication) by killing Theramenes, who had sought refuge at an altar as a suppliant.[135]

It is in this context that the ritual display of tyrant property turned ritual object resonates and unfolds its symbolic power. The episode demonstrates how wealth, the prime marker of oligarchic power, was redefined to represent the power and unity of the Athenian people and their commitment to divine *charis* ('benevolence').[136] The wealth of individuals was now displayed as the wealth of the community used in communication with the gods. The power of the few lay once more with the people. What once represented the extravagance and moral corruption of individual wealth and oligarchic power was now recast as part of a communal spectacle, and not just any kind of spectacle, but a special one that served the still-unstable

---

[130] X. *HG* 2.4.1. See also Arist. *Ath.* 35; Lys. 12.4–24.   [131] Shear 2011: in particular 188–322.
[132] Shear 2011: 259. Reclaiming of the Agora and the Acropolis: Shear 2011: 263–85.
[133] See, e.g., Shear 2011: 135–65 on the role of ritual in the process of remembering. See also Cleocritus' appeal to his fellow citizens to reunite after the Battle of Piraeus in X. *HG* 2.4.18–22.
[134] See Lys. 12.9.
[135] Theramenes was himself a member of the oligarchy who had fallen out with Critias: X. *HG* 2.3.52–56. On *hiketeia* see Gould 1973.
[136] On *charis* see Parker 1998b.

democracy as an important medium for the self-representation of inner cohesion. This public parading of symbols involved a direct inversion of religious appropriation: we since know from Xenophon that the Thirty had themselves stored the confiscated arms of those who were not on the roll of the Three Thousand in the Parthenon.[137]

Unfortunately, the fragment is vague concerning the exact quality of the objects involved and the way in which they were displayed during the procession. There are, however, other ways for us to find out to what kind of transaction Philochorus referred. Several marble *stēlai*, probably from the Agora, testify that in 402/1 BC, after the restoration of democracy, the property of the Tyrants was confiscated and sold.[138] The *stēlai* provide detailed information on several series of sales of the property of the Thirty and of their oligarchic associates by the *pōlētai* ('sellers'). The fragments list various estates, their sales price and the names of those who bought them.[139] Perhaps it was the money derived from these sales that was used to finance ritual equipment, as Michael Walbank suggested?[140]

However, if *kataskeuazein* in the last line of the fragment is taken to mean that the Athenians melted down oligarchic prestige objects into ritual equipment, as I believe Philochorus implies, the redefinition of meaning through the medium of gold, silver or bronze becomes an even more pronounced statement of symbolic discourse.[141] The inventories of the Hekatompedon list 27 silver *hydriae* for the years after the restoration of democracy that were not included in earlier records from the same temple.[142] It has been suggested that these may have been part of the *pompeia* made out of the property of the Thirty, and it is at least conceivable that some items of movable property of the tyrants were melted down to create these *hydriae*.[143]

Shear has argued that the Athenians, in the wake of the oligarchic revolutions, turned internal civil strife into external war and that they remembered the Thirty only selectively and in very restricted contexts.[144] In particular, she has shown that after the restoration of democracy, references to the Thirty were largely missing from official records. The absence of any

---

[137] X. *HG* 2.3.20.
[138] *SEG* XXXII 161. See also *Agora* XIX, P2 (70–74) and Shear 2011: 238, 246.
[139] E.g., *SEG* XXXII 161, 19–20, which mention a purchase made by a certain Meletus.
[140] Walbank 1982: 96.
[141] See [Plu.] *Moralia* 841 D for a parallel (albeit later) use of *kataskeuazein*.
[142] E.g., *IG* II² 1400, 23–32 (with *SEG* XXXIV 116); *IG* II² 1407, 14–20. See also Ferguson 1932: 113, n. 2; Linders 1987: 119. See also Harris 1995: 161–2 (V.260) with further references to the temple inventories listing the *hydriae*.
[143] See Foucart 1888: 288–9; Ferguson 1932: 113; Walbank 1982: 94–8.   [144] Shear 2011: 286–312.

direct identification of the silver *hydriae* with the property of the Thirty in the inventories fits this pattern.

The question emerges, however, of what we make out of this absence. Do we have to assume that it prevents the dynamics described here? The apparent absence of references to the Thirty in official records does not necessarily indicate their absence from popular memory. Indeed the amnesties after the restoration of democracy seem to be a good case in point, for they respond to the continuing presence of the Thirty in popular memory. The point is that one can prevent people from mentioning past ills in official contexts, but one cannot prevent them from nevertheless carrying all they know about their past in mind. Perhaps those memories that remain unarticulated are even more powerful exactly because they are suppressed? In other words, the history written out of the epigraphic evidence may not tell the whole story here; our fragment indicates that there may be another side to the dynamics of public remembering and forgetting in the wake of the reign of the Thirty at Athens than the one revealed by the official records.

Although our fragment does not refer to any specific festival, it is reasonably safe to assume that it occurred during the Panathenaia or the City Dionysia, two outstanding Athenian festivals which both involved extensive processions.[145] The simple allusion in the fragment to *pompeia* and *pompē* evokes such associations and it is unlikely that the Athenians would have bothered to invest their symbolic currency so heavily into much smaller festivals.[146] I think we can be even more specific. We know that a tenth of the property of traitors as well as of any man killed under the terms specified in the decree of Demophantus went to Athena, and it is likely that the same rule applied to the property of the Thirty and their followers.[147] This equipment would belong to Athena and would probably have been used only in her festivals. The silver *hydriae* of the treasure list mentioned above seem to confirm this as they are specifically listed as belonging to Athena Polias.[148] The *hydriae* would probably not have been used for the festival of other divinities. From this we can conclude with reasonable confidence that it was during the festival of the Panathenaia that the tyrant property turned ritual equipment was paraded.

---

[145] See Neils 1996a; Maurizio 1998.

[146] I would like to thank Peter Wilson for pointing this out to me.

[147] For the confiscation of property from traitors see [Plu.] *Moralia* 834 A–B. The decree is preserved in And. 1.96–98. Clinton 1982: 29, n. 10 argued that the decree was 'almost certainly included in the revised Solonian Code of 403/2'.

[148] See Harris 1995: 161 (V.260).

Among the different groups that marched in the processions at the Panathenaia, however, the metics (resident aliens) formed a particularly important subgroup.[149] Male metics (as well as young Athenian ephebes) were dressed in purple tunics and carried the *skaphai* (special sacrificial trays), while unmarried metic women helped the *kanēphoroi*, the Athenian maidens who carried the sacred baskets or vessels of gold and silver containing ritual equipment such as the sacrificial knife. Might the ritual equipment carried by these metics have been crafted out of the possessions of the Thirty? This proposition can be further supported by the fact that we know that *hydriae* in particular were among the ritual equipment carried in processions by female metics.[150]

If this scenario is correct, there would have been much more at stake than a simple restoration of religious equipment and temple treasures that had been seriously diminished in the years before the oligarchic revolution.[151] If it was the movable property of the Tyrants that was recast into ritual equipment, a fundamental 'recycling' of symbolic capital would lie at the heart of this transaction. Oligarchic prestige objects would have been removed from their circulation as 'political capital' first. They would have been melted down and recast into a very different, religious kind of 'symbolic currency' to be recirculated, in the Panathenaic procession, in the re-established democratic order.

If Philochorus was indeed referring to the melting and recasting of tyrant property into ritual objects to be displayed by metics during the Panathenaic procession, the whole episode takes on an even higher value, as the Thirty were infamous for killing metics of considerable wealth. The Athenian orator Lysias, who was himself a resident alien at Athens (his father had moved there from Syracuse), offered personal evidence for the hostilities of the Thirty against the metics.[152] He lost not only precious property and possessions to the Thirty, but also his brother Polemarchus, whom they executed. Apparently the Thirty even seized two golden earrings Polemarchus' wife was wearing at the time of his arrest.[153] In this scenario, then, the metics would have been displaying the repossessed and refashioned wealth of their murdered relatives.

However that may be, this episode entails an incident that was by no means unique. Rather, the incident mentioned in the fragment envisions several cultural practices concerned with the circulation of symbolic capital at the intersection of socio-political power and religious display, practices

---

[149] See Parker 2005: 170.   [150] See Miller 1992: 104.   [151] See Blamire 2001: 114–15.
[152] Lys. 12.   [153] Lys. 12.19.

that were well attested in Athens. Staying strictly within the religious realm, we have plenty of evidence for the recasting of one kind of symbolic religious currency into another.[154] We know, for example, that during the third century BC the priest of the Asclepieion at Athens was entitled to melt down those dedications that the sanctuary had received during his tenure and to have the material recast as an offering made in his name (ἐκ τῶν τύπων).[155] There was even a special class of temple inventory (the *kathairesis*) which listed objects to be removed from the sanctuary, mostly to be melted and recast into new ritual objects.[156]

The opposite procedure to the recycling of secular prestige objects into ritual equipment – the melting and use of temple inventory for worldly purposes in times of crisis and financial hardship – is also well attested in Athens.[157] The *locus classicus* here is Thucydides 2.13, in which Pericles in 434 BC speaks at great length of the possibility of using gold and silver offerings, sacred vessels and other procedural equipment, even the gold of the statue of Athena if necessary, in order to finance Athenian military operations. Indeed, even though the statue of Athena remained untouched, we know that golden *Nikai* dedicated to Athena were turned into coinage in 407/6 BC.[158]

The Thirty themselves in many ways provided the best example of a wartime process of melting and recasting of temple property to finance military operations. We know that in 404/3 BC they melted down two gold-plated *Nikai* into about 36–48 silver talents, probably to finance the 700 Laconian hoplites supporting their regime.[159] With the end of the Peloponnesian War and the restoration of democracy in Athens, there was consequently a real need to pay back at least some of the funds that had been 'borrowed' from the gods – another aspect which puts the Philochorus fragment into context.[160]

Even the very strategy the Athenians followed to repay their debt to the gods is not as singular as it might at first appear. Athenian democracy routinely confiscated property from convicted offenders. People found guilty of mutilating the herms and violating the Eleusinian Mysteries in

---

[154] Ferguson 1932: 110–27; Harris 1995: 28–39.   [155] See Aleshire 1989: 83. See also Aleshire 1992.
[156] See Aleshire 1989: 104; Harris 1995: 10–11.
[157] Several speeches by Demosthenes (*Against Androtion*, *Against Timocrates*) also addressed the issue of the melting and recasting of temple dedications. For an overview of this procedure at Athens: Ferguson 1932: 85–95; Harris 1995: 25–39; Blamire 2001 vs. Linders 1987: 117, who argues that the remelting and recasting of votives was 'a rare occurrence, the exception which proves the rule'.
[158] Hellanicus *FGrHist* 323a F26; Philochorus *FGrHist* 328 F141. See also Thompson 1965; Linders 1987: 115.
[159] *SEG* XXI 80; XXIV, 45. See also Thompson 1965; Krentz 1979: 61–3.
[160] See Arist. *Ath.* 39.6.

414/13 BC, for example, had their property confiscated and sold.[161] There was even a special group of ten officials, the *pōlētai* ('sellers', see above), elected from each of the ten *phylai*, whose job involved selling or leasing confiscated property. Most frequently this took the form of a public auction in front of the council, the outcomes of which were recorded on stone and displayed in public.[162] We have numerous fragments of such stones, which, just like our marble *stēlai*, demonstrate the popularity of this kind of procedure.[163]

The example of tyrant property turned into processional equipment ultimately confirms that Greek religion was more than a simple tool for individuals to achieve their goals. Rather, religious symbols were active players in the negotiation of socio-political power. Religious symbols, perhaps quite literally and materially in this example, shaped and were shaped by the power discourses permeating Greek culture and society.

CONCLUSION

This chapter examined the conception of religious symbols at the nexus of religious, social and political power. I illustrated that some classical scholars – most notably, perhaps, John Gould – conceived of the symbolic dimension of ancient Greek religion as a mere disguise for socio-political power. This instrumental view of the religious is based on the notion of religious symbols as, at least in principle, separate and separable from the world. Drawing on recent works in social anthropology (notably by Comaroff and Comaroff) I suggested that the symbolic dimension of ancient Greek religion should be taken to be intrinsic to and actively involved in the negotiation of socio-political power. This more dynamic conception of the circulation of religious symbols in ancient Greece also informed my reading of a fragment by Philochorus illustrating the 'recycling' of symbolic capital after the restoration of democracy at Athens in 403 BC. The same notion of religious symbols as intrinsic to the negotiation of socio-political power will be taken up in the next chapter, which investigates the place of magic within the broader religious culture of ancient Greece.

---

[161] *SEG* XIII 12–22; XIX 23–25. See also Pritchett 1953.
[162] See Langdon 1994 vs. Hallof 1990.
[163] See *Agora* XIX: 58–60 with examples. The *stēlai* set up at the Eleusinion recording the proceedings after the mutilation of the herms and the profanation of the Mysteries, for example, are discussed in Lewis 1966.

CHAPTER 4

Rethinking boundaries: the place of magic in the religious culture of ancient Greece

[T]hat heterodox and often arcane aspect of religion known as 'magic'.

Roy Kotansky[1]

The phenomenon of magic . . . cannot be separated from any serious understanding of ancient Greek religion.

Robert Fowler[2]

Religion contains magic, as one specific religious form.

Fritz Graf[3]

INTRODUCTION

In her once-influential book *Prolegomena to the Study of Greek Religion* (1903) Jane Ellen Harrison sketched a picture of ancient Greek religion in which the category of magic formed a central component of the religious. Influenced by evolutionary anthropology as practised by Frazer and others, Harrison sought to uncover an earlier, more 'primitive' stratum of ancient Greek religion, which significantly pre-dated the anthropomorphic conception of the Greek gods and goddesses living in an ordered divine society on Mount Olympus as propagated in particular by Homer and Hesiod (Olympianism).[4] This prehistoric stratum, she argued, was still visible in religious phenomena such as witchcraft, purification and mysteries, all practices that Olympianism had eventually driven underground. It was also evident in festivals such as the Thesmophoria, which were 'left almost uncontaminated by Olympian usage'.[5] Harrison, then, focused on magical elements in such festivals and practices in order to access earlier

---

[1] Kotansky 1991: 107. [2] Fowler 2000: 321. [3] Graf 1997a: 211.

[4] For a succinct formulation of this position see in particular Harrison 1905: 27–37. For the evolutionary perspective towards ancient Greek religion see also Murray 1912, later expanded into Murray 1925. The evolutionary approach ultimately goes back to Frazer's *The Golden Bough* and to Tylor, who influenced him. See Tylor 1871/1873; Frazer 1913; also Tambiah 1990: 42–54.

[5] Harrison 1903: 120.

stages in the development of ancient Greek religion – with the effect that magic became an ubiquitous feature within her oeuvre.

For Harrison magic meant almost exclusively 'a *drōmenon*, a rite which emphasises, and aims at inducing, man's collective desire for union with or dominion over outside powers', although she also occasionally discussed the symbolism of magical rituals and their indebtedness to certain kinds of belief.[6] As a *drōmenon*, magical practices featured in official contexts: the Thesmophoria, for example, was a fertility festival celebrated in autumn at which women carried magical *sacra* intended to cause nature to yield rich crops.[7] In Harrison's oeuvre, then, 'primitive religion' included an instrumental (magical) side, 'a web of practices emphasising particular parts of life', such as the importance of sowing in the agricultural cycle.[8]

Harrison's interest in magical ritual, however, was grounded in a much more fundamental difference she observed between the earlier stratum of the religious and the Olympianism that partly came to overwrite it. While the interaction with the gods of Homer and Hesiod was imagined as an exchange, a *do ut des* ('I give so that you may give'), the earlier stratum was based on the idea of *do ut abeas* ('I give so that you may keep away'):[9] '[T]he rites of the lower stratum are characterised by a deep and constant sense of evil to be removed and of the need of purification for its removal; that the means of purification adopted are primitive and mainly magical nowise affects this religious content.'[10] Magical ritual, it appears from this and other statements, was not opposed to religion: rather, it served as a practical means towards a goal that was ultimately religious in nature.

As one might expect from a so-called 'Cambridge ritualist', Harrison ultimately preferred the notion of divinity underlying magical ritual to the Homeric gods, which she criticised as being merely the product of art and literature. This focus on ritual practice as the true stuff of the religious explains the perhaps surprising fact that Harrison seems occasionally to have situated the Homeric gods themselves outside religion proper. In *Themis* she states 'these Olympians were not only non-primitive, but positively in a sense non-religious'.[11] Magical ritual, in contrast, especially the practices of sympathetic magic, was part of the 'old religion of Aversion' and reflective of a stage in the development of the religious in which magic and religion were not yet separated.[12]

---

[6] Harrison 1912: xi.   [7] See Harrison 1903: 120–62.   [8] Harrison 1912: viii.
[9] Harrison 1912: 134.   [10] Harrison 1903: ix.   [11] Harrison 1912: vii.
[12] Harrison 1903: x. See also her discussion of the role of cursing in the old religion in Harrison 1903: 138–45. The term 'sympathetic magic' was created by Frazer in his *The Golden Bough*: Frazer 1922: 12–55.

Harrison was by no means alone in including magical practices within the picture she drew of ancient Greek religion. Similar observations can be made of Rohde's *Psyche* (first published in 1890/1894), a study of ancient Greek conceptions of the immortality of the soul, which also traces an earlier stratum of the religious that included magical elements (for example, belief in ghosts and spirits and their magical powers). Implicitly, then, older scholarship seems to have promoted a perspective on ancient Greek religion that included a place for those practices, encompassing a darker and/or more instrumental side of the religious. More recently the capacity and willingness of scholars to incorporate this dimension seems to have vanished, together with the conception of the 'primitive' and interest in uncovering earlier 'stages' of the religious in ancient Greece.[13] From the days of Rohde and Harrison until relatively recently classical scholarship has perceived the category of magic as being in opposition to ancient Greek religion.

It is difficult to see why classical scholarship came to apply a hard and fast distinction between different religious practices in the ancient world. Implicit Christianising assumptions about the nature of magic and religion almost certainly played a role, as perhaps did the desire to turn the Greeks into a foundation of western culture and its values of reason and rationality. The sublime features of Homeric divinity and its worship in communal religious ritual seemed to be much more in line with this agenda than the darker and more egotistical uses of the supernatural.[14] Moreover, classical scholars could point to the ancient world itself to justify the fact that such practices as the writing of curse tablets, the wearing of protective amulets and certain kinds of healing and divination did not feature prominently in their works on Greek religion. After all, the Greeks (and Romans) themselves came to distinguish magic from communal and legitimate religious practice. In fact, ancient Greek language had several words that situated certain magical rituals and those who practised them outside religion proper – that is, outside the principles and practices of communal religious worship. In Sophocles' *Oedipus Rex*, Oedipus refers to the diviner Tiresias as 'this wizard (*magos*) hatcher of plots, this crafty

---

[13] See, e.g., Vernant's influential view (1980: 87–100) that we cannot say anything of value about Greek religion prior to the rise of the polis. See also the separation of the study of Minoan-Mycenaean religion as a subdiscipline in its own right. See, e.g., Burkert 1985: 47–53; Marinatos 1986; 1993.

[14] See also the dismissive description of Dieterich's work on the magical papyri as 'Botokudenphilologie'. The 'Botokuden' were a now-extinct tribe of Amazonian Indians. This term is first attributed to Wilamowitz in Pfister 1938: 183. It is unknown whether Wilamowitz-Moellendorff mentioned it in private conversation or somewhere in his oeuvre. On the distinction between the sublime and the archaic dimensions of ancient Greek religion, see also ch. 3.

beggar (*agurtēs*), who has sight only when it comes to profit, but in his art is blind'.[15] As Fritz Graf has rightly pointed out, Oedipus here seeks to degrade Tiresias (whom he suspects of taking Creon's side) by calling him words that set the beggar priest (*agurtēs*) and the *magos* in opposition to the diviner (*mantis*), whose position and legitimacy is officially endorsed by the polis.[16]

As will be argued below, the crucial difference between the ancient Greek distinction of magic and religion on the one hand and the way in which it came to feature in classical scholarship on the other, is that the conception of magic was part of a normative discourse from within ancient Greek society and by no means a fundamental classificatory category with an 'essence' of its own. It is only the way in which modern scholarship has turned magic into a descriptive category that has assigned to Greek religion such a quasi-dogmatic quality.[17]

There were, of course, also scholars such as Geoffrey Lloyd, who illustrated the role that magic played within the argumentative and evaluative contexts of critical inquiry.[18] In his study of the relationship between 'traditional patterns of thought' and the emerging scientific ways of reasoning Lloyd identified the Hippocratic treatise *On the Sacred Disease* (late fifth or early fourth century BC) as the context in which certain religious practices were first separated from religion under the label of magic.[19] Unfortunately, the implications of his argument for the study of Greek religion were never fully grasped.

Much subsequent scholarship has followed Harrison in assuming a fundamental and ultimately irreconcilable gap between Homeric Olympianism and its worship in official religious ritual on the one hand and those religious practices subsumed under the label of magic on the other.[20] But in contrast to older scholarship, the gap between magic and religion was now no longer constructed mainly along a temporal axis,

---

[15] S. *OT* 387–388 (transl. Lloyd-Jones 1994).

[16] Graf 1997a: 22. See also Bremmer 1993 on the different kinds of diviners.

[17] See Graf 1997a: 18. See also Bremmer 2010: 14.   [18] Lloyd 1979; also 1983.

[19] See Lloyd 1979: 15–29, 37–58. See also Dodds's famous study of the coexistence of the rational and the irrational in ancient Greek culture and society as well as Frazer's influential attempt to distinguish magic (and religion) from science. See Dodds 1951; Frazer 1922: 56–69 and the refutation of this position by Tambiah 1990: 51–4.

[20] See, e.g., Guthrie 1950: 270–7, 294–304 (who still refers to an evolutionary model to explain the fundamental difference between Homeric Olympianism and the kind of 'superstition' that informed religious phenomena such as witchcraft and curses); Mikalson 1983: 46–8, 88–9 (a study which treats magic mainly and marginally under the label of 'superstition' despite its focus on popular religion); Easterling and Muir 1985 (a collection of essays on *Greek Religion and Society* focused on civic Greek religion and from which magic is largely absent).

separating 'primitive stages' of the religious from later, more elevated ones. The difference was now believed to lie between two fundamentally different ways of relating to the divine, even though classical scholars always struggled to identify where exactly to draw the line between religion and magic as antithetical conceptions.

Intriguingly, perhaps, here too the model of polis religion proved 'good to think with'. Take for example Walter Burkert's definition of magic and religion in his study *Greek Religion*, still widely read as an authoritative introduction to the field:

Religious ritual is given as a collective institution; the individual participates within the framework of social communication, with the strongest motivating force being the need not to stand apart. Conscious magic is a matter for individuals, for the few, and is developed accordingly into a highly complicated pseudo-science. In early Greece, where the cult belongs in the communal, public sphere, the importance of magic is correspondingly minimal.[21]

Of course Burkert's book (which was first published in German in 1977) predates the formulation of polis religion by Sourvinou-Inwood and others.[22] But Burkert's conception of the religious as seen in this passage and elsewhere in his book is informed by the same assumptions about the nature of ancient Greek religion that led to the explicit formulation of polis religion about a decade later.[23] Burkert's statement nicely illustrates the fact that in the absence of a church, a dogma and an orthodoxy from ancient Greek religion, the polis came to serve as a point of reference that helped classical scholars draw the line between what constituted religion and what constituted magic. By adopting the concept of polis religion, Burkert effectively defined magical practices as being outside the scope of his study. Throughout his account of ancient Greek religion, magical beliefs and practices feature merely as an afterthought to official polis religion.[24]

A similar conception of religion and magic can also be found in Bruit Zaidman and Schmitt Pantel's study *Religion in the Ancient Greek City*, which shares with Burkert's *Greek Religion* the notion of the religious sphere as a communal and civic enterprise. But what is for Burkert a marginal and ultimately negligible pastime of individuals is for Bruit Zaidman and Schmitt Pantel a sign of final religious (and civic) decline. Magic features merely in their conclusion, in a section on continuity and change:

---

[21] Burkert 1985: 55.   [22] See also ch. 1 (with further literature).
[23] Sourvinou-Inwood's first article on polis religion was originally published in 1988.
[24] As for example reflected in the fact that Burkert has a chapter on prayer, but none on cursing: Burkert 1985: 73–5. The writing of *defixiones* ('curse tablets', 'binding spells', see below) features only in a last short paragraph of the chapter on prayer.

Over the centuries . . . the collective dimension of Greek religion with its function of providing reassurance to the civic community as a whole did gradually wither. As the repetition of ancient rituals became rigidly formulaic and meaningless, and recourse to magic and soothsayers blossomed, so at the same time the old spirit was superseded by that of personal communication with the godhead.[25]

For Burkert and Bruit Zaidman/Schmitt Pantel it was the polis, in the absence of other obvious organising principles of the religious, that served as the point of reference for the establishment of the boundedness of ancient Greek religion. Both studies illustrate that the model of polis religion, at least in its narrow formulation, cannot accommodate magical beliefs and practices, or certain mystery religions. Conceptually these religious phenomena do not fit into the framework provided by official polis religion: they are put in a special category and sidelined altogether.

In the last twenty years, however, various scholars have challenged this neat separation between religion and magic, both conceptually and with regard to the use of certain magical practices within the ancient world.[26] One way of doing this has been by demonstrating how widespread the casting of 'binding spells', *katadesmoi* (Latin: *defixiones*) was in the ancient Greek city. This practice, because of its sinister nature and the instrumental attitude towards the divine underlying it, almost always features under the rubric of magic in ancient rationalist discussions of this practice (in particular Plato, see below) as well as in modern scholarship. The popularity of *katadesmoi* in the ancient world, however, demonstrates that certain personal and instrumental uses of the divine were by no means as rare and negligible as some scholars have maintained.

Such binding spells were composed or commissioned by individuals, particularly those in situations of competition and risk, as a pre-emptive strike against their opponent in juridical affairs, in sports and theatrical competitions, against rival businesses and in matters of love.[27] However, although the use of such tablets was socially frowned upon, it would be wrong to assume that those who resorted to this practice always and necessarily saw themselves as situated outside the moral universe of the city. Occasionally it was precisely the strong sense of having been wronged that instigated the writing or commissioning of such spells. This notion is

[25] Bruit Zaidman and Schmitt Pantel 1992: 233.
[26] I.e., the essays collected in Faraone and Obbink 1991, which address and frequently challenge the neat separation between magic and religion. See also Graf 1997a: 205–33; Fowler 2000.
[27] On binding spells as pre-emptive strikes in agonistic situations see Faraone 1991b. On curse tablets and risk see Eidinow 2007a; 2007b. The question of whether these spells were composed by the cursing person or an expert is discussed in Ogden 1999: 54–60; Parker 2005: 121–2.

particularly tangible in the so-called 'prayer for justice' category of binding spells, a set of curse tablets which directly voice notions of right and wrong and combine the features of prayer and curse in various ways.[28] In certain situations (when one found oneself to be the victim of theft, for instance) and when there was little or no hope of pursuing the culprit through official legal channels, some people in the ancient world resorted to curse tablets.[29] The choice to use *katadesmoi* frequently depended on the other options available in a given situation.[30] Moreover, there was nothing magical about the practice of cursing itself, which also existed in various official (polis) contexts.[31] What gave *katadesmoi* the air of magic was merely their egotistical use outside official channels as well as the way in which they enacted a darker and more instrumental side of ancient Greek religion (see below).

Curse formulae ritually binding specific body parts of one's opponent were inscribed on lead tablets, folded and pierced with a nail.[32] They were buried underground, in graves or put into wells as preferred points of contact with the chthonic divinities.[33] They might also be deposited in sanctuaries of divinities associated with the underworld. About 1,600 curse tablets have been unearthed so far, originating from different corners of the Greek world, attesting to a cultural practice which seems to have originated in Sicily but which soon spread all over the ancient world.[34] From this evidence it emerged that it was by no means only – or even primarily – the marginal and un(der)represented within society who wrote or instigated the writing of these tablets.[35] There is plenty of evidence to

[28] Versnel 1991b. See also Gager 1992: 175–99. [29] See, e.g., SGD 58 = Eidinow 2007a: 418–19.

[30] The *katadesmos* came to Athens as a 'technology' recognised as a possibility of action available in the context of litigation, primarily because the institutions of democracy made litigation a central feature of the life of people of a certain status (see, e.g., the parody of this aspect of Athenian society in Ar. *V.*, below). See Gordon 1999b: 262–3: Eidinow 2007a: 165–90.

[31] On official polis curses see, e.g., Meiggs and Lewis 1988: 62–6 (no. 30); *IG* XI 1296; *SEG* XXVI, 1306; discussed in Graf in *ThesCRA* III. 6.g.: 250–253 (with further evidence).

[32] See Versnel 1998 for an examination of binding formulae featuring anatomical details.

[33] The technicalities involved are discussed in Faraone 1991b; Versnel 1991b: 60–3; Graf 1997a: 118–74; Ogden 1999: 3–90.

[34] The evidence is uneven in terms of its geographical and chronological distribution. About a third of the tablets are in Latin, and the rest are in Greek and the corpus includes the problematic category of the 'prayer for justice' binding spells (see above n. 28). More tablets emerge from archaeological excavations every year. A significant number of these curse tablets were also inscribed in perishable material (wax tablets) and have not survived. The most recent (non-comprehensive) collection by Eidinow can help to illustrate the popularity of the practice of ritual binding in classical Athens: Eidinow's catalogue lists 173 binding spells, of which 111 are from Athens/Attica. The overwhelming majority of these spells date from the fourth and third centuries BC. See Eidinow 2007a: 352–454. Her catalogue draws on a variety of earlier collections, including those of Wünsch 1897 (*DTAtt.*); Audollent 1904 (*DTAud.*); Jordan 1985a (SGD); 2000 (NGCT).

[35] See also Pl. *R.* 364b–c.

support the unsettling insight that citizens practised magic in the city along with everybody else.[36] The use and popularity of binding spells also cannot be read as a sign of impending socio-political decline. In Athens, at least, the writing of such spells started in the second half of the fifth century BC and peaked during the fourth, thus revealing that the practice of ritual binding, arguably the 'furthest extreme from civic norms' (Parker), was apparently part of the Greek city both in times of crisis and at the peak of her power.[37] Esther Eidinow has explained the particular popularity of curse tablets at Athens during that period in the context of political and social turbulence created by the Peloponnesian War, the collapse of the Athenian Empire and the oligarchic revolutions.[38]

In the face of such overwhelming evidence, most recent scholarship has moved away from the narrow conception of ancient Greek religion as always and necessarily confined to the communal and civic. The trend is now distinctly towards a more flexible and pluralistic depiction of the religious culture at Athens and elsewhere. One area of study that has seen a change in paradigm along these lines is mystery cults. Simon Price, for example, discussed mystery religions under the rubric of 'elective cults'.[39] Referring to religious phenomena such as Orphism, Dionysiac rituals, maenadism and the emergence of 'revisionist theogonies' he regarded religious ritual and participation both within civic religion and outside it as a matter of personal choice. This perspective allowed Price to present a finely nuanced picture of the complex relationship between civic and non-civic cults. The fruitfulness of this line of inquiry is realised in the richness and plurality of the picture of Greek religious life drawn in his account. A more complicated picture of the religious emerges in which the civic and the non-civic are variously intertwined: 'the choices which lay outside the range of cults did not just add additional options to the civic menu, but . . . sometimes incorporated critiques of the civic cults and Panhellenic

---

[36] E.g., *DTAud.* 60 = Eidinow 2007a: 394 (a judicial curse, probably written by the defendant in a pending court case. See Eidinow 2007a: 167; also Wilhelm 1904). The evidence is discussed in Ober 1989: 149; Graf 1996a: 79; Parker 2005: 128–31; Eidinow 2007a: 172–90. On the use of *defixiones* by the lower segments of Greek society (including slaves) see also Gager 1992: 151–75; Ogden 1999: 67–71.

[37] Parker 2005: 122. For the recourse to binding spells in fifth- and fourth-century BC Athens see, e.g., Costabile 2000; Parker 2005: 131–2; Eidinow 2007a: 141; 2007b.

[38] Eidinow 2007b.

[39] Price 1999: 108–25. The core of the idea of 'elective cults' goes back to the School of Rome. See, e.g., Sabbatucci 1965, who distinguished between everyday religion and religion of the abnormal case. See also Vernant 1980: 116–19 for a similar distinction applied more casually to the study of ancient Greek religion. See Edmonds 2004 on Orphic beliefs and practices and polis religion. On mystery cults see also most recently Bowden 2010.

myths or were genuine alternatives to them'.[40] This is invariably a more
interesting account of ancient Greek religion: it does not set elective cults
in a conceptual vacuum, but rather considers them in interaction with
polis religion.

Moving from mystery religions to magic – the main focus of this
chapter – Robert Parker has recently made similar efforts to include the
non-civic dimension of the religious. In *Polytheism and Society at Athens*
he dedicated a whole chapter to 'unlicensed religion', creating conceptual
space for this important aspect of religious life.[41] The main focus is on practitioners of ritual healing, initiations, divination and cursing as religious
phenomena that, in one way or another, sit uneasily between magic and
religion. The examination of the motives that prompt Athenians either to
use or condemn these practices throws light on the ambiguous nature of
the seer (*mantis*) – Parker speaks of 'polymorphousness' – a figure moving
between the opposing poles of the civic and public on the one hand and
the personal and unsanctioned on the other.[42]

Such efforts to write forms of 'unlicensed religion' and 'elective cults'
into the history of ancient Greek religion are reflected on the conceptual level in the old debate about the relationship between magic and
religion.[43] Magic and religion no longer stand in strict opposition: it has
become almost commonplace to point to the relatedness of magical and
religious practices. However, this is often done without stating exactly
what the study of magic contributes to the bigger picture of ancient Greek
religion – specifically how it relates to the principle and practices of polis
religion.

This chapter seeks to answer this question by situating magic once again
within ancient Greek religion. In contrast to older scholarship which relied
on an evolutionist conception of the 'primitive' in order to separate the
Olympianism of the Greek pantheon from the more individual and instrumental ways of relating to the divine, I argue that in order to appreciate the
full spectrum of Greek religious beliefs and practices we need to redefine
our notion of the religious culture of ancient Greece itself.

---

[40] Price 1999: 115.

[41] Parker 2005: 116–35. Bremmer 2010: 35 rightly notes that the assumption of a strict distinction in
the ancient Greek city between licensed and unlicensed beliefs and practices is anachronistic.

[42] On the ambiguous figure of the seer see also Flower 2008.

[43] The literature on this is vast. For an accessible synthesis of this debate within classical scholarship
and in the interdisciplinary study of religions more generally see Graf 1997a: 1–19; Dickie 2001:
18–46; Collins 2008. For some significant contributions to this debate within classical scholarship
see Segal 1981; Versnel 1991a; Lambert 1998; Braavig 1999; Bremmer 1999; Johnston et al. 1999;
Fowler 2000; Bremmer 2008. See also *ThesCRA* III. 6.1: 283–286.

So far we have looked at magic mainly historically, as featured in classical scholarship. In the remainder of this chapter I investigate magic as a much more fluent and unstable category of religious discourse in the ancient Greek city as it appears from a variety of perspectives, driven by different interests and from diverging points of view. I do so by focusing mainly (but not exclusively) on those aspects of magic relating to the institutional framework of the polis in the pre-Hellenistic period.[44] Throughout this chapter I promote a conception of magic as a category including a variety of discursively constructed locations of the religious, which belong firmly *within* the broader religious culture of ancient Greece. Magical beliefs and practices, I argue, shared with official polis religion a common symbolic universe but differed from it in how they related to this universe as well as in the uses to which this universe was put.

MAGIC – A RESPONSE TO CHAOS?

To start with, it may be worth revisiting an earlier line of inquiry. In Chapter 3 I investigated the symbolic dimension of ancient Greek religion ('symbolic' in the sense of a conception of religion as a system of signs, as a common symbolic 'language' shared by all Greeks). In particular I examined the way in which classical scholars have conceived of the relationship between religious symbols on the one hand and Greek politics and society on the other. I have shown that some classical scholars (Gould) follow Clifford Geertz's conception of religion as 'a response to chaos', a conception nicely summed up in Christiane Sourvinou-Inwood's succinct statement that 'Greek religion is, above all, a way of articulating the world, of structuring chaos, and making it intelligible'.[45]

Interestingly, classical scholars variously advance a similar line of argument for Greco-Roman magic. In the entry on 'magic rituals' ('magische Rituale') in the *Thesaurus Cultus et Rituum Antiquorum* (*ThesCRA*), for example, Robert Fowler made the observation that there seems to be surprisingly little variation between what different societies consider to be magic.[46] Trying to explain the similarity of phenomena subsumed under the label of magic across various cultures and societies, both historical and

---

[44] I do not discuss a variety of other religious phenomena which could fit under the rubric of magic (e.g., natural magic) and which largely operated below the level of the polis and her institutions.
[45] Sourvinou-Inwood 2000a: 19. See Hesiod's *Theogony* for a genealogy of religious powers emerging, quite literally, from Chaos.
[46] See Smith 1978b: 437 for a similar observation with regard to cross-cultural conceptions of the demonic.

contemporary, Fowler pointed to the phenomenology of religion, stating that 'all societies must have ways of apprehending and explaining the world, especially that part of it that is, precisely, unknowable and inexplicable'.[47]

This perspective is productive insofar as it raises the question of what sorts of phenomena people think demand a magical explanation. On the most general level and from the point of view of the interdisciplinary study of religions, it appears that different religious traditions refer to magic in order to explain things that are theologically difficult. It is not hard to believe in a god who makes everything turn out fine for you. It is much harder to cope with a divinity that sometimes makes things turn out well and sometimes not (hence the extensive 'problem of evil debate' in Christianity).[48] Within the context of ancient Greek religion one way of addressing this problem is to state that there are many gods pursuing different agendas, some of which may actually and occasionally harm humanity. Another is to posit that there are ways in which bad men ('magicians') can influence the world for the worse, either via a bad god (such as a *daimōn*) or with the help of more direct and instrumental magical means.

Fowler's observation is therefore certainly correct. But the question emerges of what this statement implies more deeply about the way in which magic relates to the 'world' beyond its usefulness in explaining theologically difficult phenomena. Does this mean that there are aspects of the 'world' shared by all societies – even those as disparate as ancient Greece and, let's say, early modern Europe – and which fall under the realm of magic? And, if so, what are the implications for our concepts of 'world' and 'response', be they magical or religious?

The point that magic provides a 'language' for any given society to address the contingencies of life has, of course, a long ethnographic prehistory, dating at least back to Evans-Pritchard and perhaps even to Malinowski.[49] In *Witchcraft, Oracles and Magic Among the Azande* Evans-Pritchard described a society in which accusations of magic provided a means of explaining the fortuities of Azande life.[50] In particular, adverse circumstances and misfortunes of all kinds were accounted for with reference to witchcraft; the poison oracle was used to find out who was behind a perceived misfortune. Magic here, defined as a cultural system, a symbolic 'language' responding to an intrinsically chaotic world, was a ubiquitous

---

[47] *ThesCRA* III. 6.1: 285. An early formulation of magic as a response to particular aspects of the world: Kagarow 1929: 1 ('die psychologische Grundlage des Fluchs').

[48] See, e.g., Rowe 2001; van Inwagen 2004; van Inwagen 2006. Within Christianity, at least, one way of coming to terms with this problem is to believe in an anti-God, the devil.

[49] Malinowski 1954.   [50] Evans-Pritchard 1937.

feature of Azande life. But how was it related to religion, another symbolic 'language', equally concerned with the contingencies of life?

Interestingly, Evans-Pritchard sketched a picture of a society from which religion was conspicuously absent. As C. G. Seligman noted in the foreword to this study: 'It seems, indeed, that among Azande magic and religion stand so far apart that they have almost nothing to do with each other.'[51] As a result of this remarkable separation, it follows that those who are interested in Azande religion have to look elsewhere in Evans-Pritchard's oeuvre.[52]

One may, of course, doubt whether both dimensions of Azande life were really so separate and separable. There seems, for example, a considerable quantity of religion looming in the background of how the poison oracle operates. Be that as it may, Evans-Pritchard's separation of religion and magic meant that for him the problem of how religion and magic as 'symbolic languages' responding to the contingencies of 'world' are related to each other did not arise. Thus, what purports to be a much more problematic statement for other societies (that magic is a response to the contingencies of life) is apparently unproblematic for Azande society.

In Chapter 3 I argued that some classical scholars conceptualise the layers of 'world' and of 'response' separately, with the effect that, more frequently than not, religious symbols are detached from the social actions and processes in which they derive their meaning. I further argued that this often results in assigning religious symbols a quality of their own (a *sui generis* quality). The same point applies, I believe, to the scholarly conception of magic as a symbolic language and to the way in which it is thought to relate to the world.

Take for example the following statement from Faraone and Obbink concerning the place of magic in Greek culture and society – two succinct formulations of the magic-as-a-response-to-chaos hypothesis:

Individuals in antiquity turned to such rituals in the hope of bettering their fortunes in a natural world that seemed hostile and unpredictable, in a society that competed fiercely for the use and control of limited resources and advantages . . . Indeed a close reading of the extant sources for daily life in the ancient world reveals many such common fears and persistent uncertainties that daily beset all men and women, rich and poor, slave or free. Unrequited love, sterility, impotence, gout, eye disease, bad luck at the races, or an unexpected setback in a legal case – all these and a multitude of other distresses are revealed in the texts of the magical inscriptions and papyri.[53]

---

[51] Seligman in Evans-Pritchard 1937: xvi.   [52] Evans-Pritchard 1936.
[53] Faraone and Obbink 1991: v–vi. See also Graf 1997a: 113 for a similar statement of magic as a response to the contingencies of Greek life.

There is nothing wrong with these observations except, perhaps, that they seem to presuppose the existence of 'world' prior to and – in principle at least – independent from the responses to it, be they magical or religious in nature. First, there are contingencies, some of which pertain to all human life (lovesickness, lack of offspring, disease, a general uncertainty about the future), others of which, such as an increased sense of competitiveness, seem to pertain in particular to life in ancient Greece. Second, there is magic as a means of dealing with these contingencies, of addressing them, of controlling them, of 'making sense' of them by placing them in a larger cosmology which may or may not be identical to that of (polis) religion.

To conceive of the 'world' and our 'response' to it as (at least in principle) separate and separable categories, however, raises a whole set of questions. Does magic offer the same kind of response to the same kind of world as religion – in which case there would be no obvious difference between the two? Or is it, indeed, another response to the same kind of world? The same response to another aspect of world? Another response to another aspect of world? These questions have loomed in the background of much scholarship on Greco-Roman magic – without, however, producing any satisfying results. To answer these questions in a satisfying way would require religion, magic and different kinds of 'world' to be *sui generis* categories.[54]

That things are much more complicated than this is readily acknowledged by Faraone, Obbink and other classical scholars. Yet the ultimate desire to specify some kind of difference between the two still resonates – parenthetically at least – in the familiar suggestion that magic may be a more personal and instrumental extension of ancient Greek religion: 'All these practices border ostensibly on the sphere of religion (perhaps of a private and familial sort) insofar as they document perhaps attempts on the part of individuals to influence factors in their environment that are beyond their immediate control.'[55]

If we want to understand the place of magic in Greek culture and society (and in religion as part of it) we will have to look elsewhere, beyond all separate and essentialist conceptions of the 'world' and our 'responses' to it, be they magical or religious in nature. Taking up a line of argument I advanced in Chapter 3 for religion as a symbolic system and extending it to magic: we should conceive of magic and of the 'world' to which it relates

---

[54] A *sui generis* category is a unique category with an irreducible quality (an essence) of its own. Religion as a *sui generis* category: Saler 1993: 1–4.

[55] Faraone and Obbink 1991: vi. See also Graf 1997a: 14; Dickie 2001: 25–6.

not as ultimately separate and separable categories but as an inextricable whole. That is to say, magic carves out and creates the world it refers to just as much as it is itself carved out and defined by that world.[56]

An excellent illustration of this point can be found in Richard Gordon's suggestion of the intimate relationship between magic and the marvellous.[57] Gordon rightly pointed out that in the ancient world there was no unified concept of magic. What we find instead is 'a whole gamut of representations and claims [which] competed in the market-place, each with its own agenda.'[58] If we consider in particular longer periods of time, magic appears in different modes, not necessarily reducible to a single 'ultimate' description.[59] The Hellenistic period, for example, witnessed the emergence of a strong conception of magic that differed from its classical precedents by operating with a much more clearly defined counter-cultural force.[60] At the same time, however, Gordon identified the category of the marvellous as a significant reference point of Greco-Roman conceptions of magic. What is the marvellous? In Gordon's words 'the marvellous... is in effect simply the totality of perceived infringements of culturally-stated rules for normality'.[61] Norms and normality, however, are cultural constructs, as are perceived deviations from them: 'Normality is of course neither fixed nor necessarily agreed: the marvellous is always produced within a micro-climate of evaluative assertions.'[62]

Gordon's conception of the marvellous, then, presupposes the existence of a highly complex category of 'the normal' against which it defines itself. In doing so 'the marvellous' includes both the fantastic and the strange. Good things that happen abnormally and out of the ordinary are indeed 'marvellous'. But just as magicians practise 'white magic' by relying on good or neutral deviations from the norm, they also practise 'black magic', by referring to potentially threatening or obscure and uncanny deviations from the conventional order of things – ghosts, for example, and their role in Greco-Roman magic immediately come to mind. Gordon's conception of the marvellous, it follows, is neither positively nor negatively marked,

---

[56] This is not to say that magic is merely an imaginative idiom. On the contrary! The author of this study can personally attest to the fact that magic can be quite tangible. When she was about five her beloved granddad convinced her that she had just 'sold' him a small wart on her foot for the price of two *Deutsche Mark*, whereupon it disappeared.

[57] Gordon 1999a: 168–78.

[58] Gordon 1999a: 162. See also Luck 1990: 171–204; Gordon 1997.

[59] E.g., Gordon 1999a; Moreau and Turpin 2000.   [60] See Segal 1981; Gordon 1999a.

[61] Gordon 1999a: 168. The related conception of the miraculous in different magical practices, such as healing: Weinreich 1909; Lloyd 1979: 49–58; Luck 2006: 177–84.

[62] Gordon 1999a: 168–9.

but defines itself on constantly shifting ground of evaluative assertions about what is normal and what is not.[63]

To illustrate the significance of the marvellous as a reference point for magic, however, we will look at the divinatory skills of a certain Apollonius of Tyana, a 'divine man' (*theios anēr*) who roamed the ancient world during the first century AD. The historical Apollonius lived about 150 years before Philostratus wrote his biography at the request of the empress Julia Domna. Based on the, probably fictional, notes of Damis, a pupil and admirer of the sage, Philostratus' *Vita Apollonii* offers a rich picture of the role of Hellenism in the Roman world reflected in and through the actions and comments of Apollonius as the representative and upholder of Greek *paideia*.[64] Philostratus, his biographer, recounted that during a trip to Babylon, Apollonius and his companion Damis happened upon a lioness, just killed by hunters. Philostratus carefully described the lioness through the eyes of Apollonius, Damis and of the villagers present at the scene:

It was a big animal, larger than they had ever seen, and people from the village had run together and were shouting, and so indeed were the hunters, as if they saw some great miracle in it (ὥς τι μέγα θαῦμα ἐν αὐτῷ ὁρῶντες). In fact, it really was a miracle (ἦν ἀτεχνῶς θαῦμα), since when it was cut open it had eight cubs.[65]

Philostratus followed this with a brief excursus on the breeding habits of lions and how they had three cubs in the first litter, with the number decreasing to two in the second, and to one in the third. The existence of eight cubs was certainly a significant aberration. Returning to Apollonius, Philostratus went on to describe meticulously the reaction of the sage from Tyana:

Apollonius looked into the animal, and after pondering a long time said: 'Damis, the duration of our journey to the king will be one year and eight months. He will not release us sooner, and it will not be propitious for us to leave before then. We must infer the months from the cubs, and the year from the lioness, for you have to compare units with units.'[66]

---

[63] This conception of the marvellous is ultimately derived from Todorov's discussion of Romantic literature of the fantastic (Gordon pers. comm.). See Todorov 1975.

[64] The relationship between the historical Apollonius and the main character of the *VA* has for long been a central question in scholarly works. E.g., Bowie 1978; Anderson 1986: 155–97; 1994: 26. More recent scholarship, most notably Elsner 2009, has moved more toward the appreciation of Philostratus' Apollonius in his own terms. On Philostratus' *VA* see also ch. 6.

[65] Philostr. *VA* 1.22. Here and elsewhere in this book the numeration of Philostratus' *VA* follows the one by Jones, C. 2005.

[66] Philostr. *VA* 1.22.2.

A cynical reading of this passage would accuse Apollonius of merely abusing the strange and deviant for his own purposes. But much more is at stake here. The sage from Tyana practically appropriates the strange by 'translating' it into an elaborate divinatory system of knowledge with its very own logic. According to this logic, an aberration in nature – explicitly judged here against the background of empirical conceptions of the norm and the normal – becomes meaningful in its own right as exactly that: an aberration from the norm. The marvellous as something prior to and defying understanding becomes the marvellous as something intrinsic to the act of 'making sense'.[67]

Apollonius practically projects divinatory significance and regularity on to a pre-existing concept of nature as an ordered entity. This is brought out nicely in his elaboration. For in order to underline his credentials as an expert proficient in the reading of signs he gives not only the information derived from the lioness and her cubs but explicitly spells out the relevant code: 'We must infer the months from the cubs, and the year from the lioness, for you have to compare units with units.'[68] The extent to which Apollonius' divinatory system maps on to nature as an ordered system is emphasised even more forcefully when Damis subsequently challenges his interpretation. Referring to Calchas' interpretation of the length of the Trojan War in the *Odyssey* as inferred from the number of sparrows devoured by a snake, Damis points out: 'They were eight, and the snake also caught the mother, making nine. When Calchas interpreted all that, he foretold that Troy would be taken in nine years; so maybe according to Homer and Calchas our absence will last for nine years?'[69] The sage from Tyana is quick to point out that reading cubs and reading sparrows is not the same:

It is reasonable . . . for Homer to equate the chicks with years, since they have birth and existence. But how could I equate unformed animals that have not yet been born, and perhaps might not even have survived to birth, with years? For unnatural things (τὰ γὰρ παρὰ φύσιν) cannot come about, and if they do, they are subject to swift decay.[70]

Damis' challenge of his interpretation allows Apollonius to elaborate on his reading of an accidental and strange occurrence by presenting it as part of a much broader conception of natural divination. During the course of this elaboration, a seemingly accidental occurrence acquires meaning

[67] On this point see also Gordon 1999a: 168–78.   [68] Philostr. *VA*. 1.22.2.
[69] Philostr. *VA* 1.22.2. See also Hom. *Il.* 2.299–330.   [70] Philostr. *VA* 1.22.2.

as part of a larger conception of nature as equally ordered and divinely enchanted.

The sage from Tyana here refers this sign to an event in his own life. In doing so, he claims to know not only what signifies (and what does not) but also what the application of the signification may be. Philostratus' Apollonius draws on a conception of nature as an ordered system and presents it as the ultimate source of his divinatory power. By grounding his interpretation within an argument about what is natural and what is not, Apollonius ultimately both rationalises and 'naturalises' his own power and authority as an expert reader of marvellous signs.[71] But this attempt can be successful only because 'world' and 'response' are mutually implicit. The 'miracle' of the cubs literally demands an interpretation which establishes the exact quality of its meaning and, in turn, the interpretation itself draws on the imagery provided by the cubs and turns them into an elaborate code. What is at stake in this curious incident is nothing less than a profound fusion of the categories of 'world' and 'response' via the notion of the marvellous. The world is shaped by the 'response' just as the 'response' is itself shaped by the world, is part of, and participates in, the world, *is* the world. The cubs 'make sense' only in Apollonius' interpretation.

But is this form of lion-cub divination magic or religion? As Gordon has rightly pointed out, both religion and magic share a common inter-est in the marvellous.[72] The difference between magic and religion with regard to the marvellous is merely one of perspective. In ancient Greece, as elsewhere, there was a strong tendency to monopolise legitimate reli-gious capital.[73] More frequently than not this involved a process whereby certain forms and formulations of the marvellous were 'rejected, edited out, rationalized' by the dominant religious discourse. In particular, if the marvellous was used to formulate claims to power outside and independent of the acknowledged religious authorities of mainstream religion, it appar-ently became a threat (hence the attempts of people like Apollonius to link their observation of the marvellous back to acknowledged institutions of mainstream Greek religion).[74] If the marvellous/occult is made to support a universe independent from and alternative to that of communal religious

---

[71] This makes Apollonius and his conception of nature as a universal category a prime example of Lloyd's point that the magical tradition occasionally draws upon concepts and modes of reasoning developed in critical inquiry: Lloyd 1979: 49–58.

[72] Gordon 1999a: 174.

[73] Gordon 1999a: 174; also 1999a: 163 on the monopolisation of legitimate religious capital. On symbolic capital and its role within ancient Greek religion see also chs. 3, 4 (with further references).

[74] On the marvellous as a threat see also the instances of legal persecution of magic as discussed towards the end of this chapter. For Apollonius' links to institutions of civic religion see below n. 82.

practice, it tends to be rejected. This applies to ancient Greek religion as to other religious traditions, most notably, perhaps, to Christianity. It follows that the apparent congruence Fowler noted in what different cultures consider to be magic (see above) is no more surprising than the apparent congruence in what different societies consider to be religion.

In the case of a religion like that of the ancient Greeks, especially, locating dominant discourse and religious authority is far from straightforward. For a religion that lacked a church, a dogma, a creed and even a holy literature, religious authority was largely – but by no means exclusively – vested in the political institutions of the polis.[75] During the classical period this involved a complex distribution of religious power between the *dēmos*, various priesthoods and religious specialists, such as the *chrēsmologoi* and *exēgētai*.[76] This situation did not change fundamentally during the Hellenistic and Roman periods, when the Greek world became subsumed into larger political entities and when more religious institutions and structures were added to the picture.

As a result, however, it was not always clear who could say what was part of official (religious) discourse and what was not. For some, if not most, cultural practices (such as divination) the boundary between magic, religion and their conceptions of the marvellous/occult always remained murky.[77] Much depended on whom one asked. While the emperor Domitian accused Apollonius of being a magician, certain Greek city-states seem to have embraced the sage from Tyana as a religious figure, and Philostratus' Apollonius himself certainly wants us to see him as merely a privileged reader and disseminator of divine knowledge.[78] As Robert Parker succinctly put it, 'magic differs from religion as weeds differ from flowers, merely by negative social evaluation'.[79] This should not tempt us to assume that every belief or practice could be referred to as magic. Just as there is widespread cultural agreement as to what exactly constitutes a weed and what constitutes a flower, there were certain 'generic' notions of what constituted magic in the ancient world, and those who referred to this concept – by evoking it, by criticising it, by denying it – had to 'work with' these notions.

Philostratus' Apollonius, for example, variously addresses such generic conceptions as he seeks to clear himself of suspicions of magic. Throughout the *Vita Apollonii* the sage from Tyana walks a fine line between appropriating the marvellous as a source of empowerment and presenting the charismatic authority resulting from it as divinely inspired and endorsed.

---

[75] See below with further references. [76] See Garland 1984.
[77] See Graf in *ThesCRA* III. 6.1: 290. [78] Philostr. *VA* 1.1. [79] Parker 2005: 122.

Many of his practices, in particular his skills in divination and prophecy, looked suspiciously like magic to his contemporaries.[80] He therefore makes a strong point of not accepting any money for his services, of carrying them out in the open and of presenting himself as upholding rather than inverting traditional religious customs – thereby inverting features that in the ancient world were associated with magic and its practitioners.[81] He also seems to be particularly attracted to Greek sanctuaries as 'focusing lenses' of official religious discourse.[82] Generally, he is keen to show himself as following divine orders rather than coercing the gods to act on his behalf.[83] It is in this sense that the episode discussed above, which so impressively demonstrates Apollonius' skills in evoking privileged access to a special kind of knowledge, concludes with a humble reference to the divine. Having just refuted Damis' objection to his interpretation of the marvellous sign he encourages his disciple to move on: 'So follow my reasoning, and let us depart after praying to the gods who reveal all this.'[84] Magic, the case of Apollonius confirms, is an evaluative concept from within Greek religion; it is a concept which allows the speaker to align himself/herself pragmatically on one side of an invisible and constantly renegotiated line – whatever other positions he or she may take up in other situations. We will return to this point later.

Meanwhile, let us leave the example of Apollonius and return to the question we raised at the beginning of this section concerning the nature of magic and its relationship to religion: magic, like religion, is not a category *sui generis* with an irreducible essence of its own – hence the futility of attempts to find such a general essence, applicable in all instances, and in opposition to religion. The ancient Greek conception of magic becomes tangible only when we situate it within the social (inter)actions and processes in which it derives its meaning. This focus, however, ultimately and invariably points back to the normative force and the ideological discourse of the polis.

In order to understand the consequences of this point for the way in which we conceptualise the religious in ancient Greece, we return once more to classical Athens as the typical setting of polis religion. In the following section I investigate the place of magic within what I shall refer

---

[80] E.g., Philostr. *VA.* 1.2; 4.43; 5.12; 7.11.3; 8.19.2.
[81] E.g., Philostr. *VA.* 1.11, 21.3; 4.41, 44.3; 8.7.7–12. See Kolenkow 2002 on the link between power and communality in the workings of magic and religion.
[82] E.g., Philostr. *VA.* 1.8.2, 9.1; 2.8, 22.1; 3.24.3; 4.14, 30.1; 5.5.2; 6.4.1; 8.7.7. On Apollonius' links to Greek sanctuaries, see also Kolenkow 2002: 138. On sacred space as a 'focusing lens' see Smith 1988: 53–65.
[83] See ch. 6 (with further literature).   [84] Philostr. *VA.* 1.22.2.

to as the larger religious culture of Athens. I argue that bringing magic into the picture is absolutely essential as it reveals alternative locations of the religious outside/alongside those of polis religion. Official polis discourse sought to marginalise those locations (by labelling them magic) but they were nevertheless central to the religious culture of Athens and other Greek cities. The result is a much more dynamic picture of ancient Greek religion and of Athenian polis society.

MAGIC AND THE POLIS REVISITED

Consider the following three 'fragments', all 'sites' or manifestations of Athenian culture and society during the late fifth and fourth centuries BC.

A comedy of inversion

During the Lenaean festival of 422 BC Aristophanes' *Wasps* was performed at Athens. The drama exposes the workings of Athenian public institutions (most notably perhaps the civil law courts, or *dikastai*) as biased, greedy and ultimately corrupt. The comic plot revolves around the figure of Lovecleon, a likeable elderly Athenian, who frequents the courts for money, kudos and as an entertaining pastime. He is confronted by his son Loathcleon, who is set to convince his father – by persuasion and, if necessary, by brute force – to retire.[85] The comedy features a scene in which Loathcleon stages a domestic trial in order to convince Lovecleon of the advantages of staying at home.[86] The suspect is a barky dog, which has stolen a piece of cheese. But when the dog takes the stand to defend itself it is suddenly struck silent. This surprising inversion of the ordinary is related within the drama (and outside it, in the *scholia vetera* on Aristophanes' *Wasps*) to a real-life incident: a certain Thucydides, son of Melesias and a political rival of Pericles, had apparently lost his persuasive faculties in a recent court case.[87] The drama alludes to binding spells as a cultural 'code', providing us with two divergent readings. Is the (canine/human) protagonist struck by a binding spell? Or is his silence due to a much more 'profane' sudden failure of nerve? The difference between these two interpretations of the courtroom situation hinges on the success of those who evoke the workings of magic. Magic again appears to create the 'world' it responds to just as it is itself a product of that 'world'.

---

[85] I follow Henderson's translation of the characters' names here: Henderson 1998.
[86] Ar. *V.* 826–1008.
[87] Ar. *V.* 944–949; ∑ Ar. *V.* 947b. See also Faraone 1989: 149–50.

A philosopher's vision

About forty years later, around 380 BC, Plato developed his idea of a virtuous state. The *Republic* features extensive dialogue between Socrates and various other interlocutors, both from Athens and beyond. The discussion revolves around a set of closely interrelated problems. What is justice? Who is happier, the virtuous man or the unvirtuous? And, finally, what is the best form of government for the polis? Within the context of whether justice is better than injustice, one of the speakers, Adeimantus, presents the view that some people seem to be able to make use of the gods for unjust purposes:

> Begging priests and soothsayers (ἀγύρται δὲ καὶ μάντεις) go to rich men's doors and make them believe that they by means of sacrifices and incantations (θυσίαις τε καὶ ἐπῳδαῖς) have accumulated a treasure of power from the gods that can expiate and cure with pleasurable festivals any misdeed of a man or his ancestors, and that if a man wishes to harm an enemy, at slight cost he will be enabled to injure just and unjust alike, since they are masters of spells and enchantments (ἐπαγωγαῖς τισὶ καὶ καταδέσμοις) that constrain the gods to serve their end.[88]

Given the strong sentiments voiced here against these forms of appropriating the gods, it should come as no surprise that similar activities are outlawed in Plato's ideal city as sketched in his later dialogue *Laws*.[89]

A lead tablet

Sometime towards the end of the fourth century BC a small lead tablet was deposited in a grave near the Dipylon Gate of the Kerameikos, a district in the north-east of Athens which housed one of the city's burial grounds.[90] The tablet was later found in a nearby well together with another 'binding spell' and 574 other tablets, all featuring the records of the annual evaluation of the Athenian cavalry.[91] Our tablet shows two inscriptions: one of which is upside down and consists of the misspelt beginning of

---

[88] Pl. *R.* 364b5–364c4.

[89] Pl. *Lg.* 909a–d. See also *Lg.* 933a. On Plato's representation of magic in this and other contexts see also Graf 1997a: 22–3; Motte 2000; Collins 2008: 139–41.

[90] SGD 14. Jordan 1980: 236 tentatively dated the tablet to 313–307 BC and suggested a grave as the most likely site of the original deposition of the tablet. However, I think we can be even more precise: although Diodorus Siculus recounted the installation of Demetrius at Athens under 318 BC (D. S. 18.74.3), the fact that he mentioned Eupolemus in this text (D. S. 19.77.6) means that it must have been at least as late as 313 BC. The occasion might be Cassander's loss of Caria and other conquests to Ptolemy, or Ptolemy's attempted liberation of Greek cities in 310 BC. On the tablet see also Gager 1992: 147–8 (no. 57); Eidinow 2007a: 169, 408. Other evidence from this area: Peek 1941: 89–100; Willemsen 1990.

[91] See Braun 1970: 197–269.

a name: 'Pleistea'. The other inscription lists several names, including (the now correct) Pleistarchus, Eupolemus, Cassander and Demetrius of Phalerum (all in the accusative) and 'Peiriea' (a misspelt demotic). An Athenian of the later fourth century BC would probably have had no doubt who was meant here: the Macedonian Cassander dominated Athenian politics until 307 BC, when Antigonus and Demetrius Poliorcetes liberated Athens from Macedonian rule.[92] The other names on the tablet also refer to more or less prominent individuals in Cassander's circle: Pleistarchus, his younger brother; Eupolemus, his general in Greece; and the Peripatetic philosopher Demetrius of Phalerum, head of the oligarchic regime installed by Cassander and overseer of Athens.[93] Because of the high political profile of all the individuals named here, David Jordan has suggested we take this tablet as 'the result of some Athenian's displeasure at the Makedonian domination of his city'.[94]

An instance of comic reversal; a philosophical conversation; a lead tablet deposited in a grave. Surely these are very different 'fragments' or 'sites', shedding light on (and participating in) Athenian cultural, social and intellectual life in different ways, from different perspectives and through different prisms and factions. While the tablet is a direct trace of an instance of ritual binding, Aristophanic comedy refers indirectly to the same cultural practice by appropriating it for its own comic purposes. And philosophers, even those as prominent as Plato, are hardly ever taken to represent the principles and practices of real life or, as it were, the aims and ambitions of ordinary people. The three perspectives on offer here, then, hardly add up to a single coherent picture. But one point in which these three manifestations of Athenian cultural life invariably converge is that the practice of magic – and that of casting binding spells in particular – belongs firmly within the ancient Greek city.[95] All three examples situate *katadesmoi* right at the core of Athens and her civic institutions. Moreover, they do so both spatially and ideologically: the curse tablets here appear to be an explosive force intruding into the civic institution of the *dikastai*, a force to be reckoned with in the civic arena of political antagonism,

---

[92] D. S. 18.64ff. See also Jordan 1980: 229–36; Habicht 1997: 36–66.
[93] On Pleistarchus see D. S. 19.77.6–28.2; Plu. *Demetr.* 31.4–5; Paus. 1.15.1. Eupolemus is almost unknown. From D. S. 19.77.6. we know only that he was left as the military controller of Greece in 313 BC, when Cassander had to defend Macedonia against Antigonus. On Eupolemus see also D. S. 19.68.7. On Demetrius of Phalerum see D. S. 18.74.3. See also D. S. 19.68.3, 78.4; 20.27.1, 46.2 and Str. 9.1.20; D. L. 5.75–85; Cic. *Leg.* 3.14.
[94] Jordan 1980: 234.
[95] This is nicely brought out in the title of Carastro 2006 (*La Cité des mages*).

and an economic force within the *cosmos* of Plato's *politeia*. Indeed, by making godly intervention a service people can buy, binding spells extend the regular economy into an 'economy of the occult'.[96]

Our three 'fragments' are neither special nor unrepresentative in establishing such a clear link between *katadesmoi* and the city. Other binding spells that have come down to us from classical Athens illustrate this relationship as well: the theatre spells, a small group of spells directly attacking the civic institution of the *chorēgia* immediately come to mind.[97] Indeed, examples just as revealing as our comic 'fragment' could have been drawn from the various instances of magic as it featured in Athenian tragedy. In Aeschylus' *Oresteia*, for example, the older and invariably female forces of the Furies threaten Orestes' performance before the jury of Athenian citizens through the destructive power of their binding song (ὕμνον δέσμιον).[98] For Orestes to come to rest, for justice to be served, and for the city to flourish, the Furies and their destructive force must become integrated into the city itself.

Note also the profound symbolic proximity between the practice of ritual binding and the practices of official religious discourse. Binding spells relied on a variety of notions that were fundamentally religious in nature: the more elaborate tablets which list more than just names often refer to Hermes, Hecate, or Demeter as divinities associated with the underworld – an association variously developed in Greek mythology. In doing so they played up the chthonic dimension of the Greek pantheon, which complemented and extended divine Olympianism. Some tablets draw on the Greek notion of the 'untimely dead' (ἄωροι) as able to bring the spell to the attention of those divinities. Moreover, the entire conception of ritual binding was based on the assumption that the Greek gods had the will and skill to initiate an occasionally explosive intervention into human affairs – an assumption that was carefully cultivated in many beliefs and practices of polis religion. This notion also informed the oath as a central institution of civic discourse or the various collective curses spoken on behalf of the polis.[99] The casting of binding spells in all its forms and formulations, then, drew on the same symbolic universe, the same theology,

---

[96] The conception of an 'occult economy' is borrowed from Comaroff and Comaroff 1999.

[97] For the curses relating to the theatre from Athens see *DTAtt.* 33, 34, 45. See also SGD 91 (not from Athens). These spells are discussed in Gager 1992: 42–77; Wilson 2000: 155–6; Eidinow 2007a: 156–64.

[98] A. *Eu.* 306.

[99] On the Greek oath see, e.g., Hirzel 1902; Plescia 1970; Sommerstein and Fletcher 2007. On official polis curses see *ThesCRA* III. 6.1: 250–253. The absence of this belief in the gods is discussed as a primary form of *asebeia* in Plato's *Laws* (e.g., Pl. *Lg.* 885B).

as polis religion, even if it sometimes did so in different, even opposing, ways.[100] In short, *katadesmoi* 'made sense' only within the framework of ancient Greek religion. The same point applied equally to the interpretation of portents and other forms of magical divination, the principles and practices of magical healing, to magical incantations, prayers, talismanic statues and protective or aggressive amulets.[101] In order to be effective magic depended upon a 'theology' and this 'theology' was that of official Greek religion.

Rather than separating magical beliefs and practices such as the casting of binding spells from the civic dimension of Greek life (and from the religious discourse supporting it), I suggest we follow the perspective implied in our sources and see those beliefs and practices as part of a more broadly conceived 'religious culture' of classical Athens. Such a switch in perspective is as subtle as it is revealing and productive. No longer do we assume with Burkert, Bruid Zaidman and Schmitt Pantel that the ancient Greek city consisted of just a single, civic space.[102] The presence of ritual binding in Athens and elsewhere indicates the existence of alternative locations of the religious alongside those defined by the civic compromise.

SPELLS OF POWER: THE PLACE OF RITUAL BINDING IN THE RELIGIOUS CULTURE OF ATHENS

What, then, was the place of binding spells within this more broadly perceived religious culture of classical Athens? What conceptual space did 'curse tablets' create for themselves? And how was this space related to other locations of the religious – most notably, perhaps, to those of polis religion? To start with an obvious point: like Apollonius' lion-cub divination, the cultural practice of ritual binding could provide a source of individual empowerment.[103] Those men or women who inscribed a lead tablet with a binding formula or who commissioned an expert to do so on their behalf drew on the symbolic universe of ancient Greek religion, the common 'language' shared by all Greeks, to formulate a message (a command!) which furthered their personal interest alone. This message was directed as much to the sender (the cursing person) as to its recipient(s) (the person or

---

[100] On the theology of ancient Greek religion see ch. 6 and the conclusion.
[101] Talismanic statues: Faraone 1988. Amulets: Bonner 1950; Kotansky 1994.
[102] E.g., Garland 1984 for an account of religious authority in archaic and classical Athens including the locations of official polis religion only.
[103] Magic and power: Gordon 1999a: 178; Versnel 2002a. On the representation of magical power in Greek literature see also Parry 1992: 105–24.

persons to be affected by the spell) insofar as it provided an instant sense of empowerment and a direct feeling of having achieved a goal. *Katadesmoi* were effective (in the sense of being credible) exactly because they referred to powers commonly acknowledged to be real. On some level, then, the practice of ritual binding appears simply to have been an extension of a more personal and instrumental side of the religious.

Various aspects of this cultural practice helped to carve the particular position of the curser out of the general domain of ancient Greek religion. In order to be effective, the practice of ritual binding needed to capture and bundle the fleeting and dispersed nature of religious power in the ancient world and to focus it in one particular spot. One way of achieving this was through ritual inversion. Classical scholars have variously pointed out that many aspects of the cultural practice of casting binding spells directly inverted the principles and practices of civic discourse.[104] From the point of view of Greek theology, *katadesmoi* played up certain (particularly uncanny and/or countercultural) aspects of the religious, by taking them out of the larger religious context in which these aspects were counterbalanced by opposing forces. Magic drew selectively on the general symbolic universe of ancient Greek religion only in order to carve out its own particular universe. For example, more frequently than not *katadesmoi* invoked the chthonic, not the Olympian, divinities;[105] and they frequently relied on secrecy, whereas religious rituals usually took place in the open.[106] Some *katadesmoi* featured the matronymic identification of the targeted person, thereby inverting the usual patronymic identification of the individual in all official contexts, as attested in official decrees, dedications and on tombstones.[107] Some *katadesmoi* were to be read from right to left, thus consciously upsetting the conventions of ordinary language. The principle of reversal can also be found on the level of language: some magical papyri and *katadesmoi* crafted during the Hellenistic and Roman periods featured so-called *voces magicae*, particular words which have no obvious referent in Greek language.[108] The particular place the cursing person inhabited was signified here through a break with the conventions of language as another symbolic system shared by all Greeks and with the symbolic significance of this language as a general marker of Greekness. To take up and invert

---

[104] Magical inversion: Graf 1996a: 116–38, 203–7.

[105] E.g., *DTAtt.* 100; SGD 42, 75; *DTAud.* 69. See also Graf 1997a: 121–34; Ogden 1999: 44–6; Eidinow 2007a: 147–9; Collins 2008: 67–73.

[106] On the secrecy of magic see, e.g., Dickie 2001: 39–40.   [107] E.g., Gager 1992: 239 (no. 133).

[108] *Voces magicae* and other 'alienating' elements in magical language: Graf 1996a: 195–8; Ogden 1999: 46–50.

the formulation of Walter Burkert from the beginning of this chapter: sometimes it seemed to have been exactly the point to stand apart![109]

As a set of religious beliefs and practices distinct from official Greek religion magic became subject to debate and to official control.[110] Official polis discourse responded to the spatial self-positioning of those who made use of ritual binding outside mainstream religious discourse by employing its own form of religious mapping. The labelling as magic of this and other practices perceived to be a potential threat to the civic compromise was an attempt to marginalise them, to 'locate' them (in the sense of assigning them a particular place), to control them.

The ancient Greek conception of magic can best be understood as a series of culturally and socially constructed locations of the religious. The polis controlled certain deviant religious practices by naming them, shaming them and locating them at the periphery of its own conception of religious space. Again, magic was not a substantive but a relational category: to refer to a *mantis* as a *goēs* and to ritual binding as *mageia* or *goēteia* was an expression of distance applied by those who sought to refute and control this practice, a *taxon*, a label attached to those religious practices which were perceived to be in real or imagined conflict with the polis, her institutions and her religion.[111]

In polis discourse, this distance, this spatial dislocation between those religious practices placed at the centre and those situated at the periphery, came in a variety of tropes. One way of degrading certain inclinations towards the divine perceived to be excessive was to label them 'superstitious'.[112] Another, more serious way was to label such inclinations or 'uses' of the supernatural as magic and to associate them with various marginal figures: magic was variously presented as foreign, female, non-civic and perverse. Greek tragedy is an excellent context within which to study the ideology of spatial dislocation at work. Greek drama abounds in figures practising magic in all its different varieties.[113] Euripides' *Medea*, for instance, embodies several of the negative connotations associated with magic. Medea is a plotting barbarian woman, who has come to Corinth from afar, and who employs drugs and potions in order to kill the new bride of her husband Jason and the children she had with him.[114] A similar

[109] Cf. above n. 21.
[110] Cf. ancient theories of magic: Bernand 1991: 65–83 ('religion et ligature'); Graf 2002b.
[111] See Smith 1978b: 429 for a similar point on demon worship during the Hellenistic and Roman periods.
[112] E.g., Plu. *Moralia* 164e–171f (*On Superstition*).
[113] On the negative representation of magic in Greek literature see Parry 1992: 125–45.
[114] See Martin 2005: 129–42; Carastro 2006: 156–7.

presentation of magic informs Euripides' *Iphigenia in Tauris*, in which Iphigenia is accused of having performed magic by chanting 'barbarian songs'.[115] I return once more to Aeschylus' *Oresteia*, arguably the most powerful example of the way in which polis ideology is mapped on to a real and imagined sacred landscape. In the *Eumenides* the Furies and their binding song are presented as dark and female forces. Because they are roaming and without a clearly assigned space, they can even intrude into the innermost sanctuary of the Delphic oracle. To control their destructive force requires their location within the polis. What all these examples have in common is that they illustrate how the polis sought to marginalise certain religious practices by situating them at the periphery of society. In doing so they reveal a spatial mapping of religion and magic during the fifth century BC. Over time the distance between centre and periphery shifted according to the map being used, but from the perspective of the polis at least, the centre and the periphery always remained sufficiently distinct not to overlap completely.

It appears that most of the time 'social control' exerted by public disapproval was strong enough to prevent practices such as the commissioning and ritual deposition of binding spells from becoming a real problem for social cohesion.[116] But we know of at least a few cases from classical Athens when more affirmative action was required and when certain religious practices became the subject of, and subjected to, legal action. From these cases it emerges that in contrast to Rome (where we find legislation against magic as early as the Twelve Tables in the mid-fifth century BC), magic as such appears not to have been explicitly outlawed in classical Athens.[117] We do find a few cases against the deadly effects of certain *pharmaka* (plant-based drugs) and their use in erotic magic, but, again, the production of *pharmaka* themselves was never outlawed – after all, beneficial drugs, too, were referred to by the same name.[118] In addition, we know of a few cases that seem to suggest that at Athens at least certain kinds of religious behaviour which fell under the rubric of magic were legally punishable through accusations of *asebeia* (impiety).[119] Towards the end of the fourth century BC, for

---

[115] E. *IT* 1327–1419, in particular 1336–1338. See also Dickie 2001: 42.
[116] As Parker 2005: 123 pointed out, it is difficult to establish the degree and nature of social disapproval that the polis extended to certain religious practices considered to be deviant. Officially at least, practices such as the casting of binding spells were frowned upon even though many made use of them in private.
[117] E.g., Rives 2002.
[118] E.g., Arist. *MM* 1.16.2. On *pharmaka* and their use in ancient Greek love magic: Faraone 1999 (with further evidence).
[119] Magic and Greco-Roman law: Phillips 1991; Fögen 1993; Gordon 1999a: 243–66; Collins 2008: 132–65. In this respect, the situation at Athens may have differed from that elsewhere in the Greek

example, we hear of a certain Theoris from the island of Lemnos, who was accused of impiety at Athens, convicted and finally executed together with her closest kin.[120] We hear about her case from Philochorus as well as in a speech by Demosthenes (not the prosecution speech against her) and from Plutarch's *Life of Demosthenes*.[121] While Philochorus seems to have called her a seer (*mantis*) Demosthenes referred to her as a *pharmakis* (a witch, a sorceress).[122] What exactly was her offence? The details are all fairly murky and the different ancient authors commenting on her case did not always agree. But if we can trust the information we get from Plutarch it seems that Demosthenes accused her of reckless behaviour (ῥᾳδιουργούσης) and of teaching slaves how to deceive.[123] From Demosthenes himself we learn merely that she was thought to have dispersed *pharmaka* and *epōdai* (incantations).[124]

The case of Theoris provides us with a rare instance in which certain individuals within the polis sought to draw the line between religion and magic, between acceptable and unacceptable religious practices and religious power with the help of the law courts – that is, with the aid of an official polis institution.[125] But the ancient Greek conception of *asebeia* used in this and other similar contexts seems to have been as vague as the ancient Greek conception of religion itself.[126]

This conceptual vagueness, however, had the effect of making the line between official and endorsed Greek religion and those aspects of the religious that were 'edited out' (to take up a formulation from Gordon again), between religion and magic, remain always fluid and negotiable. The few attempts to control magic with the aid of the Athenian legal institutions (in particular the *graphē asebeias*) did not help to clarify the picture conceptually or theologically. They merely dealt with those cases, which for one reason or another, warranted an official response. We know of no instance in which the Athenian law actually sought to define magic as such. The interest was merely to limit its most lethal and disagreeable

world. From the city of Teos we have evidence for legislation against the production of harmful plant-based drugs (*pharmaka*), see ML 30.

[120] On this case: Dickie 2001: 50–1; Collins 2001; 2008: 136–9. See also the in-many-ways similar case of Nino: Dickie 2001: 52–4; Eidinow 2010.

[121] Philochorus *FGrHist* 328 F60; D. 25.79–80; Plu. *Dem.* 14.4.

[122] Philochorus *FGrHist* 328 F60; D. 25.79.   [123] Plu. *Dem.* 14.4.   [124] D. 25.80.

[125] Eidinow 2010 makes a convincing case for a formative role of these trials in the development of our modern conception of magic. The persecution of witchcraft and sorcery through the law courts also informed one of Aesop's fables, which, due to its local flavour, is generally believed to originate in an early collection of those fables by the Athenian Demetrius (see Hausrath 1970, no. 56).

[126] See Cohen 1991: 203–17 for an explanation of this conceptual vagueness of *asebeia* within the context of the Athenian legal system.

social and situational effects. And in most cases this seems to have involved some tangible political antagonism in addition to what some may have perceived to be a religious problem.[127] It is in this respect, then, that the embeddedness of Greek religion in the social and political cosmos of the polis also extended to magic.

To return once more to Plato's *Laws*: Plato's discussion of certain magical practices complements the picture here insofar as in the ideal city, just as in Plato's Athens, there is no attempt to legislate against magic as such. As in the legal cases discussed above, it is the effects of certain practices (whether or not they cause serious injury or even death) and the question of *who* carried them out (whether a specialist or a lay person) that matter more than the nature of the practice itself.[128] In the *Laws*, Plato envisages a tight-knit society in which religion and the law blend almost seamlessly into each other. It is in this sense that *asebeia* comes into the picture – as a serious challenge to the very fundamentals of society – and it is in the context of *asebeia* that magical practices become legally actionable. Plato does not posit *asebeia* and magic to be completely identical.[129] Not every kind of magic constitutes *asebeia* and there are kinds of *asebeia* that do not involve the practice of magic. Plato merely presents certain practices ('charming the souls of many of the living, and claiming that they charm the souls of the dead, and promising to persuade the gods, by bewitching them, as it were, with sacrifices, prayers and incantations')[130] as a subclass of the very aspect of *asebeia* which springs from the assumption that the gods can be bribed into unjust action.[131]

Classical scholars have variously acknowledged that Plato represents an intellectualist response to magic and that his rationalist refutation of it should not be taken to represent the mainstream views of his contemporaries.[132] While this is certainly correct, it is difficult not to note the resemblance of various features in the discussion of magic in the *Laws* to how magic appears elsewhere in Greek (Athenian) culture and society. In the *Laws*, as elsewhere, magical practices are situated at the periphery of a landscape which is equally sacred and political, a tendency towards the spatial dislocation of magic that we have also seen at work in other contexts, most notably, perhaps, in Greek tragedy. In the ideal city, those convicted of impiety by magic are to be locked up in a special kind of prison, away from the city, in the wild. No free citizen will be allowed to

---

[127] Cf. 'political ramifications': Dickie 2001: 54.   [128] Pl. *Lg.* 933a–e.
[129] Saunders 1991: 301–23; Collins 2008: 139.
[130] Pl. *Lg.* 909b2–4 (here and below transl. Bury 1926).   [131] See Pl. *Lg.* 908b–e.
[132] E.g., Saunders 1991: 316–23; Graf 1997a: 35; Collins 2008: 140.

visit them and they will not receive a burial when dead.[133] Such similarities suggest that Plato was not after all as fundamentally detached from his Athenian present as some scholars have come to believe. Even if his ideal city is not identical to the Athens (or Sparta, or Crete) of Plato's present, the views expressed in the *Laws* are ultimately the product of the political imagination of a citizen of fourth-century BC Athens.[134]

It is, however, significant that the discussion of magic and impiety does not stop at laying out such a specific framework for legal action. Interestingly, Book 10 of the *Laws* ends on a much more general note: the somewhat technical distinction of different kinds of *asebeia* eventually extends into a much broader argument, proposing that all kinds of private worship of the gods be outlawed.[135] 'No one shall possess a shrine in his own house: when anyone is moved in spirit to do sacrifice, he shall go to the public places to sacrifice, and he shall hand over his oblations to the priest and priestess to whom belongs the consecration thereof.'[136] Apparently, some people's magic (and other people's religion) was indeed too close for comfort to allow for any ambiguity in the ideal city.

The attempt to distinguish between legitimate and illegitimate ways of relating to the divine is also at the heart of the second major work usually discussed in the context of rationalist or intellectualist responses to magic: the Hippocratic treatise *On the Sacred Disease*, dating from the late fifth or early fourth century BC. The author, a doctor in the Hippocratic school of healing, sought to distance his own explanation and cure of epilepsy as much as possible from other self-professed experts in ritual healing, who explained this disease as particularly 'sacred' – that is, divinely inflicted.[137] These experts to whom our author referred as 'magicians, purifiers, charlatans and quacks of our own day', apparently claimed superior insight into the nature of this disease.[138] According to our author, they argued that the disease was 'due to a defilement by a god or spirit', the result of a pollution of the body caused by blood guilt, human bewitchment or an unholy practice.[139] They maintained therefore that the sacred disease could be cured by purifications, incantation, cleansings, certain dietary restrictions and other regulations. It was against this view that the author of *On the Sacred Disease* developed his own cure based

---

[133] Pl. *Lg.* 908a–909c.
[134] The participants in the dialogue originate from Athens, Sparta and Crete.
[135] Pl. *Lg.* 909e–910d.   [136] Pl. *Lg.* 909d7–9.
[137] My interpretation of *On the Sacred Disease* is greatly influenced by Lloyd's discussion of the argument made by the Hippocratic doctor. Lloyd, G. E. R. 1987: 11–29.
[138] See Hp. *Morb. Sacr.* 2.1–5 (here and below transl. Jones 1923).
[139] See Hp. *Morb. Sacr.* 4.34–42.

on a physical, naturalistic explanation of epilepsy and its symptoms, an explanation which ultimately found the cause of the disease in nature.

In order to refute the healing techniques of his rivals, the author of *On the Sacred Disease* also referred to the concept of *asebeia*. The doctor practically set out to rebut his rivals on their very own turf. He did not acknowledge their claims to piety and to superior insight into the dealings of the divine with regard to the disease: instead, he argued that their interpretation of epilepsy and the way they cured it were actually impious (*asebēs*), since they rested on the claim that the gods were subject to human will: 'He who by purifications and magic can take away such an affection can also by similar means bring it on, so that by this argument the action of godhead is disproved.'[140] At the same time as disproving the piety of his rivals, however, the author highlighted the place of divinity in his own interpretation of the disease. Epilepsy, he argued, is indeed a divine disease, but only inasmuch as all nature is divine:

This disease styled sacred comes from the same causes as others, from things that come to and go from the body, from cold, sun, and from the changing restlessness of winds. These things are divine. So that there is no need to put the disease in a special class and to consider it more divine than the others; they are all divine and all human.[141]

What is at stake here is nothing less than the attempt to draw the line between two different interpretative universes built not only on the very same symptoms of a disease but also and ultimately legitimised with regard to the same divine pantheon. In doing so the treatise once again confirms that magic ultimately shared the same symbolic universe as official Greek religion and that all attempts to separate the two must always remain provisional and artificial. At the core of *On the Sacred Disease* was the attempt to discredit certain uses of this pantheon as impious and illegitimate.[142] The Hippocratic treatise can serve as a prime example of the forces at work within a process in which certain aspects or locations of the religious were edited out and in which legitimate religion became synonymous with polis religion. In *On the Sacred Disease* the special religious knowledge of certain individuals was set in contrast to the principles and practices of polis religion. It is in this sense, then, that our author repeatedly insisted that

---

[140] Hp. *Morb. Sacr.* 3.9–12.   [141] Hp. *Morb. Sacr.* 21.1–8.

[142] Collins 2008: 36 argued that our author was not always consistent in the accusations he levelled at his rivals. At times they were accused of being essentially powerless quacks (the gods being beyond human coercion); at other times they were apparently impious because they claimed to be able to control divinity.

proper religion should not only attribute all agency to the gods (rather than to human beings who claim to be able to manipulate them) but should also take place in the sanctuary as a specially designated religious space: 'At least it is godhead that purifies, sanctifies and cleanses us from the greatest and most impious of our sins; and we ourselves fix boundaries to the sanctuaries and precincts of the gods, so that nobody may cross them unless he be pure.'[143]

A final question concerns the agency of such intellectualist responses to magic as proposed in Plato's *Laws* and in the treatise *On the Sacred Disease*. Did the views expressed here merely reflect existing currents in Greek (Athenian) society?[144] Or did they, as Fritz Graf has suggested, actively shape the unfolding discourse on what constituted magic and on how it was related to religion?[145] Owing to the patchy record of sources that have come down to us we may perhaps never be able to answer this question fully or with absolute certainty. Be that as it may, it should by now have become clear that the views expressed here relate to a much larger societal discourse which sought to draw a line between legitimate and illegitimate religious power and between legitimate and illegitimate religious practices, a line that is ultimately impossible to draw.

CONCLUSION

This chapter brought together several lines of argument developed in previous chapters: the focus on the individual and on Greek personal religion; on religion as a symbolic way of 'making sense' (a symbolic medium of interaction); and the question of the nature and location of religious power in the ancient Greek world. The chapter focused on those beliefs and practices frequently discussed (in the ancient world as well as in modern scholarship) under the rubric of magic. I argued that sidelining these practices by putting them into a separate category is to extend the ideology of the polis into modern scholarship – or, as Fritz Graf has argued, to turn an evaluative term from within Greek religion into a descriptive one.[146]

I used the cultural practice of casting binding spells and its representation in a variety of texts and contexts (Plato, Greek drama, etc.) to demonstrate the existence in classical Athens of alternative locations of the religious in addition to official polis religion. I further argued that these alternative locations were ultimately grounded in the same symbolic universe, the

---

[143] Hp. *Morb. Sacr.* 4.53–58.
[144] As suggested by Dickie 2001: 20–7 in his discussion of Graf 1996a.
[145] Graf 1996a: 31–6; 1997a: 30–5.   [146] Graf 1997a: 18.

same 'theology' as official Greek religion: magic, I argued, makes sense only within the framework of ancient Greek religion. We need to understand one to understand the other. The same point applies, of course, just as much to the study of mystery cults, which overlapped significantly with magical beliefs and practices. Further research is needed on how various other magical practices not investigated in this chapter positioned themselves within this more broadly defined religious culture. Can the changes in such additional and alternative locations of the religious over time provide insights into changes in the dominant religious discourse, which is frequently depicted as a more or less static religious system?

Overall, the chapter illustrated the existence of multiple relationships between magic and polis religion, complicating the traditional polarity between authorised and unauthorised locations of the religious (Parker) or between elective and civic religious cults (Price). I argued for the need to embrace the existence of multiple overlapping and corresponding religious identities in the ancient Greek world, an endeavour which will find its extension in the next chapter when we discuss another key polarity in the way in which we conceive of ancient Greek religion: the polarity between the local and the universal (or panhellenic) dimensions of ancient Greek religion.

CHAPTER 5

The 'local' and the 'universal' reconsidered: Olympia, dedications and the religious culture of ancient Greece

Many are the sights to be seen in Greece, and many are the wonders to be heard: but on nothing does Heaven bestow more care than on the Eleusinian rites and the Olympic games.

Pausanias[1]

INTRODUCTION

In Chapter 1 I discussed the way in which polis religion is construed as extending to what scholars have called the 'panhellenic' dimension of ancient Greek religion.[2] I argued that the 'panhellenic' is traditionally applied to describe a dimension of the religious in ancient Greece which transcended the level of individual poleis. As such it is frequently contrasted with those religious practices that were specific to a particular polis, that found no extension on the 'panhellenic' level, and that are therefore described as representing the 'local' dimension of ancient Greek religion. We speak of 'local' and 'universal' tellings of myth, for example, of 'local' and 'panhellenic' sanctuaries, of 'local' and 'panhellenic' festivals and so forth.[3] In the absence of key organising principles of the religious such as a church, a dogma, a holy book and a creed, classical scholarship has conceptualised the fabric of ancient Greek religion around a bipolar model in which 'the local' (read: the polis) and 'the universal', or 'panhellenic' serve as opposing, yet mutually reinforcing, localisations of the religious.

The categories of the 'local' and the 'universal' are important because they determine how we contextualise Greek religious beliefs and practices and what we use as frames of reference to research Greek religious phenomena. Scholarship on the sanctuary of Zeus at Olympia is a good case in point. In

---

[1] Paus. 5.10.1 (here and below translation Jones and Ormerod 1926).   [2] See pp. 13–14.
[3] Mythology: Price 1999: 11–25. Sanctuaries: Morgan 1990: 47–8; Sinn 2000a: vii; Neer 2007: 226. Games: Instone in Verity 2007: 152, nn. 66–70.

his still authoritative study of ancient Olympia, Hans-Volkmar Herrmann distinguishes between different types of Greek sanctuaries by arguing that 'some . . . were of local significance only. Some were more important. The reputation of others again exceeded the confined boundaries of the city and the region. Some were – in contemporary terms – world famous.'[4] In Herrmann's conception of the religious landscape of ancient Greece, the 'local' and the 'universal' are made to describe the different 'catchment areas' and levels of fame of different sanctuaries in the Greek world. Donald Kyle, in his account of the festival of the Panathenaia, drew on a similar conception of the 'local' and the 'universal' when he stated that, '[i]n comparison with Panhellenic athletics at inter-state sanctuaries, I have termed the Great Panathenaia and other such local games, held in or near towns and organised by city-states with a high degree of official state involvement (e.g., administration, finance, facilities, prizes) civic athletics.'[5] Both scholars used the 'local' and the 'panhellenic' as ultimately antithetical terms to describe opposing locations of the religious. Moreover, both scholars situated the sanctuary of Zeus at Olympia and the famous Games it housed firmly on one, the 'panhellenic', side of the spectrum with the other, 'local' side represented by individual poleis.

Most recently, however, the neat separation between the 'local' and 'universal'/'panhellenic' dimensions of ancient Greek religion has become the subject of scholarly debate.[6] Michael Scott in particular has called into question the usefulness of the term 'panhellenism' in general and in particular its application to the sanctuaries of Delphi and Olympia during the archaic and classical periods.[7] He has shown that Delphi and Olympia propagated and displayed the competitive edge (and sometimes outright hostility) between individual poleis just as much as their unity, for example through the erection of monuments commemorating the victory of one Greek city over another.[8] He has further stressed that, far from bringing together visitors from 'all over Greece' (as implied in the very prefix of 'panhellenism'), the 'catchment areas' of both sanctuaries fluctuated greatly throughout their long histories.[9] Most importantly, however, he has demonstrated that every attempt to pigeonhole both sanctuaries in terms of their use does not do justice to their multiple and shifting roles as complex spaces of symbolic investment and dedicatory display.

In this chapter I seek to draw out more succinctly than Scott has done how the cultural practice of setting up dedications at Olympia challenges

---

[4] Herrmann 1972: 9 (my translation).   [5] Kyle 2007: 74.
[6] See, e.g., Kowalzig 2007: 25–6, 181–221, 396–7; Scott 2010: 270–2.
[7] Scott 2010: 250–73.   [8] E.g., Scott 2010: 169–78.   [9] Scott 2010: 256.

not just the duality between the 'local' and the 'panhellenic' but also the more general one between polis religion and Greek religion beyond the polis. I do so by considering the presence and complex interplay of two divergent religious forces at Olympia as reflected in this practice of setting up dedications: that of a multiplicity of overlapping, complementary and competing identities on the one hand and that of religious, symbolic and cultural conformism on the other. At Olympia the two forces were intricately intertwined. Overall, I argue with Scott that we need to adopt a much more flexible conception of the religious culture of ancient Greece – one in which multiple religious identities overlap, correspond and communicate with each other.[10]

Because dedications have traditionally received relatively little attention outside classical archaeology, I shall start with a general survey of the kind of information they can provide for the student of ancient Greek religion. I do so in the hope that this chapter will also show how to make use of this kind of evidence in its own right and in interaction with the literary evidence.

DEDICATIONS AND THE REPRESENTATION OF IDENTITIES AT OLYMPIA

What is a dedication?

Scott has shown that the sanctuaries of Olympia and Delphi provided a space for the display of monuments just as they housed the Games and oracles and a variety of other activities.[11] However, what kind of information can dedications provide?[12] To begin with, an examination of dedications shows not only what was considered worth representing in dedicatory form but also how this was done. Some dedications, such as the elaborate portrait statues set up at Olympia (discussed in more detail below), were specifically crafted to be situated at the sanctuary.[13] Other items were removed from their original context to serve as offerings. Among the thousands of items

---

[10] See also the concluding remarks on the relationship between magic and polis religion in the previous chapter.

[11] The literature on Olympia is vast. Some accessible general works: Finley and Pleket 1976; Raschke 1988; Sinn 2000a; Miller 2004; Kyle 2007; Swaddling 2008.

[12] The standard works on Greek dedications are Rouse 1902; Linders and Nordquist 1987; van Straten 1995: 53–100. See also *ThesCRA* I. 2.d.: 269–326 for an accessible introduction to and overview of dedications and the literature discussed in ch. 3.

[13] There is some evidence for the existence of special workshops both at Olympia and in individual poleis catering for the high level of interest in items which could serve as votives. See, e.g., Mattusch 1988: 16, 32, 167–8, 212–17; Morgan 1990: 37–9. See Heilmeyer 2004 for a discussion of the nature

classical archaeology has unearthed at Olympia are objects as diverse as jewellery, weapons and armour, miniature tripods as well as huge over-sized ones, orientalising pots, small figurines made of clay and bronze, representations of Zeus in different sizes, shapes and materials, bronze reliefs, bases of individual statues (sometimes on horseback) and of groups of statues, as well as bits and pieces of thousands of statues.[14] Some of these statues were life-sized, some larger, some smaller, made of bronze, marble, terracotta and other precious materials, such as gold, ivory and glass. Many more statues made of wood are irrevocably lost, and known to us only through descriptions in literary works.[15]

These findings are so rich that they can reveal trends and conventions in dedicatory practices over time since they vary in form, size, style and material. The dedication of weapons and armour, for example, seems to have been vastly more widespread during the first few centuries of the sanctuaries' existence than in later periods, although the practice probably never completely ceased to exist. Weapons and armour were routinely put up on so-called *tropaia*, posts made of wood, bronze or stone and displayed to commemorate victories on the battlefield, mostly of one Greek city over another.[16] The south side of the stadium was a particularly popular location for display. Large amounts of weaponry and armour ended up as filler for wells, in the south and west mounds of the stadium and elsewhere.[17] Significantly, however, when classical archaeologists excavated these sites, they found only armour and weapons of older design and fabrication, thus revealing the early popularity of this practice and its later decline.[18]

Also clearly visible in the material record is a trend towards large-scale dedications at the turn of the sixth and fifth centuries BC. Some of the most magnificent monuments, including those featuring multiple statues, date from the first half of the fifth century BC.[19] A closer look at who is actually represented by the statues, however, has revealed the increasing

---

of such workshops more generally. Heilmeyer rightly warned against envisaging all such workshops as elaborate businesses involved in the production of art. Most of them were probably more aptly described as 'working sites'.

[14] A significant and representative number of these items have been published by the Deutsches Archäologisches Institut in the series *Bericht über die Ausgrabungen in Olympia* and *Olympische Forschungen*. For a comprehensive chronological discussion see Scott 2010: 146–217. On multiple statues sharing one base (*Statuenreihe*): Ioakimidou 1997. On the significance of the tripods, which are not discussed below: Papalexandrou 2005: 9–63.

[15] Classical archaeology has also revealed a considerable number of hammered metal sheets (*sphyrēlata*), which were probably originally attached to wooden cores. See, e.g., Mattusch 1988: 182; Kunze 1994: 101–39.

[16] Mallwitz 1972: 24–34; Scott 2010: 151–2, 224–5.   [17] See Kunze 1956: 10–11; Scott 2010: 158, 169.

[18] Mallwitz 1972: 24.   [19] Mallwitz 1972: 34, 41, 94.

popularity of outstanding individuals not otherwise associated with Olympia (honorific statues) beginning in the fourth century BC.[20] During the late fourth and third centuries BC, it was the Hellenistic monarchs in particular (Philip, Alexander, Seleucus I and Antigonus Monophthalmus) who were represented at Olympia in the form of equestrian sculptures.[21]

Dedications of all kinds reveal much about those who dedicated them, their concerns and desires and their relationship to and understanding of the gods. Among the oldest items found at Olympia are thousands of little clay and bronze figurines dating mostly from the ninth and eighth centuries BC.[22] Some of them represent male animals, such as bulls and stallions, others have human shapes, of which some are shown driving chariots.[23] As the figures driving carts are not carrying armour and weapons and therefore do not represent warrior types, it might be tempting to see them as evidence for early chariot racing at Olympia by members of the aristocratic elite from the regions surrounding the sanctuary.[24]

Races involving four-horse and two-horse chariots were probably not introduced to the Games before 680 and 408 BC respectively.[25] The first (and central) competition of the Games was not the chariot race but the single foot race.[26] Archaeologists therefore interpreted the figurines as representing the aristocratic man as such, his ownership of precious farmland and his livestock.[27] They make visible the significance of early Olympia as a place of aristocratic display, a context in which some scholars have also situated the (later) establishment of the Games.[28] Despite the many fundamental changes in the socio-political structure of Greece and in the festival

---

[20] Mallwitz 1972: 63, 99–100.   [21] Hintzen-Bohlen 1992. See also Mallwitz 1972: 99.

[22] Early clay figures from Olympia: Heilmeyer 1972. Early bronze figurines: Heilmeyer 1979. Heilmeyer 1979: 14, based on research prior to 1972, counted 4,042 bronze figurines of animals and 136 fragments of carts – the largest group of items found in the sanctuary. Snodgrass 1980: 53 counted 837 terracotta figurines for Olympia.

[23] E.g., Olympia, Archaeological Museum, inv. no. B 2301 (statuette of a horse); Olympia, Archaeological Museum, inv. no. B 4804 (statuette of a bull); Olympia, Archaeological Museum, inv. no. B 1679 (figurine operating a cart). For a picture of this figurine see Yalouris and Yalouris 1987: 55, illus. c.

[24] The early history of the sanctuary and the Games is closely linked to the process of Greek state formation. See Morgan 1990: 1–105. Although dedications testify to the existence of cult activity at Olympia from the late tenth century BC, the literary evidence suggests 776 BC as the traditional date of the beginning of the historic Games, though this evidence is problematic. See Siewert 1992; Hall 2002: 241–6. See Christesen 2007 on the Olympic victor lists as historical evidence for the history of the sanctuary and its Games.

[25] See Paus. 5.8.6–11 for an account of the subsequent introduction of various contests to the Games.

[26] See Christesen 2007: 211–12. The Olympiads, the four-year periods between celebrations of the Games, were named after the winner of the short foot race.

[27] Here and above see Heilmeyer 1972: 38–40.

[28] On Olympia as the place of funerary games in honour of Pelops and on the link between aristocratic display and early Olympia see Herrmann 1972: 64–5.

structure itself, this dimension never entirely disappeared from Olympia. In the competitions involving expensive horses and in the sculptures and monuments commemorating victories in these competitions, the Greek aristocracy always reserved one area of the festival for competitive display by noble men: chariot/horse racing was practised by those with wealth.[29]

It is particularly through the various inscriptions that the outlook and motivations of those dedicating items at Olympia are revealed.[30] Some of these inscriptions were placed directly on the dedicated item.[31] Many inscriptions are also found on the bases of statues, some of which were found *in situ* – that is, on the spot where they were originally displayed – together with the dedication proper. Many more inscriptions have come down to us only indirectly, in the literary evidence, above all, perhaps, in the account of Pausanias, who visited the sanctuary during the second century AD.[32] Typically, these inscriptions included information on the dedicator (scholars distinguish between collective, state and private dedications), the occasion of the dedication and – in dedications of elaborate craftsmanship – the artist who fashioned the statue.[33] For example, we learn from such an inscription that the statues of Damaretus of Heraea and of his son Theopompus (seen by Pausanias) were fashioned by the Argive sculptors Eutelidas and Chrysothemis.[34]

Besides such 'personalised' information on specific items, the number and geographical provenance of dedications as such at different points in time provide much information about the importance of certain poleis or regions within the Greek world, their relationship to each other and their access to the sanctuary.[35] The inscriptions that were frequently engraved on the armour dedicated at Olympia, for example, mostly identified poleis

---

[29] Sinn 2000a: 43. Note though Golden 1998: 5: '[N]o games included contests reserved expressly for the rich'.

[30] See, e.g., Kunze 1956: 149–75.

[31] See, e.g., the following items from the Archaeological Museum, Olympia: inv. no. B 4687 (Corinthian helmet with dedicatory inscription); inv. no. B 5180 (fragment of protective leg armour with dedicatory inscription); inv. no. B 6081 (Corinthian helmet with anonymous dedicatory inscription).

[32] Pausanias dedicated almost two entire books (5 and 6) of his *Description of Greece* to an account of the sanctuary. Pausanias' Olympia: Newby 2005: 202–28; König 2005: 158–204; Elsner 2007: 13–19; Scott 2010: 228–33. Pausanias as a source for the study of ancient Greek religion: Pirenne-Delforge 2008.

[33] On polis dedications at Olympia (and Delphi) dating from the late sixth to the middle of the fourth century BC, see Ioakimidou 1997. On artist signatures see Robertson 1985: 178.

[34] Paus. 6.10.4.

[35] See Kilian-Dirlmeier 1985 for a comparative discussion of polis dedications of the eighth and early seventh centuries BC at the sanctuaries of Pherae, Perachora and Olympia and at the Heraion of Samos.

from the Peloponnese and the Greek mainland as places of origin.[36] They
were therefore an expression of the geographical proximity of these cities to
Olympia and the close ties they had forged with the sanctuary.[37] It is surprising to find evidence of dedications of weapons from three Boeotian cities,
Thebes, Orchomenos and Tanagra, but none from Athens – according
to Alfred Mallwitz this could be seen as indicating Spartan supremacy in
the western Peloponnese.[38]

Finally, dedications make visible the popularity of the sanctuary as a
place of symbolic investment at any given point in time. Classical archaeology has revealed a steep increase in clay and metal dedications at the
transition between the ninth and eighth centuries BC, reflecting a jump in
the popularity of the sanctuary contemporary with the emergence of the
Greek poleis.[39] The great number of multi-figure monuments dating from
the beginning of the fifth century BC, in turn, clearly demonstrates the
importance of the sanctuary in the period following the Persian Wars.[40]
By then Olympia's popularity throughout the Greek world had reached
a peak. Compared to Delphi, however, the decrease of large-scale victor
monuments at Olympia during the fourth century BC hints at a decline in
the relative importance of the sanctuary as a place of symbolic investment
of at least one kind of currency, since the sanctuary remained a popular
place for the erection of honorific monuments.[41]

Given the large number of dedications which have survived and their
rich interpretative potential, it is surprising to find that they have frequently
been left to the archaeologists to interpret. Until most recently, the practice
of setting up dedications at Olympia has received considerably less attention
in scholarly discourse than any other activity there.[42] Dedications play only
a marginal role in most modern accounts of the sanctuary and its famous
Games, yet to the ancient visitor, like Pausanias, they were among the most
striking features of the sanctuary.[43] The question thus emerges of what
dedications added to the sanctuary, how they related to the other activities
it housed and what they can contribute to our understanding of the nature
of Olympia and its role in the Greek religious landscape more generally.

---

[36] For inscriptions on weapons see above n. 31 and Kunze 1956: 35–40; 1967: 83–110.
[37] Here and in the following see Mallwitz 1972: 27–9.   [38] Mallwitz 1972: 27; Scott 2010: 158, 169.
[39] See in particular Snodgrass 1980: 49–84; Morris 1987: 191. See also the table of early clay figures
from Olympia in Heilmeyer 1972: 123. See also Heilmeyer 1979: 21.
[40] See Scott 2010: 196–203.   [41] Mallwitz 1972: 63; Scott 2010: 203–14.
[42] See Osborne 2004 on the relative scholarly neglect of votive offerings. See Scott 2010 for a comprehensive comparative study of dedications at Olympia and Delphi during the archaic and classical
period. See also Morgan 1990: 226–56, 57–105.
[43] For a criticism of this preference see Scott 2010: 5–28.

A first and obvious point is that like the Games themselves the cultural practice of setting up dedications at Olympia brought many identities within the Greek world into the sanctuary and set them in spatial and symbolic relationship to each other. However, in contrast to the Games, which did so only temporarily, the dedications added a more enduring mode of representation to the sanctuary. The victor statues, for example, depicted representatives from different parts of the Greek world who had excelled in earlier Games.[44] They thus provided not only a mirror of past victories but also a framework for the evaluation and framing of future Olympic success. Yet other forms of dedication – especially, perhaps, the honorific statues – represented individuals and their achievements not otherwise associated with Olympia. The different types of dedications turned the sanctuary into a rich 'archive', a material inventory of Olympic achievements and significant outside events, worthy of remembrance.

Moreover, some statues also represented individuals whose athletic prowess led them to cross the line between mortal beings and supernatural powers. Theogenes of Thasos, for example, was a highly successful athlete. According to Pausanias (who referred to him as Theagenes) he won over 1,400 crowns at different athletic competitions.[45] He was represented many times in statuary at various locations, including a statue crafted by Glaucias of Aegina in the Altis.[46] Some of his statues were considered to have healing powers and were worshipped like gods, and apparently Theogenes himself claimed direct descent from the demi-god Heracles.[47] Dedications thus also enacted the possible ways in which the Games could change an athlete's life.

The category of the 'local' reconsidered

In the previous section I investigated what items were displayed at Olympia and what information they can provide. In this section I illustrate some of the ways in which these dedications bring a 'local' dimension into a sanctuary that is traditionally associated with the 'panhellenic' dimension of ancient Greek religion. In doing so, the dedications illustrate the fact that the duality between the 'local' and the 'universal' is indeed a false

---

[44] On the victor statues see, e.g., Hyde 1921; Lattimore 1988; Herrmann 1988; Peim 2000; Scott 2010: 176–8. See Olympia, Archaeological Museum, inv. no. L 99 for the marble head of an athlete.
[45] Here and in the following see Paus. 6.11.5; also 6.6.5–6.   [46] Paus. 6.11.9.
[47] See Currie 2005: 120–55 with further evidence on Theagenes/Theogenes and other athletes receiving divine honours.

dichotomy and that we need to rethink the meaning of both categories as well as their relationship to each other.

A stroll through the sanctuary of Zeus at Olympia brought the ancient visitor face to face with hundreds of monuments, statues and other items dedicated to Zeus (Fig. 1). During the first few decades of the fifth century BC the number of dedications on display in the sacred grove of Zeus (Altis) increased dramatically.[48] These were not put up at random but carefully chosen and arranged in order to speak to those frequenting the sanctuary and to refer them to the events and achievements they commemorated.[49]

The placement of the dedications within the sanctuary frequently drew upon existing buildings and other infrastructure such as altars in order to make the greatest possible impact. Most notably, statues and more elaborate monuments were lined up along the various paths that led through the Altis and in front of specific buildings, facing the people walking past them. After the temple of Zeus was completed in 456 BC, for example, statues were erected on the temple steps, along the south side of the temple and along a new ceremonial pathway between the Pelopion and the temple (Fig. 2).[50] The statues erected within the sanctuary virtually competed for the attention of the onlooker. Some dedications sought to outdo neighbouring items materially and symbolically by towering on high pedestals.[51]

Who determined where a given dedication should be placed? Scott recently addressed this question in the context of the management structure and administration of the sanctuary.[52] He showed that in contrast to Delphi, whose complex administration was shared between the religious amphictyonic council, the city of Delphi and the sanctuary priests, Olympia was subject always to a single controlling polis (first by Pisa, then, after about 580 BC, by Elis (with one interruption).[53] As a result of their strong influence the positioning of dedications was more strictly regulated at Olympia than at Delphi. This influence is reflected, for example, in the more uniform treasury design at Olympia than at Delphi.[54] It also helps to explain the relative stylistic homogeneity of various Zeus statues that emerged within the space of the sanctuary, especially in the first half of the fifth century BC (see below).[55] It would be wrong, though, to assume that it

---

[48] Herrmann 1972: 124.
[49] On the placement of statues see Ridgway 1971. See also Bol 1978: 1–6 for some casual remarks on the frequency of items found at certain locations within the sanctuary.
[50] Herrmann 1972: 120–5; Scott 2010: 188–91, with fig. 7.5.
[51] See Dillon 2006: 61 on pedestals as a form of display of public honorific portrait statues.
[52] Here and below see Scott 2010: 29–40.
[53] Elis, which was in control of the sanctuary for most of its history, was about 36 km from Olympia.
[54] Scott 2010: 165–9.   [55] See Scott 2010: 173–5.

Fig. 1 Artist's impression of the sanctuary of Zeus at Olympia (the Metroon and the treasuries)

Fig. 2 Model of the area between the temple of Zeus and the Bouleuterion at Olympia

was only the controlling polis that determined who could dedicate at Olympia, as well as what, and where. Elis and Pisa were relatively weak poleis, with economies that relied, to some extent at least, on the steady stream of visitors and the commissioning of dedications, economic necessities that make it likely that they remained responsive to requests made in this area.

There is considerable evidence to suggest that dedications were grouped within the sanctuary in certain ways, hence influencing and manipulating the way in which those walking past them perceived these statues.[56] There were various criteria according to which the statues were displayed. Specific types of dedication, such as victory statues, victor statues and honorific statues, were frequently grouped together, but within a single type, quasi-contemporary monuments were sometimes set up side by side.[57] At times, statues crafted by the same (famous) sculptor stood next to each other; or the family ties and/or polis affiliations of those represented were preserved in the arrangement of their statues. In the case of monuments commemorating Olympic success, statues were also sometimes set up according to the contests in which victory had been achieved or the mythological themes represented in monumental form. No matter what ordering criteria were applied, this thematic grouping of monuments must surely have encouraged direct comparison of neighbouring objects, turning any walk through the sanctuary into an ongoing engagement with a multitude of stories, identities and events, linked up in ever-new combinations and associations depending on the path one followed and where one looked. While the visitors to the sanctuary perused the items on display, the statues gazed back on the visitors, providing a materialised audience for the activities carried out within the sanctuary.[58]

Pausanias gave vivid evidence of this. His account of the votive offerings set up at Olympia starts with a discussion of the *Zanes*, bronze statues of Zeus, some of which were grouped together in the Altis along the path leading from the Metroon to the stadium.[59] These, as Pausanias recorded, were financed by the fines imposed on cheating athletes by the Elean officials. Their inscriptions reminded all visitors to the sanctuary, but particularly the athletes, who walked past them on their way to the

---

[56] Pausanias commented explicitly at various times on the ways in which the statues were grouped within the Altis. E.g., Paus. 5.22.6 (according to relations in mythology); 5.26.2 (the offerings of a certain Micythus are explicitly not grouped together); 6.1.7 (statues of Spartan victors in chariot racing); 6.7.1 (statues of athletes from Rhodos); 6.16.4–9 (statues of Olympic victors from Elis).

[57] See Hyde 1912: 205. On the pathways through the sanctuary see also Scott 2010: 223.

[58] This is particularly true for those statues placed close to the 'processional entrance' (πομπικὴ εἴσοδος): see Bol 1978: 6.

[59] Paus. 5.21.

stadium, of the need to follow the rules. For Pausanias and the Elean officials, at least, to cheat during the Games constituted an act of impiety towards Zeus. The *Zanes* symbolically converted this lack of reverence into a statement of piety: through the penalty payments, impiety towards the father of the gods was transformed into a representation of Zeus himself.[60] Yet for Pausanias the *Zanes* represented much more than the need to stick to the rules. They also provided evidence of the skills of the artist who crafted them – the famous sculptor Celon of Sicyon created two of the first six *Zanes* erected in the 98th Olympiad, in 380 BC.

The theme of paying fines eventually brought Pausanias to consider another instance of Olympic cheating: that of the boxer Apollonius from Alexandria.[61] He had become infamous for attempting to talk himself out of the penalty for failing to arrive at Elis in the prescribed period before the beginning of the Games.[62] He blamed adverse winds while he had really been collecting a monetary prize at the Ionian Games. The naming and shaming of the athlete, however, inspired Pausanias to bring in a special piece of information: 'The name of the man, who was fined, was Apollonius, the surname was Rhantes. To have a surname is something like a local custom (ἐπιχώριον) at Alexandria.'[63] Statues and other material representations put up within the sanctuary encouraged those perusing them to consider stories that included a 'local' dimension inasmuch as they provided information peculiar to an individual, city, ethnicity or region within Greece. Such stories circulated among the visitors to Olympia, and the guides who were specifically engaged by the sanctuary would have done their bit in providing the visitors with the necessary information.[64] When Pausanias directed his interest from the *Zanes* on the path to the stadium to representations of Zeus throughout the sanctuary more generally, he mentioned also an old statue of Zeus with a sceptre offered by the Hyblaeans.[65] This led him to consider those who had put up the dedication, again followed by a piece of 'local' information. He recorded that there were, in fact, two cities called Hybla in Sicily, that the smaller one dedicated the statue, and that the people of this city were particularly reverential towards the gods (εὐσεβής) and interested in divination. The category of the 'local',

---

[60] In 5.21.16 Pausanias explicitly stated that cheating in the Games was disrespectful towards Zeus. In 6.6.6 he noted that a certain Theagenes had to pay one talent as a fine to Zeus and another talent to Euthymos, whom he had cheated of a rightful victory.

[61] Paus. 5.21.12–14.

[62] The athletes had to undergo a mandatory training period of 30 days at Elis before the beginning of the Games. See, e.g., Crowther 1991; Golden 1998: 16, who suggests that this rule might have been a strategy to exclude 'the poor or less proficient'.

[63] Paus. 5.21.12.

[64] On the guides see, e.g., Paus. 5.20.4, 21.8. See also Jones 2001.   [65] Paus. 5.23.6.

again here understood as information pertaining to a particular area within Greece, was by no means absent from Olympia. In the various statuary representations of events and identities from different parts of the Greek world and beyond 'the local' was brought into the sanctuary in various forms and formulations.

Victory monuments, for example, represented a variety of 'local' conflicts and, in doing so, brought multiple 'local' identities into the sanctuary. The most frequent scenario certainly remained the dedication put up by one Greek polis in commemoration of victory on the battlefield against another, although some victory monuments were erected by several poleis, hence embodying military alliances and their achievements. There was for example a large (4.5m high) statue of Zeus dedicated by those Greek cities that had been victorious against the Persian commander Mardonios in the Battle of Plataea in 479 BC.[66] There was also a magnificent winged Nike dating from shortly after 421 BC and set up in front of the east side of the temple of Zeus by the Messenians and the Naupaktians (the so-called Nike of Paionius). Itself already larger than life-size, the statue towered on a 9-metre high, triangular pillar. The statue was dedicated to Zeus, paid for with the spoils of warfare and crafted out of marble by the famous sculptor Paionius of Mende.[67] Significantly, however, not only polis and inter-polis relationships found their expression in joint dedications – we also hear of dedications put on display by an entire ethnos. Pausanias, for example, knew of dedications erected jointly by the entire Achaean ethnos (ἔστι δὲ καὶ ἀναθήματα ἐν κοινῷ τοῦ Ἀχαιῶν ἔθνους).[68] The statues were arranged on a semicircular platform north-east of the temple of Zeus and apparently depicted those Greeks who at Troy had cast lots in order to decide who should face Hector in single combat (see Hom. *Il.* 7.161–169).

Although most victory monuments were put up by individual poleis, some were dedicated by entities and identities above and below the polis level. Even personal dedications put up by outstanding individuals who had distinguished themselves in a military context were not unheard of at Olympia. A rare, yet very powerful, example comes from the numerous dedicated pieces of armour that were put up on display, in particular during the archaic and early classical periods. Among the items found during

---

[66] Paus. 5.23.1; Mallwitz 1972: 28–9, 34, 94.
[67] *IvO* 259 = ML 74. See Paus. 5.10.8. See also the extended discussion of the monument in Stewart 1990, vol. 1: 89–92. For an image of a reconstruction of the Nike see Scott 2010: 197, fig. 7.6.
[68] Paus. 5.25.8. See also Paus. 6.15.2 on a statue dedicated by the Aetolian ethnos.

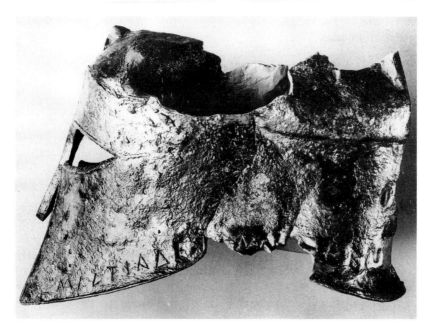

Fig. 3 Helmet dedicated by Miltiades, late sixth century BC

the excavations of the southern embankment of the stadium was a splen-
did Corinthian helmet (Fig. 3), bearing the inscription (in Attic letters):
Μιλτιάδες ἀνέ[θ]εκεν [:τ]ōι Δί ('Miltiades dedicated [me] to Zeus').[69]

This inscription is striking in its omission of a patronymic (naming of
the father), of the city of the dedicator's origin and of the occasion for the
dedication. In this it deviates markedly from the dedicatory conventions
of weapons at Olympia and elsewhere. Classical scholars have therefore
interpreted the helmet as a highly personalised dedication expressing the
self-confidence of the famous Athenian general, who had distinguished
himself in a variety of military engagements, including the famous Battle
of Marathon in 490 BC.[70] The absence of any indication of a specific
military context on the helmet itself contributes to the impression that the

---

[69] *IG* I³ 1472. For the helmet see Olympia, Archaeological Musem, inv. no. B 2600. Here and in the
following see Kunze 1956: 69–74 with tables 34–35.
[70] The helmet itself does not refer to any specific military engagement in which Miltiades was involved.
Mallwitz 1972: 32, following Kunze 1956: 71 speculates that it did not originate from the famous
Battle of Marathon but from an earlier military engagement. Cf. Gauer 1968: 23, who considers it
likely.

main focus of this dedication was the identity of the dedicator and the act of dedication itself.

It was by no means only military victories that were represented at Olympia in dedicatory form. A stroll through the Altis would also have brought the visitor face to face with events and identities that, like the victory statues, lacked any prior connection with Olympia and the Games but unlike them did not refer to a military context. From the fourth century BC onwards, honorific statues and monuments became increasingly popular. Within this group the Hellenistic monarchs featured prominently – mostly on horseback.[71] Not all statues, however, were royal: some also commemorated famous individuals who had distinguished themselves in a variety of contexts. Among them were personalities as illustrious as Gorgias of Leontini (for his eloquence and skills in persuasion) and Anaximenes of Lampsacus, the author of an elaborate universal history.[72] In many ways, it seems, a walk through the Altis would also have been a trip through the 'hall of fame' of ancient Greece.

Nonetheless, not everybody who received a statue at Olympia was a priori famous throughout the Greek world. In 5.25.2–4 Pausanias told the heartbreaking story of a chorus of thirty-five boys which, according to an old custom, was sent from the city of Messene on Sicily to the city of Rhegium in southern Italy, on the other side of the Strait of Messina. Because of bad weather, the ship carrying the boys, their teacher and a pipe player sank; everybody died. The chorus of boys who had disappeared without a trace certainly stirred a considerable amount of horror and pity.[73] It is therefore not surprising that the boys resurfaced and materialised in sculptural form at Olympia. According to Pausanias, the chorus, their teacher and the pipe player were represented as bronze statues, commissioned and dedicated to Zeus by the Messenians and crafted by Callon of Elis. As statues, those who had died prematurely found a permanent place in the space of the sanctuary and the forms of commemoration it housed. Set up during the second half of the fifth century BC, this monument was still on display at the sanctuary in the time of Pausanias, more than 500 years later![74]

This example further complicates our understanding of the presence of the 'local' at Olympia. While the tragic death of the chorus was certainly

---

[71] See for example Paus. 6.11.1.   [72] Gorgias (Paus. 6.17.7–9); Anaximenes (Paus. 6.18.2).

[73] Pausanias imaginatively described the dreadful ways in which this particular sea passage challenged those seeking to cross it, including strong winds, nasty currents and so many underwater monsters that the air was full of their smell.

[74] We can roughly date the event because we know that the sculptor who crafted the statues (Callon of Elis) was active after 496 BC: see Fowler 2005: 67.

a 'local' event in the sense that it concerned a specific place or region within Greece, its equally 'local' representation at Messene was apparently insufficient to commemorate the special circumstances of the boys' death. The sanctuary of Olympia seemed to be the more appropriate venue to commemorate the chorus, their teacher and the pipe player. The sanctuary served as a space for the display of statues and the commemoration of events and identities in instances when 'local' representation in one's city of origin was, for one reason or another, deemed insufficient. A second example from Pausanias confirms this. In 6.4.9 he recorded that Archidamus was the first Spartan king to receive a statue outside Sparta. He added that the statue of Archidamus was erected in the sanctuary because he had died outside Greece, in barbaric lands, and had missed out on a proper burial.[75] Here, as in the case of the chorus, the sanctuary served as a preferred location for the representation of those whose particular kind of death had made a commemoration by the Hellenic community desirable. Another example from Delphi supports this hypothesis. The sanctuary of Apollo featured two statues representing Cleobis and Biton, two young men from Argos, who (according to Herodotus) ranked second in Solon's list of the most blest people,[76] being renowned for their honourable death. They had – with their own hands – drawn the carriage of their mother to the local Heraion. When their proud mother asked the goddess to bestow on her sons the best divine reward possible for a human being, they died peacefully in the temple.[77] We can, of course, only speculate what may have motivated the erection of those kinds of statue representing 'local' events. In the case of Cleobis and Biton, at least, the story of their particular kind of death would have served to illustrate the Greek virtue of filial piety.

Olympia seems to have occupied a special space within the landscape of Greece. Not being a polis itself, the sanctuary conceptually transcended polis, regional and other identities within Greece while at the same time embodying them in its own physical space. Statues and monuments were only one (albeit a prominent) way in which 'local' events and identities were represented at Olympia, for there were also inscriptions featuring

---

[75] In his book on Laconia, Pausanias told us why: as an act of divine punishment the body of Archidamus was not found when he was killed in Italy helping the people of Tarentum to fight against their non-Greek neighbours (Paus. 3.10.5).

[76] Hdt. 1.31. The two *kouroi* (which are sometimes also taken to represent the Dioscuri) are now at Delphi, Delphi Museum, inv. no. 1524, 467. For a picture and discussion see, e.g., Spivey 1997: 126–32; Pedley 2002: 175–6, with illustration 6.37; Pedley 2005: 146–7.

[77] For an interpretation of this episode see Lloyd, M. 1987. See also Sansone 1991; Chiasson 2005.

treaties between individual poleis or groups of poleis.[78] Interestingly, how-ever, the material evidence frequently provided merely an entry point to the presentation of information from different corners of the Greek world: at Olympia, the visible and material referenced the invisible and discursive. The picture of Greece that emerges from a journey through the sanctu-ary is one of various, competing, sometimes even conflicting 'local' *logoi*, converging in materialised form.

Local identies, universal codes

In the section above I have investigated the presence of the local in the sanctuary of Zeus at Olympia. I have shown that the category of the 'local', traditionally equated with the polis, encompassed a variety of identities within ancient Greece, including polis identities and identities above and below the polis level. In this section I will inquire into how dedications rep-resenting 'local' identities spoke to the audience of Hellenes that gathered at Olympia.

Dedications displayed throughout the sanctuary had to strike a sub-tle balance between communicating specific information and addressing an audience from different parts of the Greek world. Different types of dedication explored different strategies in order to reach this balance and they were by no means always successful. Pausanias mentioned a statue of Theognetus of Aegina, a victor in the boys' wrestling, which featured Theognetus 'holding the fruit of the cultivated pine and a pomegranate'.[79] Yet Pausanias found himself unable to explain these peculiar insignia and suspected that 'some Aeginetans may have a local story (ἐπιχώριος λόγος) about them'.[80]

A considerable number of statues put up in the sanctuary in all periods depicted the Greek gods and they did so according to certain conventions or 'codes', which enabled those perusing the statues to iden-tify what was depicted.[81] Unsurprisingly, perhaps, for a sanctuary of Zeus, representations of the father of the gods remained particularly popular among the dedicatory objects put on display throughout Olympia's long history. They routinely featured the most important of the Greek gods in a

---

[78] *IvO* 9–11; ML 17. Crowther 2003: 64–5. See Scott 2010: 33, 159 for a discussion of the historical contexts in which they emerged in the sanctuary.

[79] Paus. 6.9.1.   [80] Paus. 6.9.1.

[81] A survey of different statuary representations of the gods (both lost and found) at Olympia: Drees 1967: 153–70.

highly formalised way, which assisted in his successful identification. Emil Kunze convincingly traced the development of representations of Zeus at Olympia over time.[82] Following works dealing with the early history of Olympia, he argued that the transition of the sanctuary from a 'local' cult place to a 'panhellenic' institution is visible in the changed representations of the father of the gods. Early bronze figurines showed Zeus as a warrior and thus pointed to the Elean aristocracy, which frequented the sanctuary during the eighth and seventh centuries BC.[83] Towards the end of the sixth century BC, however, small figurines appeared depicting Zeus with a thunderbolt in his hand (Fig. 4).[84]

Imagining the father of the gods as a fierce guardian of justice and supporter of revenge, however, is also intrinsic to Greek lyric poetry, most notably, perhaps, to Pindar.[85] This depiction of the thundering Zeus did not remain restricted to the small figurines and could soon also be found in the large bronze statues that increasingly appeared in the sanctuary during the fifth century BC.[86] Yet in Phidias' famous chryselephantine statue, we find the image of a reigning Zeus holding a sceptre, an image that can also be found in archaic poetry.[87] Because of their popularity, representations of Zeus provide a particularly tangible way of tracing the emergence of formalised representations reflecting the attributes assigned to Zeus in Greek mythology. Other gods, such as the similarly ubiquitous goddess of victory, Nike, were likewise represented at Olympia in a highly formalised style, showing the features and characteristics assigned to them by Homer, Hesiod and other poets.

Some monuments not only adhered to the set features of individual gods, which Greeks from different cities and regions would have recognised, but also evoked entire mythological narratives drawn from epic poetry. Pausanias described a monument featuring Zeus and Ganymede, which was put up by the Thessalian Gnathis and crafted by the sculptor Aristocles.[88] According to the *Iliad* the handsome prince from Troy was carried off as a boy to Mount Olympus;[89] as reparation his father Tros received a special breed of horses. One of the few virtually complete monuments we have from Olympia is a terracotta statue of a bearded Zeus with a walking stick

---

[82] Kunze 1946.   [83] See Kunze 1946: 101–4 and illuss. 5–13. Mallwitz 1972: 22–3.

[84] See, e.g., Olympia, Archaeological Museum, inv. no. 6194; Olympia, Archaeological Museum, inv. no. B 5500 (= Fig. 4); Athens, National Archaeological Museum, inv. no. 6196. See also Kunze 1946: 104–6 with illuss. 14–17.

[85] Here and below: Kunze 1946: 104–6.

[86] The development of bronze statuary in Greece: Mattusch 1988.

[87] Kunze 1946: 106–8, 110–13.   [88] Paus. 5.24.5.   [89] H. *Il* 5.265–7; 20.231–5.

Fig. 4 Zeus with thunderbolt

carrying away a smaller Ganymede who, in turn, is clutching a rooster (Fig. 5).[90] This statue is probably not the votive offering mentioned by Pausanias, but was attached to the roof of a building.[91] As such it proves the popularity of certain mythological themes and narratives in material representations at Olympia, in particular those featuring Zeus. The statues

---

[90] Olympia, Archaeological Museum, inv. no. T2, Tc 1049. See also Kunze 1940; 1956: 103–14; Mallwitz 1972: 35–7; Moustaka 1993: 42–5 with tables 33–9.

[91] See Mallwitz 1972: 36, who suggested one of the treasuries as a likely location. See also Kunze 1940; 1946: 109–10; Drees 1967: 157.

Fig. 5 Zeus and Ganymede, ca. 470 BC

set up in the sanctuaries frequently took up and extended the imagery displayed on the buildings that surrounded them.

The statues offered by a certain Micythus that were on display in various locations throughout the Altis offer another perspective on the presence of a universalising force in the sanctuary.[92] Micythus' dedications represented major and minor Greek divinities: there were statues of Amphitrite, Poseidon and Hestia, Kore (the daughter of Demeter), Aphrodite, Ganymede and Artemis and Dionysus, as well as a beardless Zeus, yet among the representations of Greek divinities were also the statues of Homer and Hesiod, the poets who had helped to shape their image and propagated their influence throughout the Greek world. There was also a statue of Orpheus, the mythical singer from Thrace, son of Apollo and a Muse, who was also considered to have shaped the image of the Greek gods and spread it throughout the Greek world.[93]

A variety of further conventions must have governed the production of the statues and their presentation within the sanctuary: the archaeological record is full of examples of typical forms and conventions visible in the bits and pieces from various statues and their change over time. Classical archaeologists have discovered a number of lightning bolts, for example, which probably once belonged to representations of Zeus, as well as fragments of wings and feathers, which in all likelihood were once part of representations of Nike.[94] 'Local' events and identities as defined above, it can be concluded, found expression in a universal visual language, and this visual language was, at least in part, propagated and spread throughout the Greek world by (epic) poetry. The imagery derived from the grand mythological narratives provided a common visual ground to which a variety of 'local' information could be attached.

Not everyone who was entitled to put up a statue at Olympia chose the 'indirect' form of representation of events and identities in the form of a divine statue and/or mythological theme. More 'personalised' and 'direct' forms of representation were certainly possible in the sanctuary, yet they, too, conformed to certain forms and conventions limiting and controlling

---

[92] Both Herodotus and Pausanias (more than 500 years later) commented on the great number of his offerings: Hdt. 7.170.4; Paus. 5.26.2–7. On the remnants of the base of the 12-figure monument see Eckstein 1969: 33–42.

[93] See Paus. 5.26.2–3. Apparently Micythus (a former slave) dedicated these statues in adherence to an oath he had made when his son was seriously ill (Paus. 5.26.5). On Micythus see also Hdt. 7.170; Str. 6.1.1 C253; D.S. 11.48.2. For the inscriptions see Hill et al. 1951: B107.

[94] Fragments of Nike representations: e.g., Olympia, Archaeological Museum, inv. nos. T 44, T 131, T 261, T 297, T 298 (all belonging to the same figure); Olympia, Archaeological Museum, inv. nos. Tc 1071, K 181; Olympia, Archaeological Museum, inv. nos. T 304, T 254. See also Bol 1978: 62–4.

the extent of personal display. At all times a significant number of statues set up within the sanctuary were victor monuments, celebrating achievement in a particular Olympic discipline. In principle every Olympic victor had the right, granted by the Elean authorities, to set up a statue to remind future generations of his achievement, and they could do so more than once. Some athletes were represented at Olympia by several statues – one for each victory![95] Yet not all those who were entitled to do so did, in fact, set up a statue as this involved considerable expense.[96] Early statues were made of wood.[97] Life-sized or near life-sized victor statues made of bronze appeared at Olympia at the transition of the sixth and fifth centuries BC, but smaller statues also continued to be set up.[98] Early examples in particular still conformed to the *kouros* type, a frontal depiction of a nude youth with the left foot slightly advanced.[99] Federico Rausa has shown that they were grouped together especially on the south side of the sanctuary, hence emphasising their likeness.[100]

Other figurines dating from the sixth and early fifth centuries BC consisted of formalised images of males engaged in a particular sporting activity (Fig. 6).[101] The spear-throwing types were remarkably similar to the figurines representing Zeus throwing his thunderbolts (see above). Other victor statues were modelled after the type of a standing youth making an offering to a divinity.[102]

In her study of Pindaric victory odes, Leslie Kurke stressed the need to reintegrate the aristocratic victor, who had excelled in agonistic

---

[95] See Paus. 6.3.11.

[96] The expenses of victory statues were not necessarily covered by the victor's city of origin, but frequently fell to the victor himself or to his family. See Dittenberger and Purgold 1896: 235; Hyde 1912: 222; Mallwitz 1972: 59–60.

[97] Pausanias identified Praxidamas of Aegina (victor in boxing in 544 BC) and Rhexibius the Opuntian (victor in 536 BC) as the first two athletes to be represented at Olympia in statuary form. See Paus. 6.18.7.

[98] Mattusch suggested that smaller figurines were probably set up on bases so that they were in sight of those strolling through the sanctuary. See Mattusch 1988: 111. Sinn 1989: 67–8 suggested that athletes may have dedicated small figurines at the sanctuary *before* the competitions ('*Bitt*-Votive' as opposed to '*Dank*-Votive').

[99] E.g., the figurine published by Sinn 1989 dating from the end of the sixth century BC. See also Mallwitz 1972: 57. Neer 2007: 230 referred to the *kouros* type as the 'all-purpose icon of the aristocracy'.

[100] Rausa 1994: 39–51. See also Neer 2007: 230.

[101] See, e.g., Olympia, Archaeological Museum, inv. no. B 26 (Fig. 6); Olympia, Archaeological Museum, inv. no. B 6767 (a discus thrower) and Mallwitz 1972: 57–60; Herrmann 1972: illuss. 3a, 3b, 5b, 5d. Thomas, R. 1981 gave a detailed survey of this type of statue.

[102] E.g., the statue of Anaxander from Sparta, a victor in the chariot race, depicted him in a position of prayer, whereas the statue of Polycles held a ribbon. See Paus. 6.1.7. See also Olympia, Archaeological Museum, inv. no. B 6300 for a sacrificing statuette dating from around 470/460 BC.

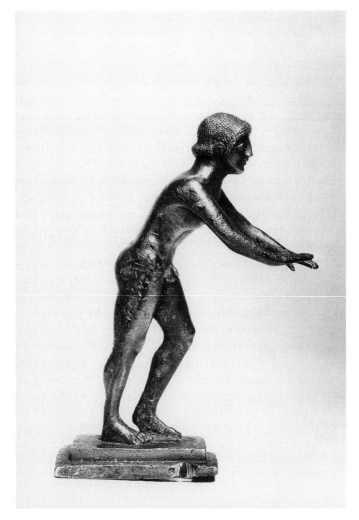

Fig. 6 Figurine of an athlete, first half of the fifth century BC

competitions, into the community of *oikos*, class and polis.[103] Victory odes, Kurke argued, helped to achieve this goal: 'the victor must be reintegrated into his house, his class *and* his city, and it is the task of Pindar's poem in performance to accomplish this reintegration'.[104] Even though Pindar himself found sculpture inferior to poetry as a medium of artistic expression

---

[103] Kurke 1991. Greek epigrams celebrating agonistic success: Ebert 1972.   [104] Kurke 1991: 6.

and heroic praise, victor statues should be considered here.[105] Like the odes, they were a form of artistic production intended to commemorate Olympic success. Like the odes, they could feature at the venue of the competition itself (Olympia) and/or in the polis community of the victor.[106] Yet, by representing the aristocratic victor in a stylised fashion, victor statues also emphasised the general equivalence of Olympic success, thus containing in their own materiality a framework for processing individual achievement. The victor statue made visible the conformity of the successful competitor to the 'type' of all Olympic victors. In his stylised replica of himself, the victor quite literally became one of the *homoioi* ('equals').[107] At Olympia past victors mingled with their peers in statuary form, yet if erected in their home city, the victor statue also projected (and hence integrated) this identity into the physical space of the polis.[108]

Sadly, most life-sized bronzes have been lost, but excavations north of the Prytaneion have produced the head of a wrestler or pancratist, dating from the fourth century BC (Fig. 7).[109] Classical scholars have sought to assign the head to one of the famous athletes known to us – a certain Satyrus, who received a statue crafted by the Athenian sculptor Silanion, being a likely candidate.[110] The head demonstrates remarkably well how far the naturalistic mode of representation had advanced by the fourth century BC.[111] The flat nose impressively recalls earlier punches and the rest of the face likewise shows the traces of heavy wear and tear.[112] However, a closer look at the head suggests once more that what we see are stereotypical rather than individual features.[113] The minute fashioning of the hair (in particular its symmetric regularity) has an ornamental touch and the section around the mouth, with the symmetrically lined beard closing the semicircle suggested by the lower lip, also demonstrates a standard design. The face is that of a typical wrestler while the crown on the head identifies the Olympic victor. Even victor monuments in the form of life-sized bronzes, it seems, tended to depict the victor engaged in his typical activity as a jumper, sprinter, or spear thrower.[114]

---

[105] See O'Sullivan 2002 on Pindar's dismissive attitude towards victor statues.

[106] See Neer 2007: 230–1.   [107] Neer 2007: 230.   [108] See Thomas, R. 1981: 20; Neer 2007: 231.

[109] Olympia, Archaeological Museum, inv. no. B 6439. This was not the original location of the statue. The head seems to have been deliberately cut from the torso: see Bol 1978: 39–43 and tables 30–2.

[110] Bol 1978: 41–2.   [111] The emergence of naturalism in Greek sculpture: Spivey 1996: 17–54.

[112] Here and in the following see Bol 1978: 40–3.

[113] Contra Hyde 1921: 56–7, who presented the pancratist's head as an example for realistic portraiture.

[114] See also, e.g., the so-called Charioteer of Delphi, a victory statue dating from ca. 474 BC that was set up in the sanctuary of Apollo at Delphi in commemoration of a victor in the Pythian Games. The Charioteer is now on display at Delphi, Delphi Museum, inv. nos. 3484, 3520, 3540. A discussion and illustration of the Charioteer: Mattusch 1988: 127–35 with illus. 6.6.

Fig. 7 Head of a wrestler, fourth century BC

The very fact that naturalistic representation gradually replaced older styles during the fifth and fourth centuries BC, however, does not mean that athletes were necessarily represented by portrait statues depicting their individual features.[115] Pliny said that only those who had won three times at Olympia were entitled to portrait statues (*iconicae*).[116] Pausanias on various occasions specified some statues as *eikones*, likenesses.[117] Yet in her account of the development of Greek bronze statuary Carol Mattusch rightly warned us not to expect too much individuality. Both victor statues

[115] The emergence of portrait statues in ancient Greece: Dillon 2006: 61–98.
[116] Plin. *HN* 34.9.16. For a critical discussion of this passage see Hyde 1921: 54–5.
[117] E.g., Paus. 6.12.5 (on the statues of Hieron of Syracuse crafted by Micon).

and honorific statues tended to follow generic types with the possible presence of a few individualised attributes, such as the depiction of age or a particular pose. Of the honorific statues, which became increasingly popular at Olympia from the fourth century BC onwards, for example, Mattusch observes:

The standard type is a standing figure; sometimes he is seated. Gestures and attributes serve as more precise references to the occupation of the individual. The head may be slightly turned, the arms engaged or extended. The simple addition of a helmet, a beard, a cloak, or a lyre gives greater specificity. The portrait statue thus served to identify a famous individual by characterizing him as a type.[118]

Representation of individuals as variations of certain types ensured their identification as a group and the general compatibility (and control) of their personal achievement, which became, in dedicatory form, the property of divinity.[119] Such statues therefore provided an important strategy for processing, containing and 'storing' individual achievement in the space of the sanctuary.

Frequently it is the votive inscriptions (*Weihinschriften*) that provide a way into the specific context of a dedication. Many statues and monuments featured quite elaborate inscriptions, which offered a variety of information on the circumstances and purpose of the dedication.[120] Pausanias frequently paused to comment on the inscriptions he found in and beyond the Altis. Take for example his account in 5.22.2–4 of a victory monument erected north-west of the Bouleuterion.[121] He described an elaborate dedication placed on a semicircular stone pedestal, featuring Zeus, Thetis and Hemera (Day) in the middle and five pairs of Greek–Trojan combatants on the side facing each other: Achilles and Memnon, Odysseus and Helenus, Alexander and Menelaus, Aeneas and Diomedes, Deiphobus and Ajax. The elegiac inscription, quoted by Pausanias, the remnants of which have also been found at Olympia together with parts of the base of the monument, addressed the onlooker as follows:[122]

Μνάματ' Ἀπολλωνίας ἀ[νακείμεθα, τὰν ἐνὶ πόντοι]
[ἰ]ονίοι Φοῖβος ϝοίκι[σ' ἀκερσεκόμας],
[οἳ γ]ᾶ[ς τέ]ρμᾳθ᾽ [ἑλόντες Ἀβαντίδος ἐνθάδε ταῦτα]
[ἔστασαν σὺν θεοῖς ἐκ Θρονίου δεκάταν].

---

[118] Mattusch 1988: 211.

[119] Not all honorific statues were dedications. The concept only applies to those statues that were set up in a sanctuary and not, for example, those that were set up in the Agora.

[120] On Olympic inscriptions see, e.g., Eckstein in Kunze 1958: 205–25; Kunze 1956: 149–75.

[121] On the monument see also Eckstein 1969: 15–22; Mallwitz 1972: 37; Mattusch 1988: 193; Ioakimidou 1997: 92–7 (with further literature).

[122] *SEG* XV 251. See also Paus. 5.22.3. On the inscription see Eckstein 1969: 16; Ioakimidou 1997: 95.

As memorials of Apollonia were we set up,
  which on the Ionian Sea Phoebus founded, he with the unshorn hair.
The Apollonians, after they seized the boundaries of the land of Abantis, here
  set up these statues with the help of the gods out of the tithe from Thronium.

The statues of this dedication have not endured, but according to Pausanias' account they drew heavily on mythological narratives known from Homer and other famous poets who had elaborated the mythological cycle associated with the Trojan War. The combatants represented are all key figures in the epic of that war. Interestingly, by referring to Apollo as 'Phoebus of the unshorn hair' (Φοῖβος ἀκερσεκόμας), the inscription itself featured a pictorial reference in the form of a Homeric epithet, thus emphasising its link to the figures towering above it, which also belonged to the world of Homer.[123] The inscription addressed the onlooker in the voice of the collective first person, thus providing a mouthpiece for the statues above it and increasing the immediacy of their communication with the onlooker. While the spectacular thirteen-figure monument would certainly have grasped the attention of everybody moving past it, the metre of the inscription provided another reference to Greek poetry and ensured remembrance of the specific information provided.

This monument also shows that 'local' identities could be inscribed in material form in a much more immediate fashion than we have so far recognised. The letter and word choice of the inscription itself, in particular the digamma in line 2 and the Doric genitive γᾶς, adhered to the 'local' customs of Apollonia in Illyria, a Corinthian colony. The epigram followed the linguistic conventions of the polis that commissioned the monument, rather than those of the artist's geographical origin (Lycius of Eleutherae in Boeotia).[124] Another example comes in the form of a grand monument erected in front of the Echo Colonnade during the third century BC, representing Ptolemy II and his wife Arsinoe.[125] Ptolemy, a Macedonian king of Egypt, had distinguished himself by expanding the Ptolemaic Empire in Asia Minor and, significantly, the columns and capitals on which the statues were placed showed distinctly Ionian features.[126] The monument communicated a regional ideology, which, quite literally and materially in this case, supported the personal identity of the statues it carried.

---

[123] E.g., Hom. *Il.* 20.39.   [124] Kunze 1956: 151 (with further examples).
[125] No inventory number. On the monument see, e.g., Herrmann 1972: 181–2; Mallwitz 1972: 63; Hintzen-Bohlen 1992: 77–81.
[126] See Mallwitz 1972: 63.

Classical archaeologists estimate that more than two dozen victor monuments sprang up within the first few decades of the fifth century BC and many more accumulated in the sanctuary over time. A conservative estimate, based on the relation between victor monuments mentioned by Pausanias and the actual bases that have come down to us, has produced the staggering number of approximately 494 victor monuments for Olympia at the time of Pausanias.[127] Victor monuments became some of the most ubiquitous and noticeable items on display within the sanctuary. From the fourth century BC on, the increasing popularity of honorific statues added to the representation of 'local' events and identities at Olympia by depicting outstanding 'local' notables not otherwise associated with the sanctuary.[128] Some scholars have estimated that overall the sanctuary housed up to 1,000 bronze statues and monuments at the time of Pausanias![129] So, was the pattern according to which items were added to the archive of significant events and identities simply cumulative?

There is considerable evidence to show that items were also removed from display within the sanctuary.[130] In particular the construction of major buildings or sites was used as an opportunity to clean up the sanctuary and to remove unwanted items. In the previous chapter I discussed the cultural practice of recycling one kind of symbolic capital into another – for example, tyrant property into ritual equipment or temple treasuries into money, etc. A similar kind of 'recycling' apparently took place at Olympia. Several bases of older monuments seem to have been reused in later times, thus providing an indication of how long the monument to which they originally belonged was on display.[131] We do not know the criteria according to which dedications were discarded, but old dedications frequently ended up as filler material in new sites. The period of time between their original dedication and the date of the site in which they were used as filler material

---

[127] Hyde 1912; Scott 2010: 150–2, 171–2. See also the critical evaluation in Bol 1978: 1 of the information on dedications provided by Polybius and Pliny and their value as comparative data for the situation at Olympia.

[128] See above n. 72.

[129] This is the estimation of Mattusch 1988: 109. See Peim 2000 for a critical assessment of the possibility of such calculations (with further literature).

[130] Fragments of old dedications were found, e.g., in various wells within the sanctuary. See Gauer 1975; Mallwitz 1988: 101–2. Older dedications were sometimes also used as filler material during major reconstructions of the sanctuary, e.g., around the middle of the seventh century BC, when 'a significant part of its gathering collection of expensive dedications was deliberately destroyed and buried as part of a levelling of the heart of the sanctuary, and replaced with a series of monumental buildings, which reorganised the focus of ritual activity in the sanctuary towards the hero cult of Pelops and (perhaps) the goddess Hera': Scott 2010: 150.

[131] The altar-like space for the priestess of Demeter on the northern mound of the stadium, e.g., was made from what was once the base of an equestrian monument. See Mallwitz 1972: 180.

gives us a good estimate of how long the statues actually stood in the sanctuary. Individual types of dedication had very different turnover rates. Small items, such as little figurines, weapons and armour in particular did not remain on display for very long. Yet, surprisingly, some fairly elaborate and costly statues were used as filler fairly soon after their dedication. The excavations of the earthwork of the second stadium dating from the middle of the fifth century BC, for example, have revealed a considerable number of distinctive locks which once adorned the heads of bronze statues.[132] As statues of this kind became popular in the sanctuary only at the end of the sixth and in the early fifth century BC, the statues must have been removed from display relatively soon after their original dedication. Had the events they commemorated, for one reason or another, become insignificant, unworthy of being recalled by the community of Hellenes gathering at Olympia? Was the past stored in the archive selected according to its ongoing relevance for present commemoration?

However that may be, a walk through the sanctuary brought the visitor to Olympia face to face with 'local' events and identities from different parts of the Greek world (and occasionally beyond).[133] The 'local' was present at Olympia in a range of forms and formulations: as stories about the events requiring a dedication; in the form of information about the artists who crafted the monuments; and in the events and identities of those represented either directly in sculptural form or indirectly via a statue depicting divinity. Yet the 'local' could also be inscribed in the styles of the sculptural production itself, by following regional rather than universal Greek conventions (see above). At Olympia, we may conclude, the category of the 'local', defined as information specific to a person, polis, area or region within Greece, was implied in the universal Greek imagery and symbolism and vice versa.

At the same time, however, 'local' events and identities 'stored' within the sanctuary were also displayed within a distinctively temporal dimension, thus encouraging an historical engagement with Greece's past as represented in the sanctuary. Some items did not simply refer to events that had occurred a long time ago. Their very shape and material were indicative of their relative age. As the styles and conventions of Greek statuary changed over time, many older items must have struck the onlooker as being distinctively old-fashioned in design. Indeed, it is not just the modern visitor browsing through the catalogues of findings from Olympia who is struck

---

[132] Here and in the following see Bol 1978: 18.
[133] On non-Greek dedications see, e.g., Paus. 5.12.5–8.

by how much dedications evolved over time: the ancient visitor, too, recognised the historical dimension of the objects on display. At various times Pausanias commented on the age or archaic style of specific items. He recorded that 'Eutelidas' statue is old and time has made the letters on the base difficult to read.' (ἔστι δὲ ἥ τε εἰκὼν ἀρχαία τοῦ Εὐτελίδα, καὶ τὰ ἐπὶ τῷ βάθρῳ γράμματα ἀμυδρὰ ὑπὸ τοῦ χρόνου).[134] He also noticed that the statue of Praxidamas of Aegina, crafted out of the wood of a fig tree, was less decayed than the one of Rhexibius from Opuntia, made of cypress wood.[135] Other items showed their relative age through their distinctly modern or antiquated decorations and designs. The famous chest of Cypselus, for example, which was kept in the temple of Hera, featured a set of inscriptions written in ancient letters, while two of the *Zanes* framing the entrance to the stadium struck Pausanias as being fairly contemporary (δύο τέχνης τῆς ἐφ' ἡμῶν ἀγάλματα).[136]

Through the 'local' events and identities that were represented at Olympia in dedicatory form, the sanctuary not only provided a space in which the community of the Hellenes could recognise itself – a space in which individual, polis and regional identities were brought together and linked in what must have seemed like a limitless array of comparable and compatible stories – but the dedications also encouraged a temporal perspective on the materialised image of a commonly inhabited past – an important dimension of the discursive establishment of identity.[137] In a nutshell, the physical space of the sanctuary provided an important context for the storage and encoding of culturally relevant information just as the institution of the Games provided a ritualised occasion and schedule for (re)visiting this information.

CONCLUSION

The case study of setting up dedications at Olympia has revealed the existence of a broader religious culture in ancient Greece, a culture which transcended the duality between the 'local' and the 'panhellenic', and between polis religion and ancient Greek religion beyond the polis, in two different ways – first, by illustrating the multiplicity of the category of the 'local', which could encompass polis identities as well as identities above or below the polis level; second, by showcasing the presence of the 'local',

---

[134] Paus. 6.15.8.   [135] Paus. 6.18.7.   [136] Paus. 5.17.6 and 5.21.16 respectively.
[137] Cf. Scott 2010: 226, who argues that because items were more frequently removed from the sanctuary of Zeus at Olympia than from the one of Apollo at Delphi, 'Olympia did not have, on display at least, the same amount of dedicatory history as the sanctuary of Delphi.'

defined here as information pertaining to a particular individual, polis or region in Greece within the physical space of an institution traditionally associated with the panhellenic side of ancient Greek religion.

Investigation of the cultural practice of setting up dedications at Olympia, however, reveals not just the coexistence of the 'local' in the 'panhellenic', but also some of the manifold ways in which they related to and were implicit within each other. We noticed the existence of two divergent forces: that of particularity, divergence and multiplicity on the one hand, and a unifying force on the other, visible, for example, in the ways in which statues drew on common mythological themes and followed similar styles in order to speak to viewers from different parts of the Greek world. Starting from the study of sanctuaries it would certainly be productive to consider the interplay of both forces at other locations or contexts of the religious – for example, in the *Histories* of Herodotus.

To sum up, the local and the universal do not serve as antipodes of the Greek religious experience, and it would be wrong to assume a strict duality between polis religion and religious beliefs and practices beyond the polis. On the most abstract level, the case study of setting up dedications at Olympia has illustrated the existence of a flexible and fluid conception of the religious culture, in which multiple identities above, below and beyond the polis level related to each other. In fact, one of the prime functions of sanctuaries such as Olympia seems to have been to mediate between different levels of Greek identity by setting them into a spatial relationship with each other. Might we call this function a form of 'panhellenism'?

CHAPTER 6

'The sex appeal of the inorganic': seeing, touching and knowing the divine during the Second Sophistic

What may generate anxiety and constitute an enigma is precisely the coming together of two opposite dimensions in a single phenomenon such as the mode of being of the thing and human sensibility.

Mario Perniola[1]

Feeling implies the union between body and spirit, mind and machine. A thinking thing can also not have a body, but a sentient thing has to have it. Who feels therefore is not God but the I.

Mario Perniola[2]

INTRODUCTION

A fragment from a (now-lost) play entitled *A Picture* by the poet Alexis features a certain Cleisophus of Selymbria, who got himself locked into a temple at Samos intending to have intercourse with the statue it housed. '[A]nd since he found that impossible on account of the frigidity and resistance of the stone (διά τε τὴν ψυχρότητα καὶ τὸ ἀντίτυπον τοῦ λίθου), he then and there desisted from that desire and placing before him a small piece of flesh (προβαλλόμενός τι σαρκίον) he consorted with that.'[3]

One might want to take this curious incident simply as what it purports to be: the product of the poetic imagination of an important advocate of Middle and New Comedy. Alternatively we might consider that the key to this odd passage is to be found in a more general but no less puzzling association between women and food in Athenaeus' *Deiphnosophistae*, the work in which it is preserved.[4] In short it might indeed be tempting to dismiss this episode as a strange but ultimately negligible incident but for the fact that Cleisophus' desire was by no means as singular as one might think. The entire story reverberates with other instances of *agalmatophilia*

---

[1] Perniola 2004: 1.   [2] Perniola 2004: 7.   [3] Ath. 13.605f.   [4] See Henry 1992.

('statue love') involving divine statues, and the similarities and differences between Cleisophus' experience and their accounts of *agalmatophilia* are as striking as they are revealing.[5]

The statue of Cleisophus' desire was perhaps a (gold and ivory) representation of the goddess Hera, who was worshipped at Samos in a lavish sanctuary.[6] This would be surprising, however, because this would be the only instance we know of when Hera was subjected to this kind of male attention. A far more frequent (and more likely) object of male veneration was Praxiteles' famous Aphrodite, a marble statue crafted around the middle of the fourth century BC and subsequently sold to the city of Cnidus, where it was displayed in the temple of the goddess.[7] But Cleisophus' experience is typical insofar as the human desire to make love to the divine statue always meets with unexpected obstacles. The agalmatophiliac's desire is diverted by the impenetrable fabric of the statue – with sometimes devastating consequences for the desiring subject. Cleisophus is lucky to have survived his erotic adventure unscathed – another young man who attempted to make love to the Aphrodite of Cnidus is said to have hurled himself over a cliff upon realising the ultimate futility of his desire.[8]

What is at stake behind this curious human/divine contact imagined here as an erotic encounter? What is the heat and *energeia* radiating from the desired, even attempted, but ultimately unsuccessful intercourse between gods' bodies and human bodies? This chapter explores what it is in the idea of *agalmatophilia* involving divine statues that inspired the poetic imagination of Alexis and other authors. To answer this question, however, we must first consider the love of statues within the context of the principles and practices of the corporeal representation of the divine in the religions of Greece and Rome more generally.

---

[5] Instances of *agalmatophilia* involving divine statues dating from the period between the first and the third centuries AD: Plin. *HN* 36.4.21; Lucian *Im.* 4; [Lucian] *Am.* 15–17; Clem. Al. *Protr.* 4.57.3; Onomarchus in Philostr. *VS* 2.18; *VA* 6.40; Val. Max. 8.11. ext. 4; Ael. *VH* 14.39. Within the modern context, the early scientific study of sexuality seems to have cultivated a fascination with the love of statues (sometimes also referred to as 'pygmalionism' or 'statuephilia'). The phenomenon is included in some medical handbooks dating from the late nineteenth/early twentieth century as a rare form of sexual deviance (e.g., Ellis 1928: 188; von Krafft-Ebing 1945: 525). Intriguingly, no single clinical case seems ever to have been recorded and the examples discussed are almost all derived from hearsay and literature, including the literature of the ancient world, see Scobie and Taylor 1975; White 1978. On 'statue love' ancient and modern, see also Hersey 2009.

[6] This seems to be the underlying assumption in Henry 1992. On the Heraion of Samos: Pedley 2005: 154–66. Evidence for the cult statue(s) of Hera on Samos: *LIMC* IV.1: 662–663; *LIMC* IV.2: 413 (illuss. 155–161).

[7] See Plin. *HN* 36.4.20–21. On the statue and the temple see Havelock 2007: 58–63.

[8] [Lucian] *Am.* 16.12–14 (see below).

THE BODY OF THE DIVINE

As Jean-Pierre Vernant so ingeniously pointed out, to give the gods a human body was a way of making the divine present in the human sphere and available for knowledge through physical experience: a body we can see and touch is a body we can think and talk about.[9] Moreover, imagining the gods in corporeal form allowed humanity to relate to divinity within the framework of bodily existence as a basic condition of human life. In their human bodies, the gods became subject to 'the same vital values, the same qualities of force, radiance, and beauty' as men.[10]

There was another dimension, too, to the corporeal existence of the divine. To locate the gods physically and materially in a specific time and space was also an important precondition of the manifold exchanges – real and symbolic – central to the cults of Greco-Roman polytheism.[11]

Yet to imagine the gods in corporeal form also posed what Vernant referred to as the 'problem of the divine body': 'Can gods who have bodies – anthropomorphic gods like those of the ancient Greeks – really be considered gods?'[12] Is not the very point of divinity to be supernatural, situated outside the human sphere and its corporeal mode of existence? In other words: what use are gods that look just like humans and are – just like us – subject to the constraints of the corporeal condition?

The answer was quite simply that the divine body was different from the human body. In order to solve the 'problem of the divine body', Greco-Roman polytheism introduced the notion of alterity to the body of the divine, hence complementing the idea of its identity to the human body. The resulting paradoxes pervaded every level of the divine existence as a corporeal existence. In Greco-Roman thought and literature, the mortality of the human body was contrasted with the immortality of the divine; like the human body, the divine body contained blood but not as a vital substance and source of energy (even bleeding gods do not die); gods enjoyed meals but without satisfying a bodily need, etc. Divine *ichōr* was like and unlike human blood; ambrosia and nectar were like and unlike human food. As Vernant succinctly put it, 'the corporeal code permits one to think of the relations between man and god under the double figures of the same and the other, or the near and the far, of contact and separation'.[13]

---

[9] Vernant 1991: 27–49. On gods' bodies see now Osborne 2011: 185–215.
[10] Vernant 1991: 47.
[11] On this point see Vernant 1991: 47; Steiner 2001: 81. Price 1984a: 143–71 has a good discussion of the similarities and differences between Greek and Roman religion.
[12] Vernant 1991: 27. See also Steiner 2001: 89.   [13] Vernant 1991: 31. See also Henrichs 2010: 29–37.

The body of the divine provided a trajectory along which a whole set of similarities and differences between the human and divine spheres could be projected and explored.

The representation of the bodies of the gods in statuary form added a further dimension to the 'corporeal code' of the divine. It extended and complicated the relationship between gods' bodies and human bodies as one of identity and alterity. Phidias' famous Athena Parthenos (438 BC), for example, a colossal chryselephantine statue, articulated the otherworldly nature of the gods through her size and the precious materials used for her fabrication.[14] However, this was only one way of representing the otherworldly nature of the gods – albeit a particularly successful one, given the statue's prestige in antiquity. Neer has recently compared the fame of Phidias' Athena Parthenos and his Zeus at Olympia with the importance of the Sistine Chapel and the *Last Supper* in Europe during the early modern period.[15]

Statues representing the Greek gods and goddesses had their very own modes of translating the otherworldly nature of the divine into the human sphere in the way in which they positioned themselves between the opposing poles of iconicity and aniconism, in their various sizes above, below and identical to the average size of the human body and in their various fabrics.[16] In Chapter 2 I discussed a text that featured a semi-iconic statue. Stories featuring the love of statues, in contrast, typically revolved around representations of the gods in the form of a naturalistic depiction of the female human body.

In the history of Greek art naturalism was an acquired taste. Statues such as the Kritios Boy (ca. 480 BC, a dedication like the ones we discussed in the previous chapter) cannot be explained without invoking a taste for naturalism.[17] The crucial step in the history of statuary representation, however, was taken in the middle of the fifth century BC, when the desire to show the body of men as they were collided with the desire to create images that had a more general, idealised force. The famous Riace bronzes (ca. 460–450 BC) were shaped by the desire to create images that were highly specific;[18] Polyclitus' Doryphorus ('spear bearer') crafted around the

---

[14] Phidias' original statue is lost, but we do have several Roman versions. See, e.g., Neer 2010: 99–102.

[15] Neer 2010: 101.   [16] See Gordon 1979; Donohue 1988; Steiner 2001: 79–134; Platt 2011: 77–121.

[17] Athens, Acropolis Museum, inv. no. 698. For an illustration see Osborne 1998: 158; Pedley 2002: 226. On naturalism and the question of why the Kritios Boy marked a distinct shift see most recently Neer 2010: 147–55.

[18] Reggio di Calabria, Museo Nazionale, no inventory numbers. For an illustration see Boardman 1993: 87 ('Warrior A'); Osborne 1998: 160–1 ('Warriors A and B').

same time (ca. 450/40 BC) showed a retreat from this desire.[19] With this turn, however, a crucial and productive tension was introduced, which remained at the heart of Greco-Roman sculptural production: subsequent developments in ancient art found ever-new compromises between the individual and the typical.

But how does naturalism apply to the principles and practices of divine representation? Vernant argued that, 'at the pivotal point of the fifth and fourth centuries, the theory of *mimēsis*, sketched out by Xenophon, and elaborated in a fully systematic way by Plato, marks the moment when in Greek culture the turn is completed that leads from the "presentification", the making present, of the invisible to the imitation of appearance'.[20] But Vernant told too simple a story here, for as Donohue and others rightly showed, the tension between 'presentification' and 'imitation' as competing and opposing principles of divine representation was never resolved: simple wooden statues (in later sources sometimes referred to as *xoana*) continued to coexist with more elaborate *agalmata*.[21] What Vernant sketched as a strict temporal succession were really two alternative principles in statuary representation of the gods.[22] The problem is that Vernant relied mainly on the textual evidence; the crisis he found in Plato was already visible in mid-fifth-century BC art. It emerged together with the development of divine representations in statuary form: as statues became more lifelike, the problem became more obvious. The theological questions raised by the two opposing forces of presentification and imitation with regard to the production and consumption of divine images could not have been more pressing. How did the divine representation position itself with regard to them?

Praxiteles' Aphrodite was crafted at a crunch point in the development of Greek sculpture, when the possibility of a full naturalistic imitation of the human body raised such questions. Unfortunately we do not have the original statue, but we do encounter the Cnidia in numerous Roman copies and variations, on coins from Cnidus and in the textual evidence. From this we can with some confidence deduce her general features. The goddess of love, sex and beauty was fully nude; she was life-sized or even a bit larger and stood in *contrapposto* with her right hand covering her pubic area. She probably held a piece of garment in her left hand draped over a vase placed

[19] A marble copy is on display in Naples, Museo Nazionale Archaeologico, inv. no. 6146. For an illustration see Osborne 1998: 163; Pedley 2002: 275.
[20] Vernant 1991: 152.   [21] Donohue 1988.   [22] See ch. 2, n. 49.

on a pedestal. The entire arrangement seems to suggest a bathing scene as the reason for her nudity.[23]

Was Praxiteles' Aphrodite the first life-sized female nude in the history of Greek art? Most classical scholars prefer to give a tentative answer to this question, arguing only that this *may* be the case.[24] The most outspoken challenge to this position comes from Mary Beard and John Henderson,[25] who have dismissed all attempts to construct a succession of Aphrodite statues in which the goddess of love gradually sheds her dress (culminating in the Cnidia). According to Beard and Henderson, such chronological reconstructions frequently misunderstand the principles and practices of imitation; they are also based on chronological claims that are ultimately untenable: 'none of the claims to relative priority between the different statue types has proved persuasive'.[26]

One might wonder whether the crux of the matter did not lie elsewhere. For in some ways it could be argued that what made Praxiteles' Aphrodite the original female nude has nothing to do with how much or how little other female statues wore but everything to do with the relationship between Praxiteles' statue and the viewer. Almost all Roman copies have developed this aspect of the statue by providing ever-new variants and variations on the same theme. The scholarly questions asked about these statues reflect just how much the question of the relationship between statue and viewer has dominated both the ancient and the modern reception of the sculptures. Is the statue protecting her modesty in covering her private parts?[27] Is Aphrodite displaying a suggestive smile? A deceitful smile? A knowing smile? Is she, in fact, deliberately posing in front of the viewer? Or is this a much more innocent scene?[28] Is she merely demonstrating some form of natural modesty, which does not rely on the presence of an onlooker?[29] A form of 'heroic' or 'epiphanic' nudity perhaps?[30] It is these kinds of question that have dominated modern scholarly debates about those statues that have survived. Surely we cannot be far off the mark if we suggest that some form of the very same ambiguity of pose and facial expression was already inherent in Praxiteles' sculpture, the very statue that inspired these copies? Moreover, the relationship between statue

---

[23] See Havelock 2007: 11–37.   [24] See, e.g., Morris 1994: 84; Blundell 1995: 194.

[25] E.g., Beard and Henderson 2001: 127–8 vs. Osborne 1994; Havelock 2007; Stewart 1990, vol. I: 149.

[26] Beard and Henderson 2001: 127.   [27] See Blinkenberg 1933: 21, 47.

[28] As argued in particular in older scholarship, e.g., Bernoulli 1873: 14–16; Blinkenberg 1933: 37, who argued that Aphrodite's nudity was due to her taking a bath.

[29] As argued by Rodenwaldt 1944: 15.

[30] See Rodenwaldt 1944: 14 ('heroische Nacktheit'); Borbein 1973: 173–4 ('das Erscheinungsbild meint Epiphanie'); Himmelmann 1990: 48–52.

and (male) viewer was also at the heart of much of the literary evidence from the late Hellenistic and Roman periods.

Stories of *agalmatophilia* featuring the Cnidia, then, were part of a much larger ancient preoccupation with the relationship between statue and (male) viewer. They depicted the seductive side of naturalism in divine representation – in such accounts both aspects of the divine body, that of 'making present' (of the divine) and of perfect *mimēsis* (of the female human body), seemed to be in conflict with each other. As stories of the human/divine encounter depicted as a bodily encounter, these accounts raised the question of the nature of the availability of the divine body. Ultimately, however, we will find that they also reasserted the notion of divine alterity by introducing and exploring a series of fundamental distinctions between the bodies of gods and those of humans. Above all, accounts of *agalmatophilia* juxtaposed the human body as an animated, organic and sentient body with the inanimate and inorganic body of the divine as a body incapable of feeling, and used the resulting paradoxes to explore the nature of the divine and its relationship to humanity. It is in particular this dichotomy between the organic and the inorganic which, I argue, proved 'good to think with' for those Greco-Roman authors interested in questions of divine ontology.

Consider, for example, the story derived from Alexis/Athenaeus as discussed above. What was behind the curious substitution of ivory and flesh? Simon Goldhill proposed that this episode turns on an opposition between the uncooked quality of sacrificial meat (and its subsequent out-of-context use) and the crafted female body of the statue. He suggested that Cleisophus' experience virtually 'cries out for a structuralist analysis along raw/cooked lines'.[31] Yet I believe that it is not only the duality between natural and man-made things, between nature and culture, that is highlighted here, but also and in particular the distinction between the organic and the inorganic: it is the inorganic coldness and rigidity of the sculptured divine body that is highlighted in the story and which disqualifies the statue from being the focus of erotic passion. The piece of flesh (σάρξ), by contrast, can bring about the desired outcome: as an organic substance it can serve as a metonymic substitute for the actual object of erotic desire.

In the remainder of this chapter I investigate how three authors drew on the distinction between organic and inorganic bodies in order to explore the nature of divine alterity and of divine ontology. I compare and contrast the way in which the same or similar incidents feature in three authors,

---

[31] Goldhill 1995: 171, n. 99 referring to Lévi-Strauss 1969.

who all wrote within sixty-odd years of each other: Philostratus in his *Life of Apollonius*, Clement of Alexandria in his *Exhortation to the Greeks* and Ps.-Lucian in *Amores*.[32] I do not necessarily intend to suggest direct influences and mutual borrowings between these and other authors although, as I will illustrate below, this seems to have been a distinct possibility between Philostratus and Clement at least. Instead, I explore them as individual contributions to a much larger discourse, one which revolved around the divine body and drew on the traditional anthropomorphism of the gods in order to respond to the challenges springing from religious and cultural change.

Our first visit takes us to Cnidus and into the realm of the erotics of hermeneutics and the hermeneutics of erotics. Ps.-Lucian's *Amores* may well be the latest of the three texts I discuss below. Classical scholars usually suggest a date somewhere around 250 AD – although Elsner has recently raised the question of whether the *Amores* might not be Lucianic rather than merely Ps.-Lucianic.[33] Be that as it may, the *Amores* is a good text to start from because Ps.-Lucian, unlike any other author, exposed the philosophical, hermeneutic and theological problems at stake in the imagination of the human/divine encounter as a bodily encounter.

THE EROTICS OF HERMENEUTICS AND THE HERMENEUTICS OF EROTICS IN PS.-LUCIAN'S AMORES

A visit to Cnidus

In *Amores*, a treatise attributed to Lucian which compares and contrasts the love of boys and the love of women, Charicles, Callicratidas and Lycinus visit the temple of Aphrodite at Cnidus.[34] The temple housed a statue of the goddess by the famous sculptor Praxiteles, a statue Pliny believed to be the most beautiful and accomplished divine sculpture in the ancient world.[35] The statue was crafted out of Parian marble and set up in the middle of the temple.[36] It featured Aphrodite showing an arrogant little smile with her lips slightly open.

---

[32] Throughout this chapter, unless otherwise noted, I use the translations of Macleod 1967 ([Lucian]); Jones, C. 2005 (Philostratus); Butterworth 1919 (Clement); Gulick 1950 (Athenaeus). The numeration of Clement's *Protrepticus* and *Stromata* follows the editions of Stählin 1905 and 1985.

[33] Elsner 2007: 119. For a more extensive discussion of the reasons to classify this text as a later imitation of Lucianic writing see also Jones 1984.

[34] [Lucian] *Am.* 13–17.   [35] See Plin. *HN* 36.4.20.

[36] In another treatise the statue is said to have been produced out of Pentelic marble: Lucian *JTr.* 10.12–14.

Fig. 8 Roman variant of Praxiteles' famous statue of Aphrodite, end of first century BC

In Ps.-Lucian's account, the goddess of love, sexuality and seduction presents herself fully to the human eye: 'Draped by no garment, all her beauty is uncovered and revealed, except insofar as she unobtrusively uses one hand to hide her private parts.'[37] Upon inspecting the statue from the front Charicles kisses Aphrodite 'with importunate lips', while Callicratidas looks on in wonder and amazement.[38] As soon as the three visitors proceed to look at her back, however, it is Charicles who stands in awe and Callicratidas who gets excited about those features of the goddess that resemble those of a boy.

A closer inspection of the sculpture, however, reveals a black stain on Aphrodite's thigh, which the visitors take to be a skilfully concealed natural defect in the marble. However, the female guard of the temple enlightens them as to the true nature of the mark: according to a popular story a young man once fell in love with the statue. After spending hours in the temple gazing at Aphrodite in quiet contemplation, he made several attempts to approach the goddess. He threw dice made from knuckle bones of a Libyan gazelle, trying to throw a constellation named after Aphrodite, and lay down in front of the statue. As his desire grew stronger, he started to write messages to Aphrodite on walls and into the bark of trees and offered to the goddess 'every beautiful treasure that his home guarded'.[39] Finally, he decided to hide behind the door of the temple in the evening, 'hardly even breathing' until he was locked in with the goddess. The next morning revealed the black mark as proof of the young man's amorous approaches. The young man is said to have hurled himself over a cliff or down into the sea, never to be seen again.

Ps.-Lucian's account focuses squarely on the body of the divine. It is prominently displayed in the beginning of the episode, when the three visitors to the temple praise Aphrodite's features and commend her beauty and bodily perfection. It also plays a key role in the subsequent account of the temple guardian describing the responses the statue evoked in the young man, resulting in his misguided attempts to approach the goddess. It is clearly the body of Aphrodite that attracts, even transfixes the gaze of Charicles, Callicratidas, Lycinus and the nameless young man in the story related by the temple attendant.

It should, of course, come as no surprise that Aphrodite featured in a treatise about love and sexuality, but we might nevertheless wonder what it was about her bodily existence that recommended itself as the focus of the story and the obsession of the perceiving subjects within it. I shall not attempt a general interpretation of the dialogue here in terms of its

---

[37] [Lucian] *Am.* 13.2–4. [38] [Lucian] *Am.* 13.8–10. [39] [Lucian] *Am.* 16.2–3.

contribution to the history of sexuality both ancient and modern.[40] What interests me is the way in which the incident at Cnidus was used by Ps.-Lucian to frame the hermeneutic set-up of the investigation at the core of his dialogue – specifically, how the discussion of Aphrodite was used as a way into the examination of the love of boys and women.

A closer look at the way in which the divine body presents itself in the *Amores* reveals its position between that of a human production and a divine representation. The most striking feature of Praxiteles' Aphrodite in the eyes of the beholders in Ps.-Lucian's account is its perfect *mimēsis* of the human body, a skill for which Praxiteles was renowned: τοσοῦτόν γε μὴν ἡ δημιουργὸς ἴσχυσε τέχνη, ὥστε τὴν ἀντίτυπον οὕτω καὶ καρτερὰν τοῦ λίθου φύσιν ἑκάστοις μέλεσιν ἐπιπρέπειν ('[s]o great was the power of the craftsman's art that the hard unyielding marble did justice to every limb').[41] At the same time, however, the statue is more than the product of human craftsmanship. The second dimension of the statue's identity and nature comes into the picture when the young man in the temple servant's account praises both Praxiteles and Zeus (ἐτιμᾶτο δ' ἐξ ἴσου Διὶ Πραξιτέλης).[42] In some sense both Zeus and Praxiteles 'fathered' Aphrodite.[43] But to acknowledge the role of both human production and divine reproduction is to acknowledge the material and the divine dimension of the sculptured divine body.[44] In Ps.-Lucian's account both dimensions of the divine body are equally the object of human admiration. But as we will see below, the tension stemming from the fact that the sculptured divine body is both a human production and represents and contains a divine essence can also become a point of contention. In the words of Claude Lévi-Strauss, the body of Aphrodite was both *cru* and *cuit*, 'raw' and 'cooked'.[45] The bodily perfection of Aphrodite, her perfect *mimēsis* of the female human body, served as proof of the superb skills of Praxiteles as the sculptor who crafted the statue. But at the same time, the bodily perfection of the divine statue, its radiance and everlasting youth, brought out its divine essence – a dimension situated quite literally beyond the human touch.[46]

The ambiguous position of Aphrodite's body between a human production and a divine representation extended also to the kind of attention

---

[40] For such an interpretation: Goldhill 1995: 46–111, in particular 102–10, in response to Foucault 1985.

[41] [Lucian] *Am.* 13.4–6.   [42] [Lucian] *Am.* 16.2.

[43] In Hesiod's *Theogony* Aphrodite is born from Uranus' severed genitals, but according to Homer she is the offspring of Zeus and Dione: see Hes. *Th.* 188–206; Hom. *Il.* 5.370–417.

[44] Steiner has taken this duality between form and content as the point of departure for her conception of the divine statue as a 'two-leveled vessel'. See Steiner 2001: 79 vs. Johnston 2008b.

[45] See Lévi-Strauss 1969.

[46] On the divine body as a 'super-body' which exceeds the human bodily ideal: Vernant 1991: 33–7.

she receives within the story. David Freedberg stressed that the ontological status of images qua images produced 'visual attention – the gaze,
look, stare'.[47] This was particularly true for the body of Aphrodite, which
inevitably attracted the gaze of the male viewers. Aphrodite's body lent
itself as the subject of both the religious and the erotic gaze. The religious
and the erotic both relied on the visual as the primary medium of interaction. Both dimensions of human life together informed the way in which
the statue was approached. Religious gazing can be oriented along the
ritualistic functions of religious objects.[48] But, as I have shown in Chapter 2, it also encompasses another way of looking on as fundamentally a
mental (cognitive) activity. Religious viewing acknowledges the difference
between the human and divine spheres and does not intend to collapse
the distinction between the viewing subject and religious object.[49] The key
here is precisely that in order to understand the otherworldly nature of the
divine, the human onlooker must, to some extent at least, remove himself
from his own personal circumstance.

Erotic gazing, in contrast, is driven by the desire to touch and to possess
(in sexual union), to traverse and penetrate – Freedberg spoke of the
'intentionality of desire'.[50] This aspect of erotic gazing is nicely highlighted
in a passage from Aelian (ca. 165/70–230/35 AD). The longing for sexual
possession here takes a distinctly material turn, when a young Athenian
aristocrat approaches the council with the intent of purchasing (!) the statue
of his desire, a representation of Good Fortune – a request that is refused.[51]

To return once more to Ps.-Lucian's account: while Charicles and Callicrates restrict their admiration and reverence of the goddess to little more
than harmless banter, the young man in the temple attendant's account
seeks the ultimate fulfilment of his desire. His various attempts to approach
Aphrodite describe a transition from passive to active, from seeing to touching, from an acknowledgement of the statue's divine essence to an obsession
with its surface. In Ps.-Lucian's account the sexual discourse highlights the
forms and conventions of the religious discourse, and vice versa.

The young man first peruses the statue in quiet contemplation:
πανήμερον ἐν τῷ ναῷ διατρίβοντα κατ' ἀρχὰς ἔχειν δεισιδαίμονος
ἁγιστείας δόκησιν ('he would spend all day in the temple and at first
gave the impression of pious awe').[52] What first looks like religious viewing
soon turns into erotic viewing when he gives up his passive, contemplative
stance and actively seeks to engage with the sculpture. The whole story
turns on the point that full disinvesting is humanly impossible.

---

[47] Freedberg 1989: 329.   [48] See Elsner 2007.   [49] See pp. 48–54 above.
[50] Freedberg 1989: 322.   [51] Ael. *VH* 9.39.   [52] [Lucian] *Am.* 15.13–14.

Consider for example the interactions between the young man and the statue prior to his getting locked up in the temple at night, all of them deeply ambiguous practices. On the one hand the giving of gifts (dedications, sacrifice), the writing of messages (e.g. in curse tablets), and the reading of auspicious signs are all well-established symbolic forms of communicating with the gods; on the other hand they are also set pieces of erotic pursuit: lovers, just like believers, tend to give gifts and write messages. And both lovers and believers tend to (over-)interpret signs! These ambiguities indicate that religious gazing, like disinvested gazing, is only an ideal: there is always an erotic gaze inherent in the religious gaze and vice versa.

Religious contemplation lapses fully into erotic pursuit when the young man seeks to gain direct (physical) access to the divine body by getting himself locked in the temple at night. That much more is at stake here than the simple amorous adventure of a somewhat boisterous young man is highlighted by the bodily transformation he has to undergo to achieve his goal. In order to spend the night with the goddess of love and sexuality, the young man seeks to escape the notice of those present: 'he slipped in behind the door and, standing invisible in the innermost part of the chamber, he kept still, hardly even breathing' (οὐδ' ἀναπνέων ἠτρέμει).[53] In order to be able to approach the statue physically, the young man has to repress the very activity that fills the human body with life. His organic body temporarily takes the form of an inorganic body, hence emphasising the fact that the young man, quite literally, seeks to transgress the ontological boundary separating gods from men.

The emergence of the stain brings about the climax of the story. The black mark serves as a focal point on the divine body, binding the gaze of those perusing the statue. It provides a *punctum* on the otherwise spotless and radiant surface of the marble, an entry point into a past story brought into the present of the onlookers.[54] In short, the stain asks for, even demands, an explanation.[55]

The stain not only marks the presence of an absence – the actual sexual act unfolds at night, hidden inside the temple, inaccessible to the human eye and hence outside the scope of the narrative[56] – but also, perhaps more importantly, it highlights as evidence of sexual pleasure both the

---

[53] [Lucian] *Am.* 16.7–8.

[54] See Hauser 2008 on the cinematographic effects of stains and their role as what Roland Barthes has called a *punctum*, a 'sting, speck, cut, little hole . . . that accident which pricks me (but also bruises me, is poignant to me)': Barthes 1981: 27.

[55] The stain on the divine statue also features in Plin. *HN* 36.4.21.

[56] The female guard of the temple recounting the incident refers to the night which the boy spent in the temple quite literally as ἄρρητος – 'unspeakable' [Lucian] *Am.* 16.9–10.

momentary satisfaction of human desire and the ultimate realisation that a true union between gods and men is impossible. For the young man's attempts to relate to the goddess as an organic body remain purely external. The human touch is confined to the surface of the statue 'like a stain on a dress' (ὥσπερ ἐν ἐσθῆτι κηλῖδα);[57] it cannot penetrate it and relate to its essence because the statue asserts its non-vital, inorganic quality.

The sexual encounter with the goddess does not result in the final fulfilment of the young man's passion but harbours the insight into the unattainable nature of the divine.[58] The stain ultimately serves to underline the fact that Aphrodite's nudity reveals much of what the female human body has to offer but – and this is the point – little if anything with regard to its divine essence. The nude divine body is nothing but extraneous clothing![59] It is presented as a body that can seduce the human eye through its perfection and physical beauty, but it is also a body which does not feel, cannot be penetrated and remains finally unavailable to the touch.[60] The desiring human gaze stays transfixed upon the surface as the very dimension of the statue, which was shaped (imagined) by man himself.[61]

As the product of a human bodily function, however, the black mark (μέλαιναν κηλῖδα) affects the purity of the body of the divine, its brilliance. As Lycinus, the viewing subject, points out, the darkness of the stain is in direct opposition to the shining quality of the marble: ἤλεγχε δ' αὐτοῦ τὴν ἀμορφίαν ἡ περὶ τἆλλα τῆς λίθου λαμπρότης ('the unsightliness of this was shown up by the brightness of the marble everywhere else').[62] The black mark makes visible the unattainable nature of the gods and condemns the human attempt to achieve such a contact by force. It is the mark of a failed and misguided attempt to approach divinity in the past and a warning to all future visitors to the temple (including Charicles and Callicratidas!) that such contact is not feasible. Finally, the spot also serves to link the frivolous, humorous and voyeuristic tone of the temple attendant's account with its deeper inquisitive content.

Death is the final and complete annihilation of the human body as an organic entity. In the temple attendant's account it is thus presented as the final consequence of the insight into the ontological unattainability of the divine. The young man ends up not only without an organic body,

---

[57] [Lucian] *Am.* 15.2.   [58] See also Steiner 2001: 192.

[59] On the semantics of nudity as a dress more generally see Bonfante 1989: 559–62.

[60] Steiner 2001: 192. See also Platt 2011: 180.

[61] This is also underlined by the inability of the viewing subjects in Ps.-Lucian's account to conceive of the statue in its entirety. In the *Amores*, all visitors to the temple (within the temple attendant's story and outside it) respond to the divine body by fetishising its parts.

[62] [Lucian] *Am.* 15.2–3.

but also without a proper name (ἡ δὲ πρᾶξις ἀνώνυμον αὐτὸν ἐσίγησεν, 'though his deed has caused him to be left nameless')[63], hence stripping away two key features that define human personal identity. The young man's end (his fall to his death from a cliff or into the sea) is a result of his attempted transgression into the sphere of the gods.[64] In annihilating his organic body, the young man takes the opposite stance to the everlasting beauty and incorruptible quality of the statue.[65] The young man's physical body – unlike that of Aphrodite – is no longer visually available.

In Ps.-Lucian's *Amores* the failed intercourse between the man and the statue marks a turning point. Starting from the question of which body part served as the focus of the young man's erotic passion, the two friends squabble about whether in the end the story supports the love of boys or the love of women. When Lycinus demands a more orderly mode of inquiry the two experts in love readily oblige. What follows is a detailed investigation of the merits of both types of sexuality, staying largely within the realm of the organic. In the ensuing debate both speakers draw upon the argument from nature to support their point of view. The transition is nicely introduced by Charicles, who invokes Aphrodite, 'the first mother and earliest root of every creature',

who in the beginning established earth, air, fire and water, the elements of the universe, and, by blending these with each other, brought to life everything that has breath (πᾶν ἐζωογόνησεν ἔμψυχον). Knowing that we are something created from perishable matter (ὅτι θνητῆς ἐσμὲν ὕλης δημιούργημα) and that the lifetime assigned each of us by fate is but short, she contrived that the death of one thing should be the birth of another and meted out fresh births to compensate for what dies, so that by replacing one another we live forever.[66]

The focus has quite literally and physically shifted between this and the previous scene – the more orderly mode of inquiry takes place outside the temple. This nicely emphasises the fact that the debate has moved from the realm of (theological) speculation and storytelling to the realm of critical inquiry into nature and the laws that govern it. In the ensuing discussion in Ps.-Lucian's account, the divine serves merely as a point of reference in the exploration of love and sexuality and no longer as the object of inquiry (and of erotic desire) in itself.

---

[63] [Lucian] *Am.* 15.11–12.

[64] Death as a result of transgression into the divine realm also features in Aelian's account of *agalmatophilia*: see above n. 51.

[65] In the words of Clement of Alexandria, an author we will discuss later in this chapter, statues 'do not partake of feeling and therefore cannot partake of death': Clem. Al. *Protr.* 10.103.2.

[66] [Lucian] *Am.* 19.3–9.

Yet the temple attendant's story does more than just set up the argument from nature. More generally, perhaps, the incident involving the young man and the statue frames the subsequent debate on a more fundamental level, by exposing a key aspect of all human knowledge. The desire of the viewing subject within Ps.-Lucian's account exposes the erotic basis of human efforts to make sense. The agalmatophiliac's gaze represents the erotic dimension included in the act of understanding. In order to know we must, to some extent at least, appropriate, transgress, possess. To quote Freedberg again, 'the hermeneutic quest is always founded on the repression and perversion of desire; the objects of understanding are always bare. The long gaze fetishises, and so, too, unequivocally does the handling of the object that signifies.'[67]

INTERLUDE: 'WHERE DID PRAXITELES SEE ME NAKED'? LOCATING THE DIVINE BODY BETWEEN ORIGINAL AND REPRESENTATION

The Greco-Roman world cultivated a certain fascination with the deceptive qualities of naturalistic art.[68] The *locus classicus* usually cited to illustrate this comes from Pliny's *Natural History*, where Pliny (23/4–79 AD) discussed a competition between Parrhasius and Zeuxis, two famous painters.[69] Zeuxis produces a picture of grapes, Parrhasius that of a drawn linen curtain. When the grapes, due to their realism, attract the attention of birds, Zeuxis considers himself the winner and orders his rival to remove the curtain to reveal his picture. Upon realising his mistake he yields the victory to Parrhasius. The episode illustrates the fact that in some instances, naturalistic art can deceive even those skilled in its production into mistaking the representation for the real thing.

Animals, too, fell victim to the misleading qualities of naturalistic images. Take the following example from Athenaeus' *Deipnosophistae*: 'a bull once mounted the bronze cow of Peirenē; and a painted bitch, pigeon, and goose were approached, in the one case, by a dog, in the other, by a pigeon, in the last, by a gander leaping upon them'.[70] *Agalmatophilia* was not restricted to humans, but could occur in other beings with organic bodies as well. It was in this sense that Valerius Maximus (early first century AD) compared the human response to Praxiteles' famous statue with similar occurrences among animals. Referring to the Aphrodite of Cnidus, he stated:

---

[67] Freedberg 1989: 317.   [68] On this point see Elsner 2007: 124–8.
[69] Plin. *HN* 35.65.   [70] Ath. 13.605e–f.

the beauty of the work is such that it was hardly safe from a libidinous embrace, so providing some excuse for the mistake of a stallion which on seeing the picture of a mare could not help neighing, or of the dogs which the sight of a dog in a painting caused to bark, or of the bull in Syracuse that was driven to erotic intercourse with a bronze cow by the stimulus of too close a likeness (*similitudinis inritamento compulsus*). For why should we be surprised that animals void of reason (*ratio*) should be deceived by art when we see a human being's sacrilegious lust excited by the outlines of voiceless stone (*muti lapidis*)?[71]

The category of the inanimate and inorganic enables us to see the commonality of man and beast as living organisms. As perceiving and sentient bodies both are able to experience desire for naturalistic representations of their bodily forms. Naturalistic art introduces an alterity in which organic bodies are opposed to inorganic bodies. But at the same time what can serve as an excuse for animals, which fall for the illusion of inorganic matter, does not necessarily apply to humans. It is via *ratio* (reason) that humans should be able to see through the illusion provided by the naturalistic representation of their body in art, hence introducing a further alterity between man and beast, between organic bodies with and without a mind. The result is a complex and sophisticated interplay of competing and complementary taxonomies in which humans are both like and unlike animals.

The reference to similar occurrences among animals and to reason as the feature that distinguishes the human body from the animal body is a significant complication of the story about the agalmatophiliac's desire, a story which, in its philosophical core, goes all the way back to Plato's theory of Ideas (Forms).[72] We will find this complication developed in more detail elsewhere. Valerius Maximus, meanwhile, touched upon this point only in passing: those humans who fall for the deceptive qualities of statues are situated on the same ontological plane as animals.

But how exactly are reason and the brain as the organ in which it is situated involved in the viewing of mimetic images? An answer to this question can be found in a text already discussed in Chapter 4: Philostratus' *Vita Apollonii*, a *vie romancée* (Flinterman) of Apollonius from Tyana (dating from the first half of the second century AD).[73]

---

[71] Val. Max. 8.11. ext. 4 (transl. Shackleton Bailey 2000).

[72] In the *Republic*, Plato describes the non-philosopher as the one who cannot distinguish between beautiful things and beauty itself, mistaking an image for the real thing: Pl. *R.* 475e–477b.

[73] Flinterman 1995: 1. On Philostratus and on the place of the *VA* in his oeuvre, see Elsner 2009; Bowie 2009. On the *VA* see also Bowie 1978; Anderson 1986: 121–239; Bowie 1994: 189–96. On Apollonius from Tyana, see also ch. 4, n. 64 (with further literature).

In Book 2 of the *Vita Apollonii* Apollonius outlines his theory of representation through art.[74] He starts by stressing the centrality of *mimēsis* to the production of paintings and sculpture. In order to create a truthful representation of an object, the artist must first create a copy of it in his mind, which he then, through his artistic skills, translates into a material image. But, significantly, it is not just those involved in the production of images that need the faculty of *mimēsis*, but those who 'consume' them too: for 'no one will praise the picture of a horse or bull if s/he has no idea of the creature represented'.[75] As Verity Platt put it, the viewer, 'in order to appreciate and respond appropriately to an image . . . must first conceive in his mind an *eidōlon* or *eikōn* of the thing represented'.[76]

Where does this leave the viewing of divine representations?[77] The problem is that we can only approximately know the gods in the various shapes in which they reveal themselves to us. These, however, never represent the full essence of the divine, which would be unbearable for humans to see. The point is that the 'original' against which we can assess the divine representation is not available to our senses. The anthropomorphism of the gods is always a compromise between the visible and the invisible, the immanent and the transcendent; it is a way of representing what is ultimately impossible to represent.

This problem of *mimēsis* with regard to divine representations is the subject of a conversation between Apollonius and Thespesion, an Egyptian, in Book 6 of the *Vita*.[78] Apollonius compares and contrasts the Egyptian worship of gods in animal form with the anthropomorphism of the Greek gods. He argues that to represent the gods in human form is 'very honourable' (κάλλιστον) and 'very pious' (θεοφιλέστατον). Animals by contrast are 'dumb' (ἄλογοι) and 'worthless' (ἄδοξοι) – to represent the gods in the form of animals is therefore inappropriate. When Thespesion wonders whether Apollonius' argument is based on such famous statues as the Olympian Zeus and the Cnidian Aphrodite, the sage explains that what is at stake here is a matter of principle rather than of particular examples: as beings on a lower ontological plane than humans, animals are fundamentally ill suited to serve as models for divine representations. Thespesion's answer comes in the form of a question and amounts to nothing less than

---

[74] Philostr. *VA* 2.22.1–5. On the centrality of viewing images to Philostratus' *VA* see Platt 2009. Throughout the *VA*, Apollonius features as an expert *exēgētēs* exemplifying and instructing in the correct viewing of art, in particular of divine representations. The various *ekphraseis* scattered throughout the text help us explore the link between vision and knowledge, between sight and *sophia*. It is in this context that the role of the mind in the viewing of images is elaborated.

[75] Philostr. *VA* 2.22.5. [76] Platt 2009: 143.

[77] On this point see Platt 2009: 149–54; Platt 2011: 320–32. [78] Philostr. *VA* 6.19.

a direct challenge to the anthropomorphism of the Greek gods and the role of *mimēsis* in the production of divine images more generally: 'your Phidias, . . . your Praxiteles, they did not go up to heaven and make a cast of the gods' forms before turning them into art, did they?'[79]

In an epigram which has come down to us as part of the so-called *Greek Anthology*, we find Aphrodite herself asking the same question: 'Paris, Anchises, and Adonis saw me naked. Those are all I know of, but how did Praxiteles contrive it?'[80] Was this perhaps the coquetry of a confident Goddess of love, evoked, as it were, by a certain erotic climate prevailing in the literature of the time?[81] Set in the context of the larger debate of the role of *mimēsis* in the creation of divine pictures, however, Aphrodite's question seems to have been part of a much larger discourse concerned with the principles and practices of divine representation and the scope and limits of *mimēsis* in particular.

The question of the model for Praxiteles' Aphrodite appeared and reappeared throughout the literature of the period.[82] According to one tradition none other than Phryne, a famous fourth-century BC courtesan widely praised for her outstanding beauty, served as Praxiteles' model.[83] This kind of guesswork reveals a wider contemporary concern with the adequacy of Greco-Roman anthropomorphism as a form of representation – a concern which at its core went back at least to Xenophanes and the fifth century BC.[84] Philostratus' Apollonius, it seems, was not alone in his concern about whose body it was that the mimetic representation of the divine body reproduced.

Let us return once more to the debate between Thespesion and Apollonius and the question of how Praxiteles derived his image of Aphrodite. The way in which the sage from Tyana responds to Thespesion's challenge is as subtle and resourceful as it is ingenious: 'Imagination (*phantasia*) created these objects . . . a more skilful artist than Imitation (*mimēsis*). Imitation will create what it knows, but Imagination will also create what it does not know, conceiving it with reference to the real.'[85] It was through the concept of *phantasia*, a form of viewing that combined imagination and reason, that the representation of the gods in human bodily form could be

---

[79] Philostr. *VA* 6.19.2.   [80] *Greek Anthology* 16.168 (transl. Paton 1918).

[81] E.g., Havelock 2007: 117–31. On the erotic in Roman Greece (and beyond) see most recently Blanshard 2010: 109–23.

[82] E.g., Ath. 13.585f. On this see also Havelock 2007: 117–31.

[83] Ath. 13.591a. On the beauty of Phryne see, e.g., Val. Max. 4.3. ext. 3b; Quint. 2.15.9. On the figure of Phryne see Raubitschek 1941: 898–903 with further references.

[84] Xenoph. fr. 5, 11, 14–16, 23.   [85] Philostr. *VA* 6.19.2.

justified.[86] The role of *phantasia* in representing what cannot ultimately be known allows us to make the divine present in the human sphere.

What was at stake here was much more than a confrontation of two opposing conceptions of divine representation and the celebration of Hellenism through the lens of another (the Egyptian) culture. Responding to Thespesion's suggestion that the Egyptian be seen as 'symbolic' (ξυμβο-λικός) and 'suggestive' (ὑπονοούμενος), Apollonius states:

> If these things gain venerability by being 'suggestive', the gods would be much more venerable in Egypt if no cult statue were set up to them at all, and you applied your divine lore in some other way, more profound and more mysterious. You could build temples and altars to them...and rather than introducing a statue, you could leave the shapes of the gods to those visiting your holy places. The mind portrays and imagines an object better than creation does (ἀναγράφει γάρ τι ἡ γνώμη καὶ ἀνατυποῦται δημιουργίας κρεῖττον), yet you have prevented the gods from seeming and being imagined as beautiful.[87]

The discussion of divine images in the context of another culture allows Apollonius to imagine a form of divine representation beyond the realm of the material and inorganic, situated solely within the organic human body as a reflecting, reasoning and imagining entity. This is a significant deviation from and inversion of the principles and practices of divine representation in Greco-Roman religion. We will find it developed in more detail in Clement's conception of the divine body.

HUMANS, ANIMALS AND STATUES: PROCREATION AND
THE ARGUMENT FROM NATURE IN PHILOSTRATUS'
LIFE OF APOLLONIUS

No group of people came to personify the changes that transformed traditional religious structures during the early Empire better than Apollonius and his like. The sage from Tyana was part of a much larger class of charismatic individuals who roamed the Greco-Roman world during the first few centuries AD. These men combined traits of the philosopher and the (Near Eastern) sage, of the Hellenic intellectual and the magician, of the doctor and the faith healer within a single person.[88] As representatives of a more personal aspect of religious experience, they added a human face to the religious diversity and syncretism of the period. Some scholars have

---

[86] Platt 2009: 153–4.   [87] Philostr. *VA* 6.19.4.   [88] Here and below see Anderson 1994.

expanded the circle of the 'holy men' to include Jesus Christ as the most successful '*theios anēr*' of the period.[89]

The emergence of religious specialists was not of course an entirely new phenomenon: it goes all the way back to certain priesthoods of traditional Greek religion. What was new was the intensity of their religious fervour as well as the prominence gained by some as people of special public interest. The variety of new divinities and cults that had been added to the traditional pantheon increased the need for professionals to instruct the people in their essentials – the chorus of competing and diverging revelations reverberates within the literature of the period. A certain Alexander, another example of the species, claimed to have direct access to Asclepius (incarnated in the form of a snake), a claim for which he was aptly scolded by Lucian, but which apparently worked on the people of Abunoteichos.[90]

Such 'religious activists' (Anderson) typically claimed association with a major philosophical figure such as Pythagoras, without however being overly restricted by the parameters set by their teaching. All of them claimed access to some kind of privileged knowledge. All of them were able to support their claims with redoubtable rhetorical skills.[91] As 'holy men' they frequently claimed some sort of direct link to divinity, the knowledge of which they set out to reveal through their constant search for more supporters, more followers and more clients.

In order to understand what was at stake in Philostratus' depiction of the sage from Tyana we need to consider Apollonius' position within the religious climate of the second century AD. Individuals such as Apollonius still operated fundamentally within the parameters of the traditional religions of Greece and Rome (broadly conceived) – for example, by drawing on shared notions of purity and pollution and by referring to the traditional gods of the Greco-Roman pantheon. However, at the same time they responded to an increased need for a more personal, spiritual religious experience: by offering personal advice and religious instructions; by serving as mediators, disseminators and propagators of divine knowledge; and by offering their services as healers and miracle workers through purifications and incantations.[92]

As a result of this balancing act between traditional religious structures and new religious needs, the relationship between these individuals and the

---

[89] E.g., Bieler 1935/1936. The scholarly debate surrounding the Hellenistic conception of the divine man ('*theios anēr*') and its application to early Christology is nicely summarised in Flinterman 2009: 170–5. On the 'divine man' see also du Toit 1997.

[90] See Lucian *Alex.* 10–14.   [91] The typical holy man is described in Anderson 1994.

[92] See also Anderson 1986: 139–48; 1994: ix; Flinterman 2009. See Fowden 1993 on the related religious phenomenon of hermeticism.

beliefs, practices and institutions of traditional Greco-Roman religion was not always clear. Their ascetic lifestyle, their particular religious fervour and their quest for a special, esoteric kind of knowledge derived directly from the gods set them apart from the traditional religious structures of Greece and Rome.[93] Their claim of special, unmediated access to the gods, independent and autonomous from the traditional religious institutions, was perceived at best as a curiosity and at worst an outright threat – as were some of their practices, such as incantations. All this must have made figures like Apollonius suspect in the eyes of some: Lucian, Origen and Cassius Dio call him a *goēs*, a dishonest magician.[94]

The tension springing from his attempt to reconcile this colourful figure with the traditional religious structures pervades every level of Philostratus' portrayal of Apollonius. He has the sage point out repeatedly that as a follower of Pythagoras he abstains from eating meat, hence opting out of the practice of blood sacrifice and its subsequent communal consumption.[95] As the author of a treatise *On Sacrifices* he also presented himself as an expert in the proper implementation of sacrificial ritual.[96]

There was also a certain ambiguity about Apollonius' own ontological status, his relationship to the gods, and the cults and religious institutions of the cities of Roman Greece. In *VA* 4.31.1 the sage declines divine honours at Olympia, yet throughout the *Vita* he encounters a variety of people (including his pupil Damis) who address him as a divine figure and praise his superhuman capacities.[97] Even though David du Toit and others rightly warned us against taking the 'divine man' terminology always and necessarily as ontological statements, Philostratus' Apollonius was an ontologically ambiguous figure, no longer fully subsumed in the religious structures from which he had originally emerged.[98]

Is there a better way to address such classificatory concerns than in the form of a story? Intriguingly, perhaps, Philostratus' *Vita* features yet another man who feels a strong attraction towards Praxiteles' famous statue.[99] In Philostratus' version of the story, the man has already made some dedications but promises more in exchange for the right to marry her. Could the institution of marriage (or the promise of dedications)

[93] Here and below see Graf 1997a: 92–6.

[94] Lucian *Alex.* 5; Origen *Cels.* 6.41; Cassius Dio 77.18.4. The tradition that links Apollonius with magic is explored in Dzielska 1986: 85–127.

[95] Apollonius' vegetarianism: e.g., Philostr. *VA* 1.8.1, 24.3, 32.2; 6.11.3; 8.7.30. His vegetarianism also featured in his speech at his trial in front of Domitian: Philostr. *VA* 8.13–15.

[96] Philostr. *VA* 3.41.1. Philostratus' Pythagoreanism: Bowie 1978: 1671–3; Flinterman 1995; 2009.

[97] A few examples: Philostr. *VA* 1.6; 2.17; 3.50; 6.39.1.

[98] Du Toit 1997; Graf 1997a: 233. [99] Philostr. *VA* 6.40.1–2.

really legitimise an otherwise impossible union? The Cnidians themselves
at least seem to have been convinced – they consented to the man's
proposal.

Before the agalmatophiliac can follow through with his plan Apollonius
intervenes. He dismisses the possibility of marrying the statue. The man's
desire appears strange to him – *atopos*, 'out of place' – the sanctuary itself in
need of purification from what he considers to be 'a lack of understanding'.
Here, as elsewhere, Apollonius refers to concepts of purity and pollution
in order to emphasise his ideas about proper and improper human action
concerning the gods.[100]

The episode at Cnidus was part of Philostratus' more broadly conceived
programme to establish the credentials of the sage vis-à-vis the divine and
the cults of the Greek cities. The sculptured body of Aphrodite serves here
as a placeholder for traditional cult. The episode at Cnidus, no matter what
the historicity of its content may have been, was introduced into the *Vita*
to allow Apollonius to present himself as an expert in and facilitator of
real and symbolic transactions between the human and the divine spheres.
Philostratus depicted him as an advocate of traditional religious practices
in the cities of Roman Greece.

The first lesson was therefore directed towards the Cnidians themselves.
Here, as elsewhere, Philostratus focused on the interaction between the
sage and the citizens of the cities of Roman Greece.[101] When the Cnidians
ask Apollonius whether he thinks they should change any of their practices
with regard to prayer or sacrifice, he pointedly answers: 'I will correct
your eyesight but the customs of the sanctuary may remain as they are.'[102]
Apollonius acts as an advisor on religious matters, someone who upholds
religious customs and corrects deviations from tradition.

What kind of vision was depicted here as an inadequate way of approach-
ing the divine body? Unlike Ps.-Lucian, Philostratus did not develop this
dimension of the story in more detail, but the Cnidian suggestion that
'the goddess would be more celebrated if she had a lover' seems to indicate
that it was indeed the belief in the erotic availability of the goddess of
love that was at the heart of the 'poor sight' both of the Cnidians and of
the nameless young man. The correct eyesight, in contrast, corresponds
to a correct kind of viewing and brings insight into the true nature of the
divine. Comparing religious and erotic viewing, it seems, was not restricted
to Ps.-Lucian alone.

---

[100] Some examples: Philostr. *VA* 1.10.2; 2.5.3, 30.1; 7.6.
[101] See Flinterman 1995: 56.   [102] Philostr. *VA* 6.40.

The second lesson, no less pointedly formulated, was directed towards the agalmatophiliac and featured the juggling of taxonomies as part of a larger argument from nature.[103] Referring to the laws of procreation, Apollonius educates the man as to his misguided desire:

Gods love gods, humans love humans, animals love animals, and in short like loves like (ὅμοια ὁμοίων ἐρᾷ) for the purpose of producing genuine offspring of its own kind. But when something alien unites with something unlike itself (τὸ δὲ ἑτερογενὲς τῷ μὴ ὁμοίῳ ξυνελθὸν), there is neither union nor love.[104]

In order to explain the ontological unavailability of the divine, the gods themselves are subject to the laws of nature. Gods, like humans and animals, need to reproduce and procreate by mating with their kind. Conceptually this seems to differ considerably from Ps.-Lucian's positioning of gods as somehow preceding the realm of nature (see above). In Philostratus' account, Apollonius forcefully dismisses all attempts to cross the boundary that separates the human from the divine as futile and ultimately contrary to nature: there can be no reproductive union between members of different species! He effectively denounces the possibility of transcending the divide between human and divine bodies as a categorical mistake.

Apollonius concludes his message by warning the man that he will 'perish throughout the world' (ἀπολεῖ ἐν ἁπάσῃ τῇ γῇ) if he does not leave the sanctuary. Unlike the case of the young man in Ps.-Lucian's *Amores*, however, physical annihilation of the organic human body is avoided and order restored when the agalmatophiliac confirms and acknowledges the vertical taxonomy of gods, men and animals by seeking forgiveness through a sacrifice, the central ritual of Greco-Roman religion.

Philostratus depicted his hero as an advocate of traditional religion and a protégé of the divine, someone who derived part of his charismatic, superhuman powers from his particular insight into the nature of the gods, but not someone who manipulated them for his own purposes. His telling of the tale involving the statue of Aphrodite at Cnidus helped Philostratus to disperse the accusation of *goēteia*. Philostratus' Apollonius is an upholder of the traditional taxonomy of gods, humans and animals, rather than an individual who challenges that order by manipulating the gods and goddesses and the religious institutions that house them. What the sage from Tyana emphasises here is the integrity of the categories of gods, humans and animals, categories which are represented as being as

---

[103] See Swain 2009 on the normative dimension of Philostratus' use of nature as a model throughout his oeuvre.
[104] Philostr. *VA* 6.40.2.

rigid and ultimately impenetrable as the materiality of stone. *Honi soit qui mal y pense!*

HUMAN BODIES AS 'LIVING AND MOVING STATUES' IN CLEMENT OF ALEXANDRIA'S *PROTREPTICUS*

With Clement of Alexandria's *Exhortation to the Greeks* (*Protrepticus*), written around 190 AD, we encounter an altogether different conception of the divine body. Clement's Christology was formulated with reference to the same themes we found elaborated in the authors discussed above, and again, we will find that Praxiteles' Aphrodite featured prominently.

In the late second century AD Alexandria was a thriving community of Romans, Egyptians and Greeks, whose cultural importance extended far beyond the boundaries of Roman Egypt. Formally part of the Roman Empire, Alexandria at the time had a distinctly Hellenic flavour: home to the Museum and the Great Library, the city provided a hub for learned minds of all kinds who came to Roman Egypt from Greece and beyond.[105] The ethnic diversity of Alexandria's inhabitants during the second century was mirrored in a multiplicity of religions.[106] As well as Jewish and pagan communities, the city housed a Christian church over which Clement apparently presided as presbyter. The *Protrepticus* was an attempt to convince his pagan fellow citizens to adopt Christianity by asserting its superiority over the pagan religions of the ancient world, and his radical redefinition of the divine body was at the heart of this enterprise.

Clement himself was probably a convert to Christianity. Classical scholars have deduced this from his detailed knowledge not only of Greek religious rituals – in particular the Eleusinian Mysteries – but also of Greek philosophy and the literature of classical Greece,[107] which suggests that he was born and raised somewhere in the centre of 'old Greece', probably in Athens.[108] Even after his conversion to Christianity Clement continued to use his classical education to his advantage: his various allusions to the literary and intellectual tradition of pre-Hellenistic Greece must have

---

[105] The Museum and the Library: Erskine 1995. Clement's Alexandria: van den Hoek 1990; Hägg 2006: 15–70.

[106] Alexandria, religious diversity, and life in Roman Egypt: Lewis 1983; Pearson 1986; Frankfurter 1998.

[107] See Clem. Al. *Protr.* 2.1ff. for a discussion of mysteries. On the Hellenism of Clement see Witt 1931; Jaeger 1961.

[108] As suggested by the sixth-century AD Epiphanius Scholasticus and generally assumed in modern scholarship. Clement received further education after his arrival at Alexandria in the Catechetical School under Pantaenus (see Scholten 1995: 32–7; Hägg 2006: 54–9).

resonated in particular with the educated elites of second-century AD Roman Egypt.[109]

The *Protrepticus*, his first work, is both a comprehensive and sometimes polemical attack on ancient Greek religion and an enthusiastic endorsement of the Christian faith. Clement did not summarily dismiss the pagan past, however, but drew on some of its elements – in particular on Greek philosophy (Plato, the Stoics) and the theological speculation included in it, which he believed reflected an early, pre-Christian stage of true insight into the nature of God – while refuting the silly stories about the gods in others.[110] Written during his tenure at Alexandria – Clement had to flee the city to escape the persecutions under Septimus Severus in 202–3 AD – the *Protrepticus* made use of the genre of exhortatory discourse for the purpose of presenting Christianity as a continuation and improvement of classical Greek *paideia*. His argument runs that:

[S]ince the Word Himself came to us from heaven, we ought no longer to go to human teaching, to Athens, and the rest of Greece, or to Ionia, in our curiosity. If our teacher is He who has filled the universe with holy powers, creation, salvation, beneficence, lawgiving, prophecy, teaching, this teacher now instructs us in all things, and the whole world has by this time become an Athens and a Greece through the Word.[111]

The *Protrepticus*, then, is at the heart of the refutation of pagan religions; at the heart of the *Protrepticus*, however, is the pagan conception of divinity.[112] Clement launched a fierce and sometimes polemical attack on the multiplicity of the divine in the Greek pantheon and belittled and denounced the gods of Greek poetry and drama.[113] Some of the points he made in this context read almost like a direct inversion of the views of Philostratus' Apollonius, discussed above. Having just exposed the lewdness of the gods as featured in Greek mythology, he states:

Such, then, is the character of the Greek gods; such, too, are the worshippers, who make a mockery of the divine, or rather, who mock and insult themselves. How

---

[109] See Brown 1988: 124–6, who speaks of 'Clement's delightful classicism' (124). On Clement's audience see also Hägg 2006: 18–19.

[110] Clem. Al. *Protr.* 5.64.1–66.5. On Clement's relationship to Greek philosophy see also Witt 1931; Muckle 1951; Lilla 1971: 9–59.

[111] Clem. Al. *Protr.* 11.112.1.

[112] See Hägg 2006 for a central outline of Clement's apophaticism (the approach of divinity through negation) as a meaningful approach towards his overall theology and philosophy.

[113] E.g., Clem. Al. *Protr.* 2.25.1–3.45.5.

much better are Egyptians, when in cities and villages they hold in great honour the irrational animals, than Greeks who worship such gods as these? For though the Egyptian gods are beasts, still they are not adulterous, they are not lewd, and not one of them seeks for pleasure contrary to its own nature.[114]

The same argument with which Philostratus' Apollonius sought to convince the Egyptians of the superiority of the Greek way of representing the gods was used by Clement to refute the very basis of Greek divine anthropomorphism. Here as elsewhere in the *Protrepticus*, Clement drew on the established Greco-Roman discourse revolving around the divine body and sought to rewrite and redirect it according to his own Christian ideology.

Nowhere is the radical break this involved more evident than in the fourth chapter, which focuses almost entirely on divine images and features a profound attack on statuary representations of the pagan gods and goddesses. What Clement was attempting here was nothing less than a radical redefinition of the divine ontology underlying the religions of Greece and Rome, and the divine body, including that of Praxiteles' Aphrodite, was at the heart of this enterprise.

Clement began by pointing out that divine images are human creations. Citing Psalm 115.4, he stated that they were 'the work of men's hands' (ἔργα χειρῶν ἀνθρώπων).[115] Even those images for which direct divine providence was claimed, such as 'heaven-sent' Pallas, which had allegedly simply dropped from the sky, or the Egyptian god Serapis, who claimed to be ἀχειροποίητον, 'made without hands',[116] were ultimately the product of human craftsmanship. As Clement pointedly asserted, statuary representations of the gods 'are bound and nailed and fastened, melted, filed, sawn, polished, carved'.[117] In short, they were created objects, and as such part of the order of things. Clement did not depict the human technical skill involved in creating a lifelike image as an object of veneration in its own right. The fact that statues were the product of human craftsmanship situated them firmly within the human realm and hence denied them a priori any transcendental value. Clement opposed the 'cooked' quality of statuary representations of the pagan gods to the new Christian divinity as a 'raw' God situated outside the realm of humanity and of creation. He asked, 'Why have you fallen into deeper darkness by going after these created things instead of the uncreated God?'[118] He aimed to replace the pagan pantheon and its multiple divinities with an alternative conception of God.

---

[114] Clem. Al. *Protr.* 2.39.3–4.   [115] Clem. Al. *Protr.* 4.46.1.   [116] Clem. Al. *Protr.* 4.48.1.
[117] Clem. Al. *Protr.* 4.51.5.   [118] Clem. Al. *Protr.* 4.56.4.

Intriguingly, perhaps, Clement achieved this mainly by drawing upon and manipulating the very same duality we have already observed as being fundamental to the discourse evolving around the divine body in the other authors. Like Ps.-Lucian he made a sharp distinction between organic bodies as sentient bodies and the inorganic bodies of those divine statues which imitated the human bodily form but could not partake in feeling.[119] In contrast to these and other authors, however, the immateriality and inorganic quality of divine representations were presented as a dead end. As human creations, the Greek gods represented in statuary form, no matter whether they are simple *xoana* or more elaborate *agalmata*, were 'senseless things' (ἀναίσθητα, 4.46.1) 'soulless' (ἄψυχα, 4.56.6), 'motionless' (ἀργά, 4.51.5), 'dumb' (κωφά, 4.51.4), made out of 'matter' (ὕλη, 4.51.6), crafted out of 'senseless wood and stone and precious gold' (4.51.2). Citing Heraclitus, he ridiculed the fact that people addressed statues in a way that these sculptured bodies, because of their inorganic qualities, could not perceive, let alone reciprocate: to worship statues was just as absurd as to chat to a house.[120] In order to refute the ontology of divine images fundamental to the pagan conception of the gods, Clement drew on the duality between organic and inorganic bodies as a central theme of discourse evolving around the divine body in the pagan religions of Greece and Rome and turned it against them. He did not conceive of the inorganic quality of divine representation as indicative of the otherworldly nature of the divine; the material dimension merely referred back to the human sphere, which had created these images in the first place.

Clement saw all organic bodies as superior to inorganic, crafted and created bodies. Having just argued that statues could not actually perceive the sacrifices offered to them, he stated that 'there is not a single living creature that is not more worthy of honour than these statues: and how it comes to pass that senseless things have been deified I am at a loss to know, and I deeply pity for their lack of understanding the men who are thus miserably wandering in error'.[121] This explained why even the humble oyster was by far superior, although it could not see, or hear. For as organic bodies 'they live and grow and are even affected by the moon'.[122]

The superiority of organic bodies over inorganic bodies sprang from the fact that they were perceptive bodies and had at least some, if not all, of the senses: 'For even though there are some living creatures which do not possess all the senses, as worms and caterpillars, and all those that appear

---

[119] In Clement's oeuvre, the distinction between the organic and the inorganic is part of a much more comprehensive framework of references to nature, on which see Murphy 1941.
[120] Clem. Al. *Protr.* 4.50.4.   [121] Clem. Al. *Protr.* 4.51.2–3.   [122] Clem. Al. *Protr.* 4.51.5.

to be imperfect from the first through the conditions of their birth, such as moles and the field-mouse . . . yet these are better than those images and statues which are entirely dumb.'[123] Whereas Ps.-Lucian and, to a different extent, Philostratus used the materiality of statuary representation of the gods to make visible the relationship between the human and the divine spheres as one of identity and alterity, Clement blatantly dismissed the inorganic and material as a valid medium for the presenting of divinity. He denied the legitimacy of material images as a means of making the divine present in the human sphere and available for human knowledge.[124]

Where, then, did this leave the possibility of being cognisant of the divine? If divinity is situated wholly outside the human sphere and the realm of the organic, how is humanity to know it? There are two ways in which Clement developed an alternative conception of divine ontology, divine representation – in particular divine corporality – and human knowledge of the divine: first, by placing God himself and the human knowledge of him fully outside the realm of the senses, and, second, by situating the divine firmly within the realm of the organic. Both aspects are, of course, related to each other and are ultimately two sides of the same coin: Clement's Christian ontology of the divine.[125]

The first way was developed by drawing on the same line of reasoning we have seen advanced by some of the other authors. Humans and animals as beings with organic bodies inhabit the same conceptual space which is set up in opposition to the inorganic: both can fall for the deceptive qualities of art. Again, it is the capacity to reason that ultimately distinguishes humans from animals:

Now craftsmanship is powerful, but it cannot beguile a rational being, nor yet those who have lived according to reason (κατὰ λόγον). It is true that, through lifelike portraiture, pigeons have been known to fly towards painted doves, and horses to neigh at well-drawn mares. They say that a maiden once fell in love with an image, and a beautiful youth with a Cnidian statue; but it was their sight (ὄψις) that was beguiled by the art. For no man in his senses (σωφρονῶν) would have embraced the statue of the goddess.[126]

The strict opposition between sight and reason serves as a placeholder for two radically different ways of making the divine present in the human sphere and available to human knowledge. As we have seen above, in the traditional Greco-Roman conception of the divine, statuary representations

---

[123] Clem. Al. *Protr.* 4.51.3–4.
[124] See also Clem. Al. *Paed.* 3.59.2 for his refutation of pagan idolatry.
[125] On which see Lilla 1971; Mortley 1973; McLelland 1976. 　　[126] Clem. Al. *Protr.* 4.57.4–5.

of the gods appealed to the senses, particularly to sight. In the *Protrepticus*, Clement opposed this with a new, internalised and abstract way of making the divine present, assigning a particular significance to the mind as an organ of the human body. It is the capacity to reason that distinguishes men from animals; the mind is also the place where the divine image is located. Directly juxtaposing the two competing ways of making the divine present in the human sphere, he stated that 'a statue is really lifeless matter shaped by a craftsman's hand; but in our view the image of God is not an object of sense made from matter perceived by the senses, but a mental object (νοητὸν δὲ τὸ ἄγαλμά ἐστιν). God, that is, the only true God, is perceived not by the senses but the mind (νοητόν, οὐκ αἰσθητόν ἐστι [τὸ ἄγαλμα] ὁ θεός, ὁ μόνος ὄντως θεός).'[127] Just as in Apollonius' conception of *phantasia*, the mind is the organ of the human body, which generates this knowledge: it houses the divine representation. It is particularly in this dismissal of the material and sensual dimension that Clement's indebtedness to Middle Platonism becomes evident. Knowledge of the divine can be reached by the mind through abstraction from the material.[128]

This brings us to the second way in which Clement sought to replace the traditional ontology of the divine with his Christian one. While God himself is unavailable to human sensory perception, he has placed his son within the realm of the organic. It is through the incarnation (sic!) of Christ, the Logos of God, and his adoption of flesh (σάρξ) that the divine becomes part of space, time and the realm of the organic: 'When at first His coming was proclaimed the message was not disbelieved; nor was He unrecognised when, having assumed the mask of manhood and received fleshly form (σαρκὶ ἀναπλασάμενος), He began to act the drama of salvation for humanity.'[129] In the *Strōmateis*, Clement pointed out that 'the knowledge of God is inaccessible to the ears and other related organs. Therefore the Son is said to be the Father's face by becoming a bearer of flesh (σαρκοφόρος γενόμενος) through the five senses, the Logos who reveals the Father's character.'[130] The concept of incarnation, of the corporality of Christ, allowed Clement to give the divine a corporeal existence and

---

[127] Clem. Al. *Protr.* 4.51.6.
[128] Clement's indebtedness to Middle Platonism: Jaeger 1961: 44–7; Lilla 1971; Hägg 2006: 71–133. The conception of transcendence in Middle Platonism: Dörrie 1957.
[129] Clem. Al. *Protr.* 10.110.2. The concept of incarnation in Clement, including the accusation of him 'dehumanising' the flesh: Chadwick 1966: 51; Hägg 2006: 194–7. On incarnation as a 'theological locus' in early Christological debates: Crisp 2007.
[130] Clem. Al. *Strom.* 5.5.33.6–34.1. Clement's doctrine of the Logos: Wolfson 1951; Dawson 1992: 183–234; Edwards 2000.

to situate it within the realm of the senses. The consequences of this look strikingly similar to that of the Greek gods: Christ eats 'not for the sake of the body, which was kept together by a holy energy, but in order that it might enter into the mind of those who were with him to entertain a different opinion of him'.[131] Yet the implications of these two forms of divine representation in the human sphere could not be more different. Both ontologies of the divine are, conceptually at least, worlds apart: they rely on different – even opposing – conceptions of the divine body.

Given the profound reorganisation between organic and inorganic bodies that is at the heart of the *Protrepticus*, it should come as no surprise that Clement made use of the infamous story involving the Aphrodite at Cnidus in the passage quoted above so as to demonstrate the futility of the traditional conception of the divine. The story was discussed in more detail earlier in the *Protrepticus*:

So the well-known Pygmalion of Cyprus fell in love with an ivory statue; it was of Aphrodite and was naked. The man of Cyprus is captivated by its shapeliness and embraces the statue. This is related by Philostephanus. There was also an Aphrodite in Cnidus made of marble and beautiful. Another man fell in love with this and has intercourse with the marble as Poseidippus relates. The account of the first author is in his book on Cyprus; that of the second in his book on Cnidus. Such strength had art to beguile that it became for amorous men a guide to the pit of destruction.[132]

Clement did not see instances of *agalmatophilia* as a way of exploring the otherworldly nature of the divine. Like Ps.-Lucian and Philostratus' Apollonius, he compared and to some extent collapsed religious and erotic gazing at divine statues, this time, however, in order to expose the error that lay behind the worship of images. Addressing his audience directly, he stated, 'but in your case art has another illusion with which to beguile; for it leads you on, though not to be in love with the statues and paintings, yet to honour and worship them'.[133] For Clement, too, there was an erotic gaze implied in the religious gaze; to worship statues as gods was not much different from 'worshipping' them as the object of erotic desire. Both were the result of an illusion evoked by the deceptive qualities of art.

At the heart of Clement's *Protrepticus*, then, is a profound reorganisation of the categories of the organic and inorganic with regard to divine representation. Again it is the mind which is at the core of this conception of the organic human body as a sentient body; its absence makes the organic

---

[131] Clem. Al. *Strom.* 6.8.71.2. [132] Clem. Al. *Protr.* 4.57.3. [133] Clem. Al. *Protr.* 4.57.5.

human body itself resemble a statue: '[B]ut as for you, while you take great pains to discover how a statue may be shaped to the highest possible pitch of beauty, you never give a thought to prevent yourselves turning out like statues owing to want of sense' (ὅπως δὲ αὐτοὶ μὴ ὅμοιοι δι' ἀναισθησίαν τοῖς ἀνδριᾶσιν ἀποτελεσθῆτε, οὐ φροντίζετε).[134]

According to the same logic, then, it is the organic human body as the true and only carrier of the divine image which itself becomes an *anathema* (dedication) to God:

For we, yes we, are they who, in this living and moving statue (ἐν τῷ ζῶντι καὶ κινουμένῳ τούτῳ ἀγάλματι), man, bear about the image of God, an image which dwells with us, is our counsellor, companion, the sharer of our hearth, which feels with us, feels for us. We have been made a consecrated offering (ἀνάθημα) to God for Christ's sake.[135]

With this conversion of humans and statues, however, we seem to have come full circle in the encounter between gods' bodies and human bodies, organic and inorganic bodies and bodies available and unavailable to the touch.

CONCLUSION

This chapter moved beyond archaic and classical Greece as the traditional focus of ancient Greek polis religion and focused on the religion of the so-called 'Second Sophistic', a period extending roughly from the first to the third century AD.[136] It was a period of cultural revival and recovery of the Greek cities, shaped in many ways by a self-conscious reorientation towards the classical past.

I compared and contrasted the way in which the human desire to make love to Praxiteles' Aphrodite of Cnidus featured in Philostratus' *Life of Apollonius*, Clement of Alexandria's *Exhortation to the Greeks* and Ps.-Lucian's *Amores*. I showed that the story of the human/divine encounter, imagined as an erotic encounter, proved 'good to think with' for these authors. I argued that what was ultimately at stake in accounts of *agalmatophilia* was a profound concern with divine ontology, divine representation and human knowledge of the divine. These are all-important concepts that had

---

[134] Clem. Al. *Protr.* 4.62.3.   [135] Clem. Al. *Protr.* 4.59.2.

[136] The reorientation of this period encompassed much more than just rhetoric and political oratory, as the term 'Second Sophistic' suggests. It included culture, and religion in particular. See Whitmarsh 2001: 42–5; Elsner 2009: 9. On the period of the Second Sophistic more generally see, e.g., Bowersock 1969; Anderson 1993; Swain 1996; Goldhill 2001a.

begun to shift by the second century AD. At the transition between the traditional religions of Greece and Rome and the new Christian creed, the body of Aphrodite – and the curious human responses it evoked – quite literally and materially negotiated the frictions resulting from religious, societal and cultural change.

At the same time the story of *agalmatophilia* as told and retold by our authors also reveals much that is well known from the religion of earlier periods. It illustrates the fact that the fundamental vertical dichotomy between the human and the divine spheres that was central to archaic and classical Greek religion was still in place and operational during the second century AD. It also showcases the ongoing interest in the divine body (and in divine representations more generally) as a manifestation of divine alterity. What remains to be done then in terms of a conclusion is to think about what the study of accounts of 'statue love' contributes to our knowledge of the religious culture of ancient Greece.

The study of 'statue love' brings out a general dimension of ancient Greek religion which at its core goes all the way back to the classical period: the existence of a Greek discourse about the nature of the divine and its availability to human knowledge. Accounts of *agalmatophilia*, no matter who told them and how they were told, revolve around a common set of themes: the human desire to possess the divine body, the transgressive act involved in overcoming the boundary between the human and the divine and the negative consequences following from it. In these accounts, the distinction between the organic and the inorganic helps to challenge (and ultimately reassert) the ontological unavailability of the divine. In flagging these issues, the study of 'statue love' concludes our study of ancient Greek religion beyond the polis by bringing together a variety of concepts outlined in the previous chapters, especially, perhaps, those of the cognitive and symbolic dimensions of ancient Greek religion.

At their very core, accounts of *agalmatophilia* tell a story that problematises the relationship between gods' bodies and human bodies and in doing so explores the principles and practices of divine representation. This is a story that revolves around a body that has been crafted (imagined) by human hand, but which ultimately remains unavailable to the human touch; the gods, even in their human shapes, can never fully be known. In the literature of Roman Greece we find the story in a variety of contexts that all possess a certain searching quality as to where exactly the boundary runs between the sphere of the gods and that of humans. In fact, what we find here is a discourse, a conversation about divine ontology and its availability to human knowledge revolving around the nude body of Aphrodite.

A key feature of this discourse is its versatility: it permeates not just the material but also the literary evidence; not just comedy, but also philosophy and historiography; the works not only of those who still thought from within traditional Greco-Roman polytheism but also of those who opposed it. By bringing together a variety of authors and genres, writing in different traditions and from different, even opposing, points of view, accounts of *agalmatophilia* ultimately reveal the existence of a religious discourse which, in the absence of a better word, one might want to call theological in nature.

Traditionally, classical scholarship has mainly looked for the theological dimension of ancient Greek religion within the genres of Greek tragedy and philosophy.[137] The reason for this is that the relatively contained and self-reflective universe of these two discourses (tragedy and philosophy) is much more in line with the conception of theology as a systematic and explicitly formulated body of knowledge.[138] Yet the question emerges whether this conception of theology is too narrowly grounded in Christianity to allow us to conceive of other forms of theological reflection in other religious traditions, such as those of Greece and Rome; most recent scholarship seems to have acknowledged this by also using the term outside these contexts.[139]

Can there ever be more convincing proof of the existence of a theological dimension in ancient Greek religion than the vigour and rigour with which Clement sought to replace the 'pagan' conception of the divine body with a new, Christian one? The variety of ways in which the authors discussed this position themselves with regard to the same kind of questions suggests that in ancient Greece religious concepts and the speculative dimension of religion more generally were part of a larger conversation about the nature of the gods and their availability to human knowledge, a conversation which in many ways drew on, continued, inverted and revised archaic and classical Greek conceptions about the nature of the gods and their availability to human knowledge. The fact that accounts of *agalmatophilia* were part of an ongoing and much older religious conversation is nicely highlighted by the fact that they revolved around a divine body which was crafted much earlier, around the middle of the fourth century BC.

---

[137] E.g., Jaeger 1947; Lloyd 1979: 11; Bodéüs 2000; Drozdek 2007 (philosophy); Lloyd-Jones 1956: 57; Mikalson 1991: 235; Parker 1997: 150; Zelenak 1998: 68 (tragedy). Some scholars have also demonstrated the existence of systematic belief for individual authors, such as Herodotus: e.g., Harrison 2000.

[138] On systematic Christian theology see, e.g., Chopp and Taylor 1994; Webster 2009: 1–18.

[139] E.g., Parker 1996: 211; Graf 1997a: 34; Price 1999: 127; Henrichs 2010: 21–9.

Accounts of *agalmatophilia* have not only further substantiated the existence of theological discourse in the ancient world, but they have also illustrated once again the centrality of divine representations (statues) to this discourse. In particular they have illuminated a religious culture in which symbolic bodies could – to some extent at least – serve as place-holders for human and divine bodies, a culture which we also discussed in Chapter 5.

This culture, however, extended almost seamlessly from the realm of religion to the realm of 'magic' as discussed in Chapter 4. It was, for example, at work in the various dolls that have been found with needles stuck into their bodies or with their limbs mutilated into twisted positions.[140] Most of these dolls, we learn from the instructions for their production in the magical papyri, served as symbolic substitutes for human bodies. They allowed those skilled in their production to control the very real body, mind and soul of the victim they represented.

An erotic binding spell now in the *Bibliothèque Nationale* in Paris, for example, gives detailed instructions for the fabrication of two figurines out of wax or clay, representing a female figure (the beloved other) and a male figure (Ares).[141] The figure of Ares holds a sword in its left hand pointed at the right side of the female figurine in a kneeling position with her arms fastened behind her back. The ultimate purpose behind the elaborate rites described in this papyrus, far too detailed to be described fully here, was to make the real woman think of no man other than the lover-magician. The figure of Ares, as well as the other deities and demons invoked in the prayers and recitations accompanying the ritual practices involving the dolls, was supposed to help the lover-magician achieve his goal.

Albeit impressive, this is just one example of how the gods could be instrumentalised for particular purposes, a way of referring to the supernatural which, as we have argued in Chapter 4, is not fully absent from official religious ritual either. Accounts of *agalmatophilia* (and Greek theological discourse) seem to reflect on this religious culture insofar as they – rather physically – raise the question of the availability of the divine to the satisfaction of human needs.

---

[140] On these dolls see, e.g., Graf 1997a: 137–42; Eidinow 2007a: 142–52.
[141] *PGM* IV: 296–466. See also Graf 1997a: 137–40.

Conclusion

> I was therefore compelled reluctantly to face the question, what mean-
> ing did I attach to the word religion?
>
> Jane Ellen Harrison[1]

Overall, a more complex view than previously held of the nature and the
location of religious power in the ancient Greek world has been proposed.
Religion, I argue, did not just map on to the structures of Greek culture
and society but was actively involved in shaping this society and in the
negotiation of its structures over time. As I have demonstrated (in particular
in Chapters 3 and 4), religion was not, or not only, a tool for individuals
to achieve their ambitions. It was also a matter of personal contemplation
(see Chapter 2) and, more generally, a symbolic medium, a 'language' that
created the world to which it related as well as being defined/shaped by
that world. Seen from this perspective, a more complex picture of the
religious dimension of the ancient Greek world emerges, a picture that
captures those aspects of the religious supporting the dominant order but
also including those alternative locations of the religious that drew on,
complemented and sometimes even challenged official polis discourse.

Stress has been laid on the variety of the ways in which ancient Greek
religion was like as well as unlike other religious traditions, both ancient and
modern. It is a much-repeated truism that ancient Greek religion differed
from most modern religions insofar as it had no structured community
of believers (no church) and no systematic and authoritative statement of
belief (no creed) and no holy text. In the absence of such traditional loci of
religious authority it can be difficult to identify and describe the structures
of ancient Greek religion. However, if we base our conception of ancient
Greek religion exclusively on its civic, official and communal religious
aspects, we run the real risk of ascribing to it a degree of conformity,

---

[1] Harrison 1912: vii.

inner coherence and boundedness, of assigning it a quasi-dogmatic quality which it never really had and which is more reminiscent of religions such as Christianity than of the vibrancy and plurality of religious life in the ancient world. Some of the most interesting and productive questions about ancient Greek religion, as I hope has been demonstrated, lie just beyond the communal and civic, in the interplay of polis religion and those religious strategies, discourses and institutions beyond the polis.

Which theoretical conceptions caused polis religion to take over in the first place? I think the appeal of the polis-centred perspective for the student of ancient Greek religion lay first and foremost in the need to identify a centre, a common core for a religion that lacked the obvious organising principles of most other religions (see above). Together with the conception of religion – derived from older scholarship and the sociology of religion – as always and in all aspects a communal and collective enterprise, the polis provided this common core around which Greek religious beliefs and practices were organised. The approaches to Greek religion by Burkert and the so-called Paris School, in particular, presupposed the existence of a more or less static and coherent cultural system, provided by the polis and her institutions. The polis approach towards the study of ancient Greek history more generally, as discussed in the introduction to this study, will have contributed to the assumption that the polis served as the unifying factor for all areas of Greek life including that of religion. The result of this focus, however, was a somewhat lopsided interest in those aspects of the religious, which map on to the structures of Greek politics and society, and the relative neglect of others which either challenge it or are situated above or below the radar of the polis.

Throughout the individual chapters, therefore, I have propounded the necessity of expanding our conception of the religious to embrace a broader religious culture, and have done so, overall, by illustrating the exemplary rather than the general and comprehensive. As a result, however, some of the aspects of the religious, which polis religion explains rather well, have largely been outside the scope of this study. There is, for example, very little on religious festivals as such (apart from the interest in religious processions in Chapter 3), because festivals were one of the principal ways in which polis religion expressed and articulated itself.[2] There is also little, if anything, on sacrifice as the central constitutive ritual of ancient Greek polis religion, although the institution of blood sacrifice is currently subject to much

---

[2] E.g., Burkert 1985: 225–46; Price 1999: 11–46; Parker 2005: 155–383; Evans 2010: 50–62.

debate as scholars seek to move beyond the complementary positions of Burkert and Vernant.[3] I have instead sought to illustrate in particular those areas of the religious which the model of polis religion does not explain, or at least not sufficiently, including those of personal religion, the cognitive dimension of ancient Greek religion, Greek theology and 'magic'.

More research is needed to explore the place within this revised conception of the religious of other beliefs, practices and institutions not discussed here. Mystery religions are one example; another would be diverse religious concepts such as death and piety that cannot fully be associated with either civic or personal religion. The role of myth within this expanded conception of the religious will in particular have to be revisited. Myth is central to polis religion, but usually only insofar as aetiological myths can provide interesting insights into the religious practices they purport to explain (which, as I have argued in Chapter 1, are always in some way related to the polis). The same applies to foundation stories, which may explain a given city or its political and religious institutions. However, the question emerges of how other, non-aetiological stories about the Greek gods and goddesses fit into the picture. Surely intricate ideas about the nature of the supernatural are expressed in other myths, which are not – or at least not primarily – polis-specific? Where do we place local traditions as reflected, for example, in the material evidence and myths which illustrate Near Eastern influences? What do we do with mythological narratives expressive of other identities above and below the level of the polis? To assess the way in which Greek mythology maps on to the revised religious landscape within and beyond polis religion will be a productive avenue for future research.

The more comprehensive exploration of the religious in ancient Greece requires us to revisit some central tenets in the study of ancient Greek religion. For example, we will need to take a fresh look at the way in which we conceive of the unity and diversity of ancient Greek religion, and in particular to rethink what we regard as being at the centre of the religious culture of ancient Greece and what we think constituted its periphery. No longer can we assume with the polis model that it is always and necessarily the civic dimension of ancient Greek religion that defined what was at its core. What we need is a conception of ancient Greek religion which allows for multiple locations of the religious inside and outside those of polis religion, one that embraces multiple centres and peripheries.

---

[3] See, e.g., Parker 2011: 124–70; Faraone and Naiden (2012).

This leads us to an important caveat: we must avoid the temptation to structure ancient Greek religion around a set of simple dualities: between centre and periphery, for example, or between belief and practice; or, as Chapter 5 has shown, between the local and the universal/panhellenic. On the most abstract level this also applies to the study of ancient Greek religion beyond polis religion itself. In moving towards a broader conception of the religious culture of ancient Greece we should not assume a simple duality between civic religion and Greek religion beyond the polis either. The reality of lived religion was much more complicated than that.

A central focus throughout this book has been on religious representations. Several chapters have focused on the modes and modalities in which the supernatural manifested itself in the human sphere – through oracles and the oracular, for example, or through statues and divine representations and manifestations of all kinds (Chapters 2, 4 and 6). As a result, the picture of ancient Greek religion that emerges from this study is one of a vibrant symbolic medium of interaction.

In the last chapter of the book I extended this conception of religion as a symbolic 'language' and argued for the existence of a theology of ancient Greek religion. Not, of course, a theology in the form of a definite and binding formula as in revealed religions such as Christianity, but as a form of theological speculation that evolved in narrative and episodic form and was descriptive rather than prescriptive. The conception of a theology, or theologies, of ancient Greek religion is, I think, a productive one. It warrants further exploration beyond the context in which it was considered in Chapter 6.

In particular, we should investigate if and how speculation about the nature of the gods and their availability to human knowledge as it featured broadly in Greek thought and literature relates to the much more clearly defined theological universe of Greek tragedy and philosophy.[4] We must also consider what authorities were underwriting this theology and how various forms of magic related to it beyond the contexts considered in Chapter 4. Overall, the goal will be to describe the systematic nature of Greek theological speculation as it emerges in a variety of overlapping themes that resurface time and again within the religious discourse of the Greco-Roman world (for example, the question of divine ontology, the presence of the gods in the human sphere, and the question of the scope and limits of human knowledge of the divine).

---

[4] On the theologies of Greek tragedy and oratory see also Parker 1997.

Again, as I have argued in Chapter 1, we should expect to find multiple theologies as well as frictions, gaps and inconsistencies in the way these theologies took shape. All this makes it necessary to consider alternative conceptions of theological speculation beyond the familiar Christianising discourse. Perhaps the interdisciplinary perspective will be able to offer invaluable guidance in further developing this aspect of ancient Greek religion beyond the polis?

Bibliography

The following bibliography includes titles referred to in this book as well as a number of other works the reader may find useful.

Adler, F., et al. (1892) *Die Baudenkmäler von Olympia: Olympia* II. Berlin

Akujärvi, J. (2005) *Researcher, Traveller, Narrator: Studies in Pausanias' Periegesis.* Stockholm

Alcock, S. and Osborne, R. (eds.) (1994) *Placing the Gods: Sanctuaries and Sacred Space in Ancient Greece.* Oxford

Alcock, S., Cherry, J. F. and Elsner, J. (eds.) (2001) *Pausanias: Travel and Memory in Roman Greece.* Oxford

Aleshire, S. (1989) *The Athenian Asklepieion: The People, their Dedications, and the Inventories.* Amsterdam

(1992) 'The economics of dedication at the Athenian Asklepieion', in T. Linders and B. Alroth (eds.), *Economics of Cult in the Ancient Greek World.* Uppsala, 85–99

(1994) 'Towards a definition of "state cult" for ancient Athens', in Hägg, 9–16

Alroth, B. (1989) *Greek Gods and Figurines: Aspects of Anthropomorphic Dedications.* Uppsala

Alroth, B. and Hellström, P. (eds.) (1996) *Religion and Power in the Ancient Greek World.* Uppsala

Anderson, B. (1991) *Imagined Communities: Reflections on the Origins and Spread of Nationalism*, rev. edn. London

Anderson, G. (1976) *Lucian: Theme and Variation in the Second Sophistic.* Leiden

(1982) 'Lucian: a sophist's sophist', *YClS* 27, 61–92

(1986) *Philostratus: Biography and Belles Lettres in the Third Century* AD. London

(1989) 'The *pepaideumenos* in action: sophists and their outlook in the early empire', *ANRW* II, 33.1, 79–208

(1993) *The Second Sophistic: A Cultural Phenomenon in the Roman Empire.* London

(1994) *Sage, Saint, and Sophist: Holy Men and their Associates in the Early Roman Empire.* London

(1996) 'Philostratus on Apollonius of Tyana: the unpredictable on the unfathomable', in G. L. Schmeling (ed.), *The Novel in the Ancient World.* Leiden, 613–18

Andresen, J. (ed.) (2001) *Religion in Mind: Cognitive Perspectives on Religious Belief, Ritual, and Experience.* Cambridge

Ankarloo, B. and Clark, S. (eds.) (1999) *Witchcraft and Magic in Europe*, vol. II: *Ancient Greece and Rome*. London

Appadurai, A. (ed.) (1986) *The Social Life of Things: Commodities in Cultural Perspective*. Cambridge

Arafat, K. W. (1996) *Pausanias' Greece: Ancient Artists and Roman Rulers*. Cambridge

Asad, T. (1983) 'Anthropological conceptions of religion: reflections on Geertz', *Man* 18, 237–59

   (1993) *Genealogies of Religion: Discipline and Reasons of Power in Christianity and Islam*. Baltimore, MD

Assmann, J. (1997) *Das kulturelle Gedächtnis: Schrift, Erinnerung und politische Identität in frühen Hochkulturen*. Munich

Audollent, A. (1904) *Defixionum Tabellae*. Paris

Aune, D. E. (1980) 'Magic in early Christianity', *ANRW* II, 23.2, 1507–57

Babcock, B. A. (ed.) (1978) *The Reversible World: Symbolic Inversion in Art and Society*. Ithaca, NY

Baitinger, H. (2001) *Die Angriffswaffen aus Olympia* (Olympische Forschungen XXIX). Berlin

Barb, A. A. (1994) 'The survival of magic arts', in A. Momigliano (ed.), *The Conflict between Paganism and Christianity in the Fourth Century*. Oxford, 100–25

Barber, E. J. W. (1992) 'The peplos of Athena', in Neils, 103–18

Barringer, J. (2005) 'The temple of Zeus at Olympia: heroes and athletes', *Hesperia* 74, 211–41

   (2008) *Art, Myth, and Ritual in Classical Greece*. Cambridge

Barry, J., Hester, M. and Roberts, G. (eds.) (1996) *Witchcraft in Early Modern Europe: Studies in Culture and Belief*. Cambridge

Barthes, R. (1981) *Camera Lucida: Reflections on Photography*, transl. R. Howard. London (French orig. 1980)

Bartsch, S. (2006) *The Mirror of the Self: Sexuality, Self-Knowledge, and the Gaze in the Early Roman Empire*. Chicago, IL

Bartsch, S. and Elsner, J. (2007) 'Introduction: eight ways of looking at an ekphrasis', *CPh* 102, i–vi

Bauer, D. F. (1962) 'The function of Pygmalion in the Metamorphoses of Ovid', *TAPhA* 99, 1–21

Baumgarten, A. I. (2002) *Sacrifice in Religious Experience*. Leiden

Bean, G. E. and Cook, J. M. (1952) 'The Cnidia', *ABSA* 47, 171–212

Beard, M. and Henderson, J. (2001) *Classical Art: From Greece to Rome*. Oxford

Beard, M. and North, J. (eds.) (1990) *Pagan Priests: Religion and Power in the Ancient World*. Ithaca, NY

Beard, M., North, J. and Price, S. (1998) *Religions of Rome* (2 vols.). Cambridge

Beck, R. (2006) *The Religion of the Mithras Cult in the Roman Empire: Mysteries of the Unconquered Sun*. Oxford

Bell, C. (1989) 'Religion and Chinese culture: toward an assessment of "popular religion"', *HR* 29, 35–57

Belting, H. (1994) *Likeness and Presence: A History of the Image before the Era of Art*, transl. E. Jephcott. Chicago, IL (German orig. 1990)

Bendlin, A. (2000) 'Looking beyond the civic compromise: religious pluralism in late republican Rome', in E. Bispham and C. J. Smith (eds.), *Religion in Archaic and Republican Rome and Italy*. Edinburgh, 115–35

Bengtson, H. (1977) *Griechische Geschichte*, 5th edn. Munich

Benko, S. (1984) *Pagan Rome and the Early Christians*. Bloomington, IN

Bérard, C. and Bron, C. (1989) *A City of Images: Iconography and Society in Ancient Greece*, transl. D. Lyons. Princeton, NJ (French orig. 1984)

Berger, P. L. (1969) *The Sacred Canopy: Elements of a Sociological Theory of Religion*. Garden City, NY

Bergquist, B. (1967) *The Archaic Greek Temenos: A Study of Structure and Function*. Lund

Bernand, A. (1991) *Sorciers grecs*. Paris

Bernoulli, J. J. (1873) *Aphrodite: ein Baustein zur griechischen Kunstmythologie*. Leipzig

Berthiaume, G. (1982) *Les Rôles du mágeiros: étude sur la boucherie, la cuisine et le sacrifice dans la Grèce ancienne*. Leiden

Betz, H. D. (1983) 'Gottmensch II (Griechisch-römische Antike und Urchristentum)', *Reallexikon für Antike und Christentum* 12, 244–312

(ed.) (1986) *The Greek Magical Papyri in Translation* (2 vols.). Chicago, IL

(1991) 'Magic and mystery in the Greek magical papyri', in Faraone and Obbink, 244–59

(2003) *The 'Mithras Liturgy'*. Tübingen

Bieler, L. (1935/1936) *ΘΕΙΟΣ ΑΝΗΡ: das Bild des 'göttlichen Menschen' in der Spätantike und Frühchristentum* (2 vols.). Vienna

Bill, C. P. (1901) 'Notes on the Greek *theoros* and *theoria*', *TAPhA* 32, 196–204

Billault, A. (2000) *L'Univers de Philostrate*. Brussels

Blamire, A. (2001) 'Athenian finance, 454–404 BC', *Hesperia* 70, 99–126

Blanck, H. (1969) *Wiederverwendung alter Statuen als Ehrendenkmäler bei Griechen und Römern*. Rome

Blanshard, A. (2010) *Sex: Vice and Love from Antiquity to Modernity*. London

Blinkenberg, C. (1933) *Knidia: Beiträge zur Kenntnis der praxitelischen Aphrodite*. Copenhagen

Blundell, S. (1995) *Women in Ancient Greece*. Cambridge, MA

Boardman, J. (ed.) (1993) *The Oxford History of Classical Art*. Oxford

Bodéüs, R. (2000) *Aristotle and the Theology of the Living Immortals*, transl. J. Garrett. New York (French orig. 1992)

Böhm, S. (1990) *Die 'nackte Göttin': zur Ikonographie und Deutung unbekleideter weiblicher Figuren in der frühgriechischen Kunst*. Mainz

Bol, R. (1978) *Grossplastik aus Bronze in Olympia* (Olympische Forschungen IX). Berlin

(1984) *Das Statuenprogramm des Herodes-Atticus-Nymphäums* (Olympische Forschungen XV). Berlin

(1989) *Argivische Schilde* (Olympische Forschungen XVII). Berlin

Bonfante, L. (1989) 'Nudity as a costume in classical art', *AJA* 93, 543–70

Bonnechere, P. (2003) *Trophonios de Lébadée: cultes et mythes d'une cité béotienne au miroir de la mentalité antique*. Leiden

Bonner, C. (1932) 'Witchcraft in the lecture room of Libanius', *TAPhA* 63, 34–44

(1950) *Studies in Magical Amulets, Chiefly Graeco-Egyptian*. Ann Arbor, MI

Borbein, A. H. (1973) 'Die griechische Statue des 4. Jahrhunderts v. Chr.: formanalytische Untersuchungen zur Kunst der Nachklassik', *JDAI* 88, 43–212

Borell, B. and Rittig, D. (eds.) (1998) *Orientalische und Griechische Bronzereliefs aus Olympia: der Fundkomplex aus Brunnen* (Olympische Forschungen xxvi). Berlin

Borg, B. (ed.) (2004) *Paideia: The World of the Second Sophistic*. Berlin

Bourdieu, P. (1977) *Outline of a Theory of Practice*, transl. R. Nice. Cambridge (French orig. 1972)

Bowden, H. (2005) *Classical Athens and the Delphic Oracle: Divination and Democracy*. Cambridge

(2010) *Mystery Cults of the Ancient World*. Princeton, NJ

Bowersock, G. W. (1969) *Greek Sophists in the Roman Empire*. Oxford

(1989) 'Philostratus and the Second Sophistic', in P. E. Easterling and B. M. W. Knox (eds.) *The Cambridge History of Greek Literature*, vol. I, pt. 4: *The Hellenistic Period and the Empire*. Cambridge, 95–8

(1990) *Hellenism in Late Antiquity*. Ann Arbor, MI

(2002) 'Philosophy in the Second Sophistic', in G. Clark and T. Rajak (eds.), *Philosophy and Power in the Graeco-Roman World: Essays in Honour of Miriam Griffin*. Oxford, 157–70

Bowie, E. L. (1974) 'Greeks and their past in the Second Sophistic', in M. Finley (ed.), *Studies in Ancient Society*. London, 166–209

(1978) 'Apollonius of Tyana: tradition and reality', in *ANRW* II, 16.2, 1652–99

(1991) 'Hellenes and Hellenism in writers of the early Second Sophistic', in S. Saïd (ed.), ΕΛΛΗΝΙΣΜΟΣ: *quelques jalons pour une histoire de l'identité grecque*. Leiden, 183–204

(1994) 'Philostratus: writer of fiction', in J. R. Morgan and R. Stoneman (eds.), *Greek Fiction: The Greek Novel in Context*. London, 181–99

(1996) 'Past and present in Pausanias', in J. Bingen (ed.), *Pausanias historien*. Geneva, 207–30

(2009) 'Philostratus: the life of a sophist', in Bowie and Elsner, 19–32

Bowie, E. L. and Elsner, J. (eds.) (2009) *Philostratus*. Cambridge

Boyer, P. (2001) *Religion Explained: The Evolutionary Origins of Religious Thought*. New York

Boys-Stones, G., Graziosi, B. and Vasunia, P. (eds.) (2009) *The Oxford Handbook of Hellenic Studies*. Oxford

Braavig, J. (1999) 'Magic: reconsidering the grand dichotomy', in Jordan et al., 21–54

Bradley, K. (1997) 'Law, magic, and culture in the apologia of Apuleius', *Phoenix* 51, 203–23

Bradley, R. (1990) *The Passage of Arms: An Archaeological Analysis of Prehistoric Hoards and Votive Deposits*. Cambridge

Branham, R. B. (1989) *Unruly Eloquence: Lucian and the Comedy of Traditions*. Cambridge, MA

Branquinho, J. (ed.) (2001) *The Foundations of Cognitive Science*. Oxford

Brashear, W. (1995) 'The Greek magical papyri: an introduction and survey; annotated bibliography (1928–1994)', *ANRW* II, 18.5, 3380–684

Braun, K. (1970) 'Der Dipylon-Brunnen B1: die Funde', *MDAI(A)* 85, 129–296

Bremmer, J. N. (1993) 'Prophets, seers, and politics in Greece, Israel, and early modern Europe', *Numen* 40, 150–83

(1994) *Greek Religion*. Oxford

(1998a) 'Aspect of the Acts of Peter: women, magic, place and date', in J. N. Bremmer (ed.), *The Apocryphal Acts of Peter: Magic, Miracles and Gnosticism*. Leuven, 1–20

(1998b) '"Religion", "ritual" and the opposition "sacred vs. profane": notes towards a terminological genealogy', in F. Graf (ed.), *Ansichten griechischer Rituale: Geburtstags-Symposium für Walter Burkert*. Stuttgart, 9–32

(1999) 'The birth of the term "magic"', *ZPE* 126, 1–12

(2002) 'Orphism, Pythagoras, and the rise of the immortal soul', in J. N. Bremmer, *The Rise and Fall of the Afterlife: The 1995 Read-Tuckwell Lectures at the University of Bristol*. New York, 11–26

(2008) 'Appendix II: magic and religion', in J. N. Bremmer, *Greek Religion and Culture, the Bible and the Ancient Near East*. Leiden, 347–52 (first published in Bremmer and Veenstra, 267–71)

(2010) '*Manteis*, magic, mysteries and mythography: messy margins of *polis* religion?', *Kernos* 23, 13–35

Bremmer, J. N. and Veenstra, J. R. (eds.) (2002) *The Metamorphosis of Magic from Late Antiquity to the Early Modern Period*. Leuven

Briggs, R. (1996) *Witches and Neighbours: The Social and Cultural Context of European Witchcraft*. London

Brown, P. (1970) 'Sorcery, demons and the rise of Christianity from late antiquity into the Middle Ages', in M. Douglas (ed.), *Witchcraft Confessions and Accusations*. London, 17–45

(1971) 'The rise and function of the holy man in late antiquity', *JRS* 61, 80–101

(1972) *Religion and Society in the Age of Saint Augustine*. London

(1981) *The Cult of the Saints: Its Rise and Function in Latin Christianity*. Chicago, IL

(1982) *Society and the Holy in Late Antiquity*. Berkeley, CA

(1988) *The Body and Society: Men, Women and Sexual Renunciation in Early Christianity*. New York

Bruit Zaidman, L. (2001) *Le Commerce des dieux: eusebeia, essai sur la piété en Grèce ancienne*. Paris

Bruit Zaidman, L. and Schmitt Pantel, P. (1992) *Religion in the Ancient Greek City*, transl. P. Cartledge. Cambridge (French orig. 1989)

Brulotte, E. L. (1994) '"The pillar of Oinomaos" and the location of the stadium I at Olympia', *AJA* 98, 53–64

Bruneau, P. (1970) *Recherches sur les cultes de Delos à l'époque hellénistique et à l'époque impériale*. Paris

Buck, C. D. (1953) '*Theoros*', in G. E. Mylonas and D. Raymond (eds.), *Studies Presented to David Moore Robinson*, vol. II. St Louis, MO, 443–4

Buck, R. J. (1979) *A History of Boeotia*. Edmonton, AB

Buell, D. K. (1999) *Making Christians: Clement of Alexandria and the Rhetoric of Legitimacy*. Princeton, NJ

Bulloch, A. W., Gruen, E., Long, A. A. and Stewart, A. F. (eds.) (1993) *Images and Ideologies: Self-Definition in the Hellenistic World*. Berkeley, CA

Burckhardt, J. (1943) *Kulturgeschichte Griechenlands*, abridged edn. Berlin

Burkert, W. (1962) ΓΟΗΣ: zum griechischen "Schamanismus"', *RhM* 105, 36–55

    (1983a) *Homo Necans: The Anthropology of Ancient Greek Sacrificial Ritual and Myth*. Berkeley, CA (German orig. 1972)

    (1983b) 'Itinerant diviners and magicians: a neglected element in cultural contacts', in R. Hägg (ed.), *The Greek Renaissance of the Eighth Century BC: Tradition and Innovation*. Stockholm, 115–19

    (1985) *Greek Religion*, transl. J. Raffan. Oxford (German. orig. 1977)

    (1987) 'Offerings in perspective: surrender, distribution, exchange', in Linders and Nordquist, 43–50

    (1995) 'Greek poleis and civic cults: some further thoughts', in Hansen and Raaflaub, 201–10

    (2006) 'Orphism and Bacchic mysteries: new evidence and old problems of interpretation', in F. Graf (ed.), *Kleine Schriften III: Mystica, Orphica, Pythagorica*. Göttingen, 152–72 (first published in W. H. Wuellner (ed.) (1977) *Protocol of the 28th Colloquy of the Center for Hermeneutical Studies in Hellenistic and Modern Culture*. Berkeley, 1–10)

Burriss, E. E. (1928) 'Some survivals of magic in Roman religion', *CJ* 24, 112–23

    (1931) *Taboo, Magic, Spirits: A Study of Primitive Elements in Roman Religion*. New York

Bury, R. G. (ed.) (1926) *Plato: Laws, Books VII–IIX*. Cambridge, MA

Butterworth, G. W. (ed.) (1919) *Clement of Alexandria: Exhortation to the Greeks, the Rich Man's Salvation, to the Newly Baptized*. Cambridge, MA

Buxton, R. (1981) 'Introduction', in Gordon, ix–xvii.

    (ed.) (2000) *Oxford Readings in Greek Religion*. Oxford

Carapanos, C. (1878) *Dodone et ses ruines*. Paris

Carastro, M. (2006) *La Cité des mages: penser la magie en Grèce ancienne*. Grenoble

Cartledge, P. (1985) 'The Greek religious festivals', in Easterling and Muir, 98–127

    (1994) 'The Greeks and anthropology', *Anthropology Today* 10, 3–6

Casanova, J. (1994) *Public Religions in the Modern World*. Chicago, IL

Cawkwell, G. (1996) 'The end of Greek liberty', in R. W. Wallace and E. M. Harris (eds.), *Transitions to Empire: Essays in Graeco-Roman History 360–146 BC in Honor of E. Badian*. Norman, OK, 98–121

Chadwick, H. (1966) *Early Christian Thought and the Classical Tradition: Studies in Justin, Clement, and Origen*. Oxford

Chiasson, C. C. (2005) 'Myth, ritual and authorial control in Herodotus' story of Cleobis and Biton (Hist. 1.31)', *AJPh* 126, 41–64

Chopp, R. and Taylor, M. (eds.) (1994) *Reconstructing Christian Theology*. Minneapolis, MN

Christesen, P. (2007) *Olympic Victor Lists and Ancient Greek History*. Cambridge

Ciraolo, L. and Seidel, J. (eds.) (2002) *Magic and Divination in the Ancient World*. Leiden

Clark, R. J. (1968) 'Trophonios: the manner of his revelation', *TAPhA* 99, 63–75

Clinton, K. (1982) 'The nature of the late fifth-century revision of the Athenian law code', *Hesperia*, Supplement 19, 27–37

Cohen, D. (1988) 'The prosecution of impiety in Athenian law', *ZRG* 105, 695–701

  (1991) *Law, Sexuality, and Society: The Enforcement of Morals in Classical Athens*. Cambridge

Cohen, E. (1992) 'Pilgrimage and tourism: convergence and divergence', in A. Morinis (ed.), *Sacred Journeys: The Anthropology of Pilgrimage*. New York, 47–61

Cole, S. G. (1995) 'Civic cult and civic identity', in M. H. Hansen (ed.), *Sources for the Ancient Greek City State*. Copenhagen, 292–325

Coleman, S. and Elsner, J. (1995) *Pilgrimage Past and Present: Sacred Travel and Sacred Space in the World Religions*. London

Collins, D. (2001) 'Theoris of Lemnos and the criminalization of magic in fourth-century Athens', *CQ* 51, 477–93

  (2003) 'Nature, cause, and agency in Greek magic', *TAPhA* 133, 17–49

  (2008) *Magic in the Ancient World*. Malden, MA

  (2009) 'Magic', in Boys-Stones et al., 541–51

Comaroff, J. and Comaroff, J. L. (1991) *Of Revelation and Revolution*, vol. I: *Christianity, Colonialism and Consciousness in South Africa*. Chicago, IL

  (1997) *Of Revelation and Revolution*, vol. II: *The Dialectics of Modernity on a South African Frontier*. Chicago, IL

  (1999) 'Occult economies and the violence of abstraction: notes from the South African postcolony', *American Ethnologist* 26, 279–303

Connor, W. R. (1987) 'Tribes, festivals and processions: civic ceremonial and political manipulation in archaic Greece', *JHS* 107, 40–50

  (1988) '"Sacred" and "secular": *hiera kai hosia* and the classical Athenian concept of the state', *AncSoc* 19, 161–88

Cornford, F. M. (1914) *The Origin of Attic Comedy*. London

Corrington, G. P. (1986) *The 'Divine Man': His Origin and Function in Hellenistic Popular Religion*. New York

Corso, A. (2007) 'The cult and political background of the Knidian Aphrodite', in E. Hallager and J. Jensen (eds.), *Proceedings of the Danish Institute at Athens* 5, 173–97

Costabile, F. (1999) 'Defixiones da locri epizefiri: nuovi dati sui culti sulla storia e sulle istituzioni', *Minima Epigraphica et Papyrologica* 2, 23–76

  (2000) 'Defixiones dal kerameikós di Atene II', *Minima Epigraphica et Papyrologica* 4, 37–122

Cox, P. (1983) *Biography in Late Antiquity: A Quest for the Holy Man*. Berkeley, CA

Crisp, O. D. (2007) 'Incarnation', in J. Webster, K. Tanner and I. Torrance (eds.), *The Oxford Handbook of Systematic Theology*. Oxford, 160–75

Crowther, N. B. (1991) 'The Olympic training period', *Nikephoros* 4, 161–6

   (2003) 'Elis and Olympia: city, sanctuary and politics', in D. J. Phillips and D. Pritchard (eds.), *Sport and Festival in the Ancient Greek World*. Swansea, 61–73

Csapo, E. (2005) *Theories of Mythology*. London

Culianu, I. (1980) 'Iatroi kai manteis: sulle strutture dell'estatismo Greco', *Studi Storico-Religiosi* 4, 287–303

Cunningham, G. (1999) *Religion and Magic: Approaches and Theories*. Edinburgh

Currie, B. (2005) *Pindar and the Cult of Heroes*. Oxford

Darnton, R. (1984) *The Great Cat Massacre and other Episodes in French Cultural History*. New York

Davies, O. and Turner, D. (eds.) (2002) *Silence and the Word: Negative Theology and Incarnation*. Cambridge

Davis, N. Z. (1974) 'Some tasks and themes in the study of popular religion', in C. E. Trinkaus and H. A. Oberman (eds.), *The Pursuit of Holiness in Late Medieval and Renaissance Religion*. Leiden, 307–36

   (1982) 'From popular religion to religious cultures', in S. E. Ozment (ed.), *Reformation Europe: A Guide to Research*. St Louis, MI, 321–43

   (2005) 'Clifford Geertz on time and change', in Shweder and Good, 38–44

Dawson, D. (1992) *Allegorical Readers and Cultural Revision in Ancient Alexandria*. Berkeley, CA

Day, J. W. (2010) *Archaic Greek Epigram and Dedication: Representation and Reperformance*. Cambridge

Demoen, K. and Praet, D. (eds.) (2009) *Theios Sophistes: Essays on Flavius Philostratus' Vita Apollonii*. Leiden

Dening, G. (1988) *History's Anthropology: The Death of William Gooch*. Lanham, MD

   (2003) 'The Comaroffs out of Africa: a reflection out of Oceania', *AHR* 108, 471–8

Detienne, M. (1963) *De la pensée religieuse à la pensée philosophique: la notion du daimôn dans le pythagorisme ancien*. Paris

Detienne, M. and Vernant, J.-P. (1978) *Cunning Intelligence in Greek Culture and Society*, transl. J. Lloyd. Chicago, IL (French orig. 1974)

   (1989) *The Cuisine of Sacrifice among the Greeks*, transl. J. Lloyd. Chicago, IL (French orig. 1979)

Deubner, L. (1932) *Attische Feste*. Berlin

Dickie, M. (1991) 'Heliodorus and Plutarch on the evil eye', *CPh* 86, 17–29

   (2000) 'Who practised love-magic in classical antiquity and in the late Roman world?', *CQ* 50, 563–83

   (2001) *Magic and Magicians in the Greco-Roman World*. London

Dietrich, B. (1965) *Death, Fate and the Gods: The Development of a Religious Idea in Greek Popular Belief and in Homer*. London

   (1986) *Tradition in Greek Religion*. New York

Dignas, B. (2002) *Economy of the Sacred in Hellenistic and Roman Asia Minor.* Oxford

Dignas, B. and Trampedach, K. (eds.) (2008) *Practitioners of the Divine: Greek Priests and Religious Officials from Homer to Heliodorus.* Cambridge, MA

Dillery, J. (2005) 'Chresmologues and manteis: independent diviners and the problem of authority', in Johnston and Struck, 167–231

Dillon, M. (ed.) (1996) *Religion in the Ancient World: New Themes and Approaches.* Amsterdam

(1997) *Pilgrims and Pilgrimage in Ancient Greece.* London

Dillon, S. (2006) *Ancient Greek Portrait Sculpture: Contexts, Subjects, and Styles.* Cambridge

Dittenberger, W. and Purgold, K. (eds.) (1896) *Olympia: die Ergebnisse der von dem deutschen Reich veranstalteten Ausgrabung,* vol. v: *Die Inschriften.* Berlin

Dodds, E. R. (1947) 'Theurgy and its relationship to Neoplatonism', *JRS* 37, 55–69

(1951) *The Greeks and the Irrational.* Berkeley, CA

(1965) *Pagan and Christian in an Age of Anxiety: Some Aspects of Religious Experience from Marcus Aurelius to Constantine.* Cambridge

(1977) *Missing Persons: An Autobiography.* Oxford

Donohue, A. A. (1988) *XOANA and the Origins of Greek Sculpture.* Atlanta, GA

(2005) *Greek Sculpture and the Problem of Description.* Cambridge

Dörrie, H. (1960) 'Die Frage nach dem Transzendenten im Mittelplatonismus', in E. R. Dodds et al. (eds.), *Les Sources de Plotin: dix exposés et discussions.* Geneva, 193–223

Dougherty, C. and Kurke, L. (eds.) (2003) *The Cultures within Ancient Greek Culture.* Cambridge

Dover, K. J. (1978) *Greek Homosexuality.* London

Drees, L. (1967) *Olympia: Götter, Künstler und Athleten.* Stuttgart

Drozdek, A. (2007) *Greek Philosophers as Theologians: The Divine Arche.* Burlington, VT

DuBois, P. (1996) 'Archaic bodies-in-pieces', in Kampen, 55–64

Durand, J.-L. (1986) *Sacrifice et labeur en Grèce ancienne: essai d'anthropologie religieuse.* Paris

Durand, J.-L. and Schnapp, A. (1989) 'Sacrificial slaughter and initiatory hunt', in Bérard and Bron, 53–70

Durkheim, E. (1912) *Les Formes élémentaires de la vie religieuse.* Paris (*The Elementary Forms of Religious Life*: *A Study in Religious Sociology,* transl. K. Fields. New York, 1995)

Dzielska, M. (1986) *Apollonius of Tyana in Legend and History.* Rome

Easterling, P. and Muir, J. (eds.) (1985) *Greek Religion and Society.* Cambridge

Ebert, J. (1972) *Griechische Epigramme auf Sieger an gymnischen und hippischen Agonen* (2 vols.). Berlin

Eckstein, F. (1969) *Anathemata: Studien zu den Weihgeschenken strengen Stils im Heiligtum von Olympia.* Berlin

Edelstein, L. (1967) 'Greek medicine in its relation to religion and magic', in O. Temkin and C. L. Temkin (eds.), *Ancient Medicine: Selected Papers of Ludwig Edelstein*. Baltimore, MD, 205–46

Edmonds, R. G. (2004) *Myths of the Underworld Journey: Plato, Aristophanes, and the 'Orphic' Gold Tablets*. Cambridge

Edwards, M. (2000) 'Clement of Alexandria and his doctrine of the logos', *VChr* 54, 159–77

Ehrenberg, V. (1960) *The Greek State*. Oxford

Eickelman, D. F. (1985) *Knowledge and Power in Morocco: The Education of a Twentieth-century Notable*. Princeton, NJ
 (2005) 'Clifford Geertz and Islam', in Shweder and Good, 63–75

Eidinow, E. (2007a) *Oracles, Curses, and Risk Among the Ancient Greeks*. Oxford
 (2007b) 'Why the Athenians began to curse', in R. Osborne (ed.), *Debating the Athenian Cultural Revolution: Art, Literature, Philosophy, and Politics 430–380 BC*. Cambridge, 44–71
 (2010) 'Patterns of persecution: witchcraft trials in classical Athens', *P&P* 208, 9–35

Eitrem, S. (1991) 'Dreams and divination in magical ritual', in Faraone and Obbink, 175–87

Elbourne, E. (2003) 'Word made flesh: Christianity, modernity, and cultural colonialism in the work of John and Jean Comaroff', *AHR* 108, 435–59

Elderkin, G. (1936) 'An Athenian maledictory inscription on lead', *Hesperia* 5, 43–9
 (1937) 'Two curse inscriptions', *Hesperia* 6, 382–95

Ellis, H. (1928) *Studies in the Psychology of Sex*, vol. 1. New York

Elsner, J. (1995) *Art and the Roman Viewer: The Transformation of Art from the Pagan World to Christianity*. Cambridge
 (1997) 'The origins of the icon: pilgrimage, religion, and visual culture in the Roman east as "resistance" to the centre', in S. Alcock (ed.), *The Early Roman Empire in the East*. Oxford, 178–99
 (2007) *Roman Eyes: Visuality and Subjectivity in Art and Text*. Princeton, NJ
 (2009) 'A protean corpus', in Bowie and Elsner, 3–18

Elsner, J. and Rutherford, I. (eds.) (2005) *Pilgrimage in Graeco-Roman and Early Christian Antiquity: Seeing the Gods*. Oxford

Engle Merry, S. (2003) 'Hegemony and culture in historical anthropology: a review essay on Jean and John L. Comaroff's *Of Revelation and Revolution*', *AHR* 108, 460–70

Erskine, A. (1995) 'Culture and power in Ptolemaic Egypt: the museum and library of Alexandria', *G&R* 42, 38–48

Evans, A. et al. (1908) *Anthropology and the Classics: Six Lectures Delivered Before the University of Oxford*. Oxford

Evans, N. (2010) *Civic Rites: Democracy and Religion in Ancient Athens*. Berkeley, CA

Evans-Pritchard, E. E. (1936) 'Azande theology', *Sudan Notes and Records* 19, 1–46
 (1937) *Witchcraft, Oracles and Magic among the Azande*. Oxford

Faraone, C. (1985) 'Aeschylus' ὕμνος δέσμιος (*Eum.* 306) and Attic judicial curse tablets', *JHS* 105, 150–4

 (1988) 'Hermes but no marrow: another look at a puzzling magical spell', *ZPE* 72, 279–86

 (1989) 'An accusation of magic in classical Athens (Ar. *Wasps* 946–948)', *TAPhA* 119, 149–61

 (1991a) 'Binding and burying the forces of evil: the defensive use of "voodoo dolls" in ancient Greece', *ClAnt* 10, 165–205

 (1991b) 'The agonistic context of early Greek binding spells', in Faraone and Obbink, 3–32

 (1992) *Talismans and Trojan Horses: Guardian Statues in Ancient Greek Myth and Ritual.* Oxford

 (1993) 'Molten wax, spilt wine and mutilated animals: sympathetic magic in Near Eastern and early Greek oath ceremonies', *JHS* 113, 60–80

 (1994) 'Deianira's mistake and the demise of Heracles: erotic magic in Sophocles' *Trachiniae*', *Helios* 21, 115–36

 (1999) *Ancient Greek Love Magic.* Cambridge, MA

Faraone, C. and Naiden, F. (eds.) (2012) *Greek and Roman Animal Sacrifice: Ancient Victims, Modern Observers.* Cambridge

Faraone, C. and Obbink, D. (eds.) (1991) *Magica Hiera: Ancient Greek Magic and Religion.* Oxford

Farnell, L. R. (1889) 'The origins and earliest development of Greek sculpture', *Archaeological Review* 2, 167–84

Farrington, A. (1997) 'Olympic victors and the popularity of the Olympic Games in the Imperial period', *Tyche* 12, 15–46

Feeney, D. (1998) *Literature and Religion at Rome: Cultures, Contexts, and Beliefs.* Cambridge

Felten, F. (1982) 'Weihungen in Olympia und Delphi', *MDAI(A)* 97, 79–97

Ferguson, W. S. (1932) *The Treasurers of Athena.* Cambridge, MA

Fernandez, J. W. (1982) *Bwiti: An Ethnography of the Religious Imagination in Africa.* Princeton, NJ

Festugière, A.-J. (1954) *Personal Religion Among the Greeks.* Berkeley, CA

 (1972) *Études de religion grecque et hellénistique.* Paris

Finley, M. I. (1973) *The Ancient Economy.* Berkeley, CA

 (1985) 'Foreword', in Easterling and Muir, xiii–xx

Finley, M. I. and Pleket, H. W. (1976) *The Olympic Games: The First Thousand Years.* London

Flint, V. I. J. (1999) 'The demonisation of magic and sorcery in late antiquity: Christian redefinitions of pagan religions', in Ankarloo and Clark, 277–348

Flinterman, J.-J. (1995) *Power, Paideia & Pythagoreanism: Greek Identity, Conceptions of the Relationship between Philosophers and Monarchs and Political Ideas in Philostratus' Life of Apollonius.* Amsterdam

 (2009) '"The ancestor of my wisdom": Pythagoras and Pythagoreanism in *Life of Apollonius*', in Bowie and Elsner, 155–75

Flower, M. (2008) *The Seer in Ancient Greece.* Berkeley, CA

Fögen, M. T. (1993) *Die Enteignung der Wahrsager: Studien zum kaiserlichen Wissensmonopol in der Spätantike.* Frankfurt

Fontenrose, J. (1978) *The Delphic Oracle: Its Responses and Operations with a Catalogue of Responses.* Berkeley, CA

Fornara, C. W. and Yates, D. C. (2007) 'FGrHist 328 (Philochorus) F181', *GRBS* 47, 31–7

Foucart, P. (1888) 'Les victoires en or de l'Acropole', *BCH* 11, 283–93

Foucault, M. (1985) *The History of Sexuality*, vol. 11: *The Use of Pleasure*, transl. R. Hurley. London (French orig. 1984)

Fowden, G. (1993) *The Egyptian Hermes: A Historical Approach to the Late Pagan Mind.* Princeton, NJ

Fowler, H. (2005) *A History of Greek Sculpture.* Norwood, MA

Fowler, R. L. (2000) 'Greek magic – Greek religion', in Buxton, 317–43 (first published in *ICS* 20 (1995), 1–22)

Fox, R. L. (1986) *Pagans and Christians in the Mediterranean World: From the Second Century* AD *to the Conversion of Constantine.* London

Francis, J. A. (1998) 'Truthful fiction: new questions to old answers on Philostratus' *Life of Apollonius*', *AJPh* 119, 419–41

Frankenberry, N. K. and Penner, H. H. (1999) 'Clifford Geertz's long-lasting moods, motivations, and metaphysical conceptions', *JR* 79, 617–40

Frankfurter, D. (1994) 'The magic of writing and the writing of magic: the power of the word in Egyptian and Greek traditions', *Helios* 21, 189–221

(1995) 'Narrating power: the theory and practice of the magical *Historiola* in ritual spells', in M. Meyer and P. Mirecki (eds.), *Ancient Magic and Ritual Power.* Leiden, 457–76

(1998) *Religion in Roman Egypt: Assimilation and Resistance.* Princeton, NJ

Fraser, P. (1972) *Ptolemaic Alexandria* (2 vols.). Oxford

Frazer, J. G. (1913) *The Golden Bough: A Study in Magic and Religion.* London

(1922) *The Golden Bough: A Study in Magic and Religion*, abridged edn. New York

Freedberg, D. (1989) *The Power of Images: Studies in the History and Theory of Response.* Chicago, IL

Freitag, K., Funke, P. and Haake, M. (eds.) (2006) *Kult – Politik – Ethnos: Überregionale Heiligtümer im Spannungsfeld von Kult und Politik.* Stuttgart

Friedrich, P. (1978) *The Meaning of Aphrodite.* Chicago, IL

Frontisi-Ducroux, F. (1996) 'Eros, desire, and the gaze', in Kampen, 81–100

Furtwängler, A. (1890) *Die Bronzen und die übrigen kleineren Funde von Olympia* (2 vols.). Berlin

Fustel de Coulanges, N. D. (1864) *La Cité antique.* Paris

Gadamer, H.-G. (1970) 'Über das Göttliche im frühen Denken der Griechen', in K. Gaiser (ed.), *Das Altertum und jedes neue Gute: Festschrift Wolfgang Schadewaldt.* Stuttgart, 397–414

Gager, J. (ed.) (1992) *Curse Tablets and Binding Spells from the Ancient World.* Oxford

Gaifman, M. (2006) 'Statue, cult, and reproduction', *Art History* 29, 258–79

(2010) 'Aniconism and the notion of the "primitive" in Greek antiquity', in Mylonopoulos, 63–86

Gallagher, E. V. (1982) *Divine Man or Magician? Celsus and Origen on Jesus.* Chicago, IL

Gallet de Santerre, H. (1959) *La Terrasse des lions, le Létoon et le monument de granit à Délos: publication topographique et architecturale.* Paris

García Teijeiro, M. (1993) 'Religion and magic', *Kernos* 6, 123–38

Garland, R. (1984) 'Religious authority in archaic and classical Athens', *ABSA* 79, 75–132

(1985) *The Greek Way of Death.* London

(1992) *Introducing New Gods: The Politics of Athenian Religion.* London

(1996) 'Strategies of religious intimidation and coercion in classical Athens', in Alroth and Hellström, 91–9

Gauer, W. (1968) *Weihgeschenke aus den Perserkriegen.* Tübingen

(1975) *Die Tongefässe aus den Brunnen unterm Stadion-Nordwall und im Südost-Gebiet* (Olympische Forschungen VIII). Berlin

Geertz, A. W. (2004) 'Cognitive approaches to the study of religion', in P. Antes, A. W. Geertz and R. R. Warne (eds.), *New Approaches to the Study of Religion*, vol. II: *Textual, Comparative, Sociological, and Cognitive Approaches.* Berlin, 347–99

Geertz, A. W. and Jensen, J. (eds.) (2010) *Religious Narrative, Cognition, and Culture: Image and Word in the Mind of Narrative.* London

Geertz, C. (1960) *The Religion of Java.* Glencoe, IL

(1963a) *Agricultural Involution, the Processes of Ecological Change in Indonesia.* Berkeley, CA

(1963b) *Peddlers and Princes.* Chicago, IL

(1968) *Islam Observed: Religious Development in Morocco and Indonesia.* Chicago, IL

(1973) *The Interpretation of Cultures: Selected Essays.* New York

(1980) 'Blurred genres: the refiguration of social thought', *The American Scholar* 49, 165–79

Gehrke, H.-J. (1986) *Jenseits von Athen und Sparta: das Dritte Griechenland und seine Staatenwelt.* Munich

Gellner, D. N. (1999) 'Religion, politics, and ritual: remarks on Geertz and Bloch', *Social Anthropology* 7, 135–53

Giangrande, G. (1978) 'Hermes and the marrow: a papyrus love spell', *AncSoc* 9, 101–16

Ginzburg, C. (1980) *The Cheese and the Worms: The Cosmos of a Sixteenth-Century Miller*, transl. A. and J. Tedeschi. Baltimore, MD (Italian orig. 1976)

Girard, R. (1977) *Violence and the Sacred*, transl. P. Gregory. Baltimore, MD (French orig. 1972)

Gladigow, B. (1979) 'Der Sinn der Götter: zum kognitiven Potential der persönlichen Gottesvorstellung', in P. Eicher (ed.), *Gottesvorstellung und Gesellschaftsentwicklung.* Munich, 41–62

(1985/1986) 'Präsenz der Bilder – Präsenz der Götter', *Visible Religion* 4/5, 114–33

Golden, M. (1998) *Sport and Society in Ancient Greece.* Cambridge

Goldhill, S. (1994) 'The naïve and the knowing eye: ecphrasis and the culture of viewing in the Hellenistic world', in S. Goldhill and R. Osborne (eds.), *Art and Text in Ancient Greek Culture*. Cambridge, 197–222

(1995) *Foucault's Virginity: Ancient Erotic Fiction and the History of Sexuality.* Cambridge

(1996) 'Refracting classical vision: changing cultures of viewing', in T. Brennan and M. Jay (eds.), *Vision in Context: Historical and Contemporary Perspectives on Sight*. New York, 16–28

(ed.) (2001a) *Being Greek under Rome: Cultural Identity, the Second Sophistic and the Development of the Empire*. Cambridge

(2001b) 'Setting an agenda: "everything is Greece to the wise"', in Goldhill 2001a, 1–26

(2001c) 'The erotic eye: visual stimulation and cultural conflict', in Goldhill 2001a, 154–94

(2007) 'What is ekphrasis for?', *CPh* 102, 1–19

Goldhill, S. and Osborne, R. (eds.) (1999) *Performance Culture and Athenian Democracy*. Cambridge

Goldman, A. (1986) *Epistemology and Cognition*. Cambridge, MA

Goodrum, M. R. (2002) 'Biblical anthropology and the idea of human prehistory in late antiquity', *History and Anthropology* 13, 69–78

Gordon, R. (1972) 'Fear or freedom? Selective continuity in religion during the Hellenistic period', *Didaskalos* 4, 48–60

(1979) 'The real and the imaginary: production and religion in the Graeco-Roman world', *Art History* 2, 5–34

(ed.) (1981) *Myth, Religion, and Society: Structuralist Essays by M. Detienne, L. Gernet, J.-P. Vernant and P. Vidal-Naquet*. Cambridge

(ed.) (1987) 'Aelian's peony: the location of magic in Graeco-Roman tradition', *Comparative Criticism* 9, 59–95

(1997) 'Reporting the marvellous: private divination in the Greek magical papyri', in Schäfer and Kippenberg, 65–92

(1999a) 'Imagining Greek and Roman magic', in Ankarloo and Clark, 161–275

(1999b) 'What's in a list? Listing in Greek and Graeco-Roman malign magical texts', in Jordan et al., 239–77

Gould, J. (1973) 'Hiketeia', *JHS* 93, 74–103

(2001) 'On making sense of Greek religion', in J. Gould, *Myth, Ritual, Memory, and Exchange: Essays in Greek Literature and Culture*. Oxford, 203–34 (first published in Easterling and Muir 1985, 1–33)

Graf, F. (1985a) *Griechische Mythologie: eine Einführung*. Munich

(1985b) *Nordionische Kulte: Religionsgeschichtliche und epigraphische Unter-suchungen zu den Kulten von Chios, Erythrai, Klazomenai und Phokaia*. Rome

(1991) 'Prayer in magic and religious ritual', in Faraone and Obbink, 188–213

(1994) *La Magie dans l'antiquité gréco-romaine: idéologie et pratique*. Paris

(1995a) 'Excluding the charming: the development of the Greek concept of magic', in Meyer and Mirecki (eds.), 29–42

(1995b) 'Umzüge und Prozessionen in der alten Welt', in F. Graf and E. Hornung (eds.), *Wanderungen*. Munich, 85–112

(1996a) *Gottesnähe und Schadenzauber: die Magie in der griechisch-römischen Antike*. Munich (see also Graf 1997a)

(1996b) '*Pompai* in Greece: some considerations about space and ritual in the Greek *polis*', in R. Hägg (ed.), *The Role of Religion in the Early Greek Polis*. Stockholm, 55–65

(1997a) *Magic in the Ancient World*, transl. F. Philip. Cambridge, MA (French orig. 1994)

(1997b) 'How to cope with a difficult life: a view of ancient magic', in Schäfer and Kippenberg, 93–114

(1999) 'Magic and divination', in Jordan et al., 283–98

(2001) 'Der Eigensinn der Götterbilder in antiken religiösen Diskursen', in G. Boehm (ed.), *Homo Pictor*. Munich, 227–43

(2002a) 'Augustine and magic', in Bremmer and Veenstra, 87–103

(2002b) 'Theories of magic in antiquity', in Meyer and Mirecki, 92–104

(2003) 'Initiation: a concept with a troubled history', in D. B. Dodd and C. Faraone (eds.), *Initiation in Ancient Greek Rituals*. London, 3–24

Graf, F. and Johnston, S. I. (2007) *Ritual Texts for the Afterlife: Orpheus and the Bacchic Gold Tablets*. London

Green, P. (1990) *Alexander to Actium: The Historical Evolution of the Hellenistic Age*. Berkeley, CA

(2004) *From Ikaria to the Stars: Classical Mythification, Ancient and Modern*. Austin, TX

Greenblatt, S. (1988) *Shakespearean Negotiations: The Circulation of Social Energy in Renaissance England*. London

(1990) 'Culture', in F. Lentricchia and T. McLaughlin (eds.), *Critical Terms for Literary Study*. Chicago, IL, 225–32

(1997) 'The touch of the real', *Representations* 59, 14–29

Gregory, C. A. (1980) 'Gifts to men and gifts to gods: gift exchange and capital accumulation in contemporary Papua', *Man* 15, 626–52

Griffiths, G. J. (2005) 'Hellenistic religions', in L. Jones, vol. VI, 3900–13

Gross, K. (1992) *The Dream of the Moving Statue*. New York

Grote, G. (1862) *History of Greece*, vol. I: *From the Earliest Period to the Close of the Generation Contemporary with Alexander the Great*. London

Guinan, A. G. (2002) 'A severed head laughed: stories of divinatory interpretation', in Ciraolo and Seidel, 7–40

Gulick, C. B. (ed.) (1950) *Athenaeus: The Deipnosophists*, vol. VI. Cambridge, MA

Günther, R. (1964) 'Der politisch-ideologische Kampf in der römischen Religion in den letzten zwei Jahrhunderten v. u. Z.' *Klio* 42, 209–97

Guthrie, S. (2001) 'Why gods? A cognitive theory', in J. Andresen (ed.) *Religion in Mind: Cognitive Perspectives on Religious Belief, Ritual, and Experience*. Cambridge, 94–111

(2007) 'Anthropology and anthropomorphism in religion', in Whitehouse and Laidlaw, 37–62

Guthrie, W. K. C. (1935) *Orpheus and Greek Religion: A Study of the Orphic Movement.* London

(1950) *The Greeks and Their Gods.* London

Habicht, C. (1957) 'Eine Urkunde des Akarnanischen Bundes', *Hermes* 85, 86–122

(1970) *Gottmenschentum und griechische Städte.* Munich

(1985) *Pausanias' Guide to Ancient Greece.* Berkeley, CA

(1997) *Athens from Alexander to Anthony*, transl. D. Schneider. Cambridge, MA (German orig. 1995)

Hägg, H. F. (2006) *Clement of Alexandria and the Beginnings of Christian Apophaticism.* Oxford

Hägg, R. (ed.) (1994) *Ancient Greek Cult Practice from the Epigraphical Evidence: Proceedings of the Second International Seminar on Ancient Greek Cult.* Stockholm.

Hall, E. (1989) *Inventing the Barbarian: Greek Self-Definition through Tragedy.* Oxford

Hall, J. (1997) *Ethnic Identity in Greek Antiquity.* Cambridge

(2002) *Hellenicity: Between Ethnicity and Culture.* Chicago, IL

Halliwell, S. (2005) 'Review of R. G. Edmonds: *Myths of the Underworld Journey: Plato, Aristophanes, and the 'Orphic' Gold Tablets'*, *Notre Dame Philosophical Reviews* 2005 (http://ndpr.nd.edu)

(2008) *Greek Laughter: A Study of Cultural Psychology from Homer to Christianity.* Cambridge

Hallof, K. (1990) 'Der Verkauf konfiszierten Vermögens vor den Poleten in Athen', *Klio* 72, 402–26

Halperin, D. M. (1990) 'Sex before sexuality: pederasty, politics, and power in classical Athens', in M. Duberman, M. Vicinus and G. Chauncey (eds.), *Hidden from History: Reclaiming the Gay and Lesbian Past.* New York, 37–53

(1992) 'Plato and the erotics of narrativity', in J. C. Klagge and N. D. Smith (eds.), *Methods of Interpreting Plato and his Dialogue.* Oxford, 93–130

Hammond, D. (1970) 'Magic: a problem in semantics', *American Anthropologist* 72, 1349–56

Hankinson, R. J. (1998) 'Magic, religion, and science', *Apeiron* 31, 1–34

Hansen, M. H. (1994) 'Poleis and city-states, 600–323 BC: a comprehensive research programme', in D. Whitehead (ed.), *From Political Architecture to Stephanus Byzantius: Sources for the Ancient Greek Polis.* Stuttgart, 9–17

(ed.) (2000) *A Comparative Study of Thirty City-State Cultures: An Investigation Conducted by the Copenhagen Polis Centre.* Copenhagen

(2006) *Polis: An Introduction to the Ancient Greek City-State.* Oxford

Hansen, M. H. and Nielsen, T. H. (eds.) (2004) *An Inventory of Archaic and Classical Poleis.* Oxford

Hansen, M. H. and Raaflaub, K. (eds.) (1995) *Studies in the Ancient Greek Polis.* Stuttgart

Harris, D. (1995) *The Treasures of the Parthenon and Erechtheion.* Oxford

Harrison, J. E. (1903) *Prolegomena to the Study of Greek Religion.* Cambridge
  (1905) *The Religion of Ancient Greece.* London
  (1912) *Themis: A Study of the Social Origins of Greek Religion.* Cambridge
Harrison, T. (2000) *Divinity and History: The Religion of Herodotus.* Oxford
  (2006) 'Religion and the rationality of the Greek city', in S. Goldhill and
  R. Osborne (eds.), *Rethinking Revolutions through Ancient Greece.* Cambridge,
  124–40
Hauser, K. (2008) 'Stained clothing, guilty hearts', in M. Uhlirova (ed.), *If Looks
  Could Kill.* London, 68–75
Hausmann, U. (ed.) (1977) *Der Tübinger Waffenläufer.* Tübingen
Hausrath, A. (1970) *Corpus Fabularum Aesopicarum*, vol. 1. Leipzig
Havelock, C. M. (2007) *The Aphrodite of Knidos and Her Successors: A Historical
  Review of the Female Nude in Greek Art.* Ann Arbor, MI
Heesterman, J. C. (1993) *The Broken World of Sacrifice: An Essay in Ancient Indian
  Ritual.* Chicago, IL
Heffernan, J. (1993) *Museum of Words: The Poetics of Ekphrasis from Homer to
  Ashbery.* Chicago, IL
Heilmeyer, W.-D. (1972) *Frühe Olympische Tonfiguren* (Olympische Forschungen
  VII). Berlin
  (1979) *Frühe Olympische Bronzefiguren: die Tiervotive* (Olympische Forschungen
  XII). Berlin
  (2004) 'Ancient workshops and ancient "art"', *OJA* 23, 403–15
Henderson, J. (ed.) (1998) *Aristophanes: Clouds, Wasps, Peace.* Cambridge, MA
Henrichs, A. (1993) '"He has a god in him": human and divine in the modern
  perception of Dionysos', in T. Karpenter and C. Faraone (eds.), *Masks of
  Dionysos.* Ithaca, NY, 13–43
  (2003) 'Writing religion: inscribed texts, ritual authority, and the religious dis-
  course of the polis', in H. Yunis (ed.), *Written Texts and the Rise of Literate
  Culture in Ancient Greece.* Cambridge, 38–58
  (2010) 'What is a Greek god', in J. Bremmer and A. Erskine (eds.), *The Gods of
  Ancient Greece: Identities and Transformations.* Edinburgh, 19–39
Henry, M. (1992) 'The edible woman: Athenaeus's concept of the pornographic',
  in A. Richlin (ed.), *Pornography and Representation in Greece and Rome.*
  Oxford, 250–68
Herington, C. J. (1955) *Athena Parthenos and Athena Polias: A Study in the Religion
  of Periclean Athens.* Manchester
Herrmann, H.-V. (1966) *Die Kessel der Orientalisierenden Zeit*, pt. 1: *Kesseltaschen
  und Reliefuntersätze* (Olympische Forschungen VI). Berlin
  (1972) *Olympia: Heiligtum und Wettkampfstätte.* Munich
  (1979) *Die Kessel der orientalisierenden Zeit*, pt. 2: *Kesselprotomen und Stab-
  dreifüsse* (Olympische Forschungen XI). Berlin
  (1988) 'Die Siegerstatuen von Olympia', *Nikephoros* 1, 119–83
Hersey, G. L. (2009) *Falling in Love with Statues: Artificial Humans from Pygmalion
  to the Present.* Chicago, IL

Hill, G. F., Meiggs, R. and Andrewes, A. (eds.) (1951) *Sources for Greek History: Between the Persian and Peloponnesian Wars, Collected and Arranged by G. F. Hill*, new edn. (ed. R. Meiggs and A. Andrews). Oxford

Himmelmann, N. (1990) *Ideale Nacktheit in der griechischen Kunst*. Berlin

Hintzen-Bohlen, B. (1992) *Herrscherrepräsentation im Hellenismus: Untersuchungen zu Weihgeschenken, Stiftungen und Ehrenmonumenten in den mutterländischen Heiligtümern Delphi, Olympia, Delos, und Dodona*. Vienna

Hirzel, R. (1902) *Der Eid: ein Beitrag zu seiner Geschichte*. Leipzig

van den Hoek, A. (1990) 'How Alexandrian was Clement of Alexandria', *The Heythrop Journal* 31, 179–94

Hölscher, F. (2010) 'Gods and statues – an approach to archaistic images in the fifth century BCE', in Mylonopoulos, 105–20

Hölscher, T. (2002) 'Rituelle Räume und politische Denkmäler im Heiligtum von Olympia', in H. Kyrieleis (ed.), *Olympia 1875–2000: 125 Jahre Deutsche Ausgrabungen*. Mainz, 331–45

Homolle, T. (1879) 'Statues trouvées à Délos', *BCH* 3, 99–110

Hönle, A. (1972) *Olympia in der Politik der griechischen Staatenwelt: von 776 bis zum Ende des 5. Jahrhunderts*. Bebenhausen

Hornblower, S. and Spawforth, A. (eds.) (2003) *The Oxford Classical Dictionary*, 3rd edn. rev. Oxford

Hughes, D. D. (1991) *Human Sacrifice in Ancient Greece*. London

Hull, J. M. (1974) *Hellenistic Magic and the Synoptic Tradition*. London

Humphreys, S. C. (1978) *Anthropology and the Greeks*. London

Hunter, R. L. (ed.) (2005) *The Hesiodic Catalogue of Women: Constructions and Reconstructions*. Cambridge

Hutton, W. (2005a) *Describing Greece: Landscape and Literature in the Periegesis of Pausanias*. Cambridge

   (2005b) 'The construction of religious space in Pausanias', in Elsner and Rutherford, 291–317

Hyde, W. W. (1912) 'The positions of victor statues at Olympia', *AJA* 16, 203–29

   (1921) *Olympic Victor Monuments and Greek Athletic Art*. Washington, DC

Instone, S. (2009) *Greek Personal Religion: A Reader*. Oxford

van Inwagen, P. (ed.) (2004) *Christian Faith and the Problem of Evil*. Grand Rapids, MI

   (2006) *The Problem of Evil*. Oxford

Ioakimidou, C. (1997) *Die Statuenreihen griechischer Poleis und Bünde aus spätarchaischer und klassischer Zeit*. Munich

Jacobson, R. (1987) 'The statue in Pushkin's poetic mythology', in K. Pomorska and S. Rudy (eds.), *Language in Literature: Roman Jakobson*. Cambridge, MA, 318–67

Jaeger, W. (1947) *The Theology of the Early Greek Philosophers*. Oxford

   (1961) *Early Christianity and Greek Paideia*. Cambridge, MA

Jameson, M. H. (1997) 'Religion in the Athenian democracy', in I. Morris and K. Raaflaub (eds.), *Democracy 2500? Questions and Challenges*. Dubuque, IA, 171–95

(1999) 'The spectacular and the obscure in Athenian religion', in Goldhill and Osborne, 321–40

Janowitz, N. (2001) *Magic in the Roman World: Pagans, Jews and Christians*. London

Jantzen, U. (ed.) (1976) *Neue Forschungen in griechischen Heiligtümern*. Tübingen

Janzen, D. (2004) *The Social Meanings of Sacrifice in the Hebrew Bible: A Study of Four Writings*. Berlin

Jeanmaire, H. (1951) *Dionysos: histoire du culte de Bacchus*. Paris

Johns, C. (1982) *Sex or Symbol? Erotic Images of Greece and Rome*. London

Johnston, S. I. (1999) *Restless Dead: Encounters between the Living and the Dead in Ancient Greece*. Berkeley, CA

(2001) 'Charming children: the use of the child in ancient divination', *Arethusa* 34, 97–117

(2008a) *Ancient Greek Divination*. London

(2008b) 'Animating statues: a case study in ritual theory', *Arethusa* 41, 445–77

Johnston, S. I. and Struck, P. (eds.) (2005) *Mantikē: Studies in Ancient Divination*. Leiden

Johnston, S. I. et al. (1999) 'Panel discussion: *Magic in the Ancient World* by Fritz Graf', *Numen* 46, 291–325

Jones, C. (1984) 'Tarsos in the *Amores* ascribed to Lucian', *GRBS* 25, 177–81

(1986) *Culture and Society in Lucian*. Cambridge, MA

(1996) 'The Panhellenion', *Chiron* 26, 29–56

(2001) 'Pausanias and his guides', in Alcock et al., 33–9

(ed.) (2005) *Philostratus: The Life of Apollonius of Tyana* (2 vols.). Cambridge, MA

Jones, L. (ed.) (2005) *Encyclopedia of Religion*, 2nd edn. (15 vols.). Detroit, MI

Jones, W. H. S. (ed.) (1923) *Hippocrates*, vol. II. Cambridge, MA

Jones, W. H. S. and Omerod, H. A. (ed.) (1926) *Pausanias: Description of Greece*, vol. II. Cambridge, MA

De Jong, A. (1997) *Traditions of the Magi: Zoroastrianism in Greek and Latin*. Leiden

Jordan, D. R. (1975) 'A curse tablet from a well in the Athenian agora', *ZPE* 9, 245–8

(1980) 'Two inscribed lead tablets from a well in the Athenian Kerameikos', *MDAI(A)* 95, 225–39

(1985a) 'A survey of Greek defixiones not included in the special corpora', *GRBS* 26, 151–97

(1985b) 'Defixiones from a well near the southwest corner of the Athenian agora', *Hesperia* 54, 205–55

(1988) 'New archaeological evidence for the practice of magic in classical Athens', in *Praktika of the 12th International Congress of Classical Archaeology, Athens, September 4–10 1983*, vol. IV. Athens, 273–7

(1994) 'Inscribed lead tablets from the games in the sanctuary of Poseidon', *Hesperia* 63, 111–26

(1995) 'A curse tablet against opponents at law', in A. Boegehold (ed.), *The Lawcourts at Athens: Sites, Buildings, Equipment, Procedure and Testimonia*. Princeton, NJ, 55–7

(2000) 'New Greek curse tablets (1985–2000)', *GRBS* 41, 5–46

(2004) 'Towards the text of a curse tablet from the Kerameikos', in A. P. Matthaiou and G. E. Malouchou (eds.), Ἀττικαὶ Ἐπιγραφαί· Πρακτικὰ Συμποσίου εἰς μνήμην Adolf Wilhelm (1864–1950). Athens, 291–312

Jordan, D. R. and Rotroff, S. I. (1999) 'A curse in a chytridion: a contribution to the study of Athenian pyres', *Hesperia* 68, 147–54

Jordan, D. R., Montgomery, H. and Thomassen, E. (eds.) (1999) *The World of Ancient Magic: Papers from the First International Samson Eitrem Seminar at the Norwegian Institute at Athens, 4–8 May 1997*. Bergen

Kagarow, E. G. (1922) 'Form und Stil der Texte der Fluchtafeln', *Archiv für Religionswissenschaft* 21, 494–7

(1929) *Griechische Fluchtafeln*. Paris

Kampen, N. (ed.) (1996) *Sexuality in Ancient Art: Near East, Egypt, Greece, and Italy*. Cambridge

(1997) 'Epilogue: gender and desire', in Koloski-Ostrow and Lyons, 267–77

Katz, M. A. (1989) 'Sexuality and the body in ancient Greece', *Métis* 4, 155–79

Kavoulaki, A. (1999) 'Processual performance and the democratic polis', in Goldhill and Osborne, 293–320

Keaney, J. (1991) *Harpocration: Lexeis of the Ten Orators*. Amsterdam

Kearns, E. (2010) *Ancient Greek Religion: A Sourcebook*. Malden, MA

Kee, H. C. (1986) *Medicine, Miracle and Magic in New Testament Times*. Cambridge

Keesling, C. (2003) *The Votive Statues of the Athenian Acropolis*. Cambridge

Kelly, J. D. and Kaplan, M. (1990) 'History, structure, and ritual', *Annual Review of Anthropology* 19, 119–50

Kenney, J. P. (1987) 'Divinity and the intelligible world in Clement of Alexandria', *Studia Patristica* 21, 308–15

Keuls, E. C. (1985) *The Reign of the Phallus: Sexual Politics in Ancient Greece*. New York

Kilian-Dirlmeier, I. (1985) 'Fremde Weihungen in griechischen Heiligtümern vom 8. bis zum Beginn des 7. Jahrhunderts v. Chr.', *JRGZ* 32, 215–54

Kindt, J. (2006) 'Delphic oracle stories and the beginning of historiography: Herodotus' *Croesus logos*', *CPh* 101, 34–51

(2007) 'Apollo's oracle in Euripides' *Ion*: ambiguous identities in fifth-century Athens', *AN* 6, 1–30

(2008) 'Oracular ambiguity as a mediation triple', *Classicum* 334, 23–7

(2009) 'Religion', in Boys-Stones et al., 364–77

(2011) 'Ancient Greece', in T. Insoll (ed.), *The Oxford Handbook of the Archaeology of Ritual and Religion*. Oxford, 696–709

Kingsley, P. (1995) *Ancient Philosophy, Mystery, and Magic: Empedocles and Pythagorean Tradition*. Oxford

Kippenberg, H. G. (1985/1986) 'Introduction: approaches to iconology', *Visible Religion* 4/5, vii–x

Kirch, P. V. and Sahlins, M. (1992) *Anahulu: The Anthropology of History in the Kingdom of Hawaii*. Chicago, IL

Kirk, G. S. (1985) *The Songs of Homer*. Cambridge

Kluckhohn, C. (1961) *Anthropology and the Classics*. Providence, RI

Koenigs, W. (1984) *Die Echohalle* (Olympische Forschungen xiv). Berlin

Kolenkow, A. B. (2002) 'Persons of power and their communities', in Ciraolo Seidel, 133–44

Koller, H. (1957) '*Theoros* und *Theoria*', *Glotta* 36, 273–86

Koloski-Ostrow, A. O. and Lyons, C. L. (eds.) (1997) *Naked Truths: Women, Sexuality, and Gender in Classical Art and Archaeology*. London

König, J. (2005) *Athletics and Literature in the Roman Empire*. Cambridge

Konstan, D. (1994) *Sexual Symmetry: Love in the Ancient Novel and Related Genres*. Princeton, NJ

Koskenniemi, E. (1991) *Der philostrateische Apollonios*. Helsinki

Koster, W. (ed.) (1978) *Scholia in Aristophanem II.1: Scholia in Vespas, Pacem, Aves et Lysistratam. Fasc.1 continens scholia vetera et recentiora in Aristophanis Vespas*. Groningen

Kotansky, R. (1991) 'Incantations and prayers for salvation on inscribed Greek amulets', in Faraone and Obbink, 107–37

(1994) *Greek Magical Amulets: The Inscribed Gold, Silver, Copper and Bronze Lamellae*, pt. 1: *Published Texts of Known Provenance*. Opladen

(1995) 'Greek exorcistic amulets', in Meyer and Mirecki, 243–77

Kowalzig, B. (1995) 'Mapping out communitas: performances of theoria in their sacred and political context', in Elsner and Rutherford, 41–72

(2007) *Singing for the Gods: Performances of Myth and Ritual in Archaic and Classical Greece*. Oxford

von Krafft-Ebing, R. (1945) *Psychopathia Sexualis: A Medico-Forensic Study*, transl. F. Klaf. New York (German orig. 1886)

Krentz, P. (1979) '*SEG* XXI, 80 and the rule of the thirty', *Hesperia* 48, 54–63

Kunze, E. (1940) 'Zeus und Ganymedes: eine Terrakottagruppe aus Olympia', in *Hundertstes Winckelmannsprogramm der archäologischen Gesellschaft zu Berlin*. Berlin, 25–50

(1946) 'Zeusbilder in Olympia', *A&A* 2, 95–113

(1956) *Bericht über die Ausgrabungen in Olympia*, vol. v. Berlin

(1958) *Bericht über die Ausgrabungen in Olympia*, vol. vi. Berlin

(1961) *Bericht über die Ausgrabungen in Olympia*, vol vii. Berlin

(1967) *Bericht über die Ausgrabungen in Olympia*, vol. viii. Berlin

(1991) *Beinschienen* (Olympische Forschungen xxi). Berlin

(1994) *Bericht über die Ausgrabungen in Olympia*, vol. ix. Berlin

Kuper, A. (1999) 'Clifford Geertz: culture as religion and as grand opera', in *Culture: The Anthropologist's Account*. Cambridge, 75–121

Kurke, L. (1991) *The Traffic in Praise: Pindar and the Poetics of the Social Economy*. Ithaca, NY

Kurtz, D. C. and Boardman, J. (1971) *Greek Burial Customs*. London

Kyle, D. G. (1996) 'Gifts and glory: panathenaic and other Greek athletic prizes', in Neils, 106–36

(2007) *Sport and Spectacle in the Ancient World*. Malden, MA

Kyrieleis, H. (2003) *Bericht über die Ausgrabungen in Olympia*, vol. XII. Berlin

(2006) *Anfänge und Frühzeit des Heiligtums von Olympia: die Ausgrabungen am Pelopion 1987–1996* (Olympische Forschungen XXXI). Berlin

Lalonde, G. V., Langdon, M. K. and Walbank, M. (1991) *The Athenian Agora*, vol. IXX: *Inscriptions – Horoi, Poletai Records, Leases of Public Lands*. Princeton, NJ

Lambert, M. (1998) 'Magic and religion', *Scholia* 7, 136–42

Lamour, D. H. J. (1999) *Stage and Stadium: Drama and Athletics in Ancient Greece*. Hildesheim

Langdon, M. (1994) 'Public auctions in ancient Athens', in R. Osborne and S. Hornblower (eds.), *Ritual, Finance, Politics: Athenian Democratic Accounts Presented to David Lewis*. Oxford, 253–65

Langdon, S. (1987) 'Gift exchange in the Geometric sanctuaries', in Linders Nordquist, 107–13

Lapatin, K. (2001) *Chryselephantine Statuary in the Ancient Mediterranean World*. Oxford

Laskaris, J. (2002) *The Art is Long: On the Sacred Disease and the Scientific Tradition*. Leiden

Latte, K. (1920) *Heiliges Recht: Untersuchungen zur Geschichte der sakralen Rechtsformen in Griechenland*. Tübingen

Lattimore, S. (1988) 'The nature of early Greek victor statues', in S. J. Bandy (ed.), *Coroebus Triumphs: The Alliance of Sport and the Humanities*. San Diego, CA, 245–56

Lawson, E. T. and McCauley, R. (1990) *Rethinking Religion: Connecting Cognition and Culture*. Cambridge

Lazzarini, M. L. (1976) *Le formule delle dediche votive nella Grecia arcaica*. Atti della Accademia Nazionale dei Lincei, 373. Memorie. Classe di Scienze Morali, Storiche e Filologiche, ser. 8, vol. IXX, fasc. 2. Rome

Lechat, H. (1889) 'Inscription imprécatoire trouvée à Athènes', *BCH* 13, 77–80

Lenz, F. (1964) 'Die Selbstverteidigung eines politischen Angeklagten: Untersuchungen zu der Rede des Apollonios von Tyana bei Philostratos', *Altertum* 10, 95–110

Lévi-Strauss, C. (1969) *The Raw and the Cooked: Introduction to a Science of Mythology*, vol. I: transl. J. and D. Weightman. New York (French orig. 1964)

Lewis, D. L. (1966) 'After the profanation of the mysteries', in E. Badian (ed.), *Ancient Society and Institutions: Studies Presented to Victor Ehrenberg on his 75th Birthday*. Oxford, 177–91

Lewis, N. (1983) *Life in Egypt under Roman Rule*. Oxford

Lhôte, E. (2006) *Les Lamelles oraculaires de Dodone*. Geneva

Liebeschuetz, J. (1979) *Continuity and Change in Roman Religion*. Oxford

Lilla, S. R. C. (1971) *Clement of Alexandria: A Study in Christian Platonism and Gnosticism*. Oxford

Lindbeck, G. A. (1984) *The Nature of Doctrine: Religion and Theology in a Postliberal Age*. London

Linders, T. (1987) 'Gods, gifts, society', in Linders and Nordquist, 115–22

Linders, T. and Nordquist, G. (eds.) (1987) *Gifts to the Gods: Proceedings of the Uppsala Symposium 1985*. Uppsala

Linforth, I. M. (1941) *The Arts of Orpheus*. Berkeley, CA

Lissarrague, F. (1994) 'Women, boxes, containers: some signs and metaphors', in E. D. Reeder (ed.), *Pandora: Women in Classical Greece*. Princeton, NJ, 91–101

Lloyd, G. E. R. (1979) *Magic, Reason, and Experience: Studies in the Origin and Development of Greek Science*. Cambridge

  (1983) *Science, Folklore and Ideology*. Cambridge

  (1987) *The Revolutions of Wisdom: Studies in the Claims and Practice of Ancient Greek Science*. Berkeley, CA

Lloyd, M. (1987) 'Cleobis and Biton (Herodotus 1.31)', *Hermes* 115, 22–8

Lloyd-Jones, H. (1956) 'Zeus in Aeschylus', *JHS* 76, 55–67

  (1971) *The Justice of Zeus*. Berkeley, CA

  (ed.) (1994) *Sophocles: Ajax, Electra, Oedipus Tyrannus*. Cambridge, MA

Loraux, N. (1993) *The Children of Athena: Athenian Ideas about Citizenship and the Division between the Sexes*, transl. C. Levine. Princeton, NJ (French orig. 1984)

Lowe, J. E. (1929) *Magic in Greek and Latin Literature*. Oxford

Luck, G. (1962) *Hexen und Zauberei in der römischen Dichtung*. Zurich

  (1990) *Magie und andere Geheimlehren in der Antike*. Stuttgart

  (2000) *Ancient Pathways and Hidden Pursuits: Religion, Morals, and Magic in the Ancient World*. Ann Arbor, MI

  (2006) *Arcana Mundi: Magic and the Occult in the Greek and Roman Worlds*, 2nd edn. Baltimore, MD

Lycan, W. G. (ed.) (1999) *Mind and Cognition: An Anthology*, 2nd edn. Malden, MA

Maas, M. (1992) 'Frühe Weihgaben in Delphi und Olympia als Zeugnisse für die Geschichte der Heiligtümer', in J.-F. Bommelaer (ed.), *Delphes: centenaire de la 'grande fouille' réalisée par l'École Française d'Athènes*. Leiden, 85–93

Mack, B. (1987) 'Introduction: religion and ritual', in R. G. Hamerton-Kelly (ed.), *Violent Origins: Walter Burkert, René Girard, and Jonathan Z. Smith on Ritual Killing and Cultural Formation*. Stanford, CA, 1–70

Macleod, M. D. (ed.) (1967) *Lucian*, vol. VIII. Cambridge, MA

Macmullen, R. (1966) *Enemies of the Roman Order: Treason, Unrest, and Alienation in the Empire*. Cambridge, MA

  (1981) *Paganism in the Roman Empire*. New Haven, CT

  (1984) *Christianizing the Roman Empire AD 100–400*. New Haven, CT

Malinowski, B. (1954) *Magic, Science, Religion and Other Essays*. New York (first published 1948)

Mallwitz, A. (1972) *Olympia und seine Bauten*. Munich

  (1988) 'Cult and competition locations at Olympia', in Raschke, 79–109

Mallwitz, A. and Herrmann, H.-V. (1980) *Funde aus Olympia*. Athens

Marcadé, J. (1969) *Au musée de Délos: étude sur la sculpture hellénistique en ronde bosse découverte dans l'île.* Paris

Marinatos, N. (1986) *Minoan Sacrificial Ritual: Cult Practice and Symbolism.* Athens

(1993) *Minoan Religion: Ritual, Image, and Symbol.* Columbia, SC

(1995) 'What were Greek sanctuaries? A synthesis', in Marinatos and Hägg, 228–33

Marinatos, N. and Hägg, R. (eds.) (1995) *Greek Sanctuaries: New Approaches.* London

Martin, L. H. (1987) *Hellenistic Religions: An Introduction.* New York

Martin, M. (2005) *Magie et magiciens dans le monde gréco-romain.* Paris

Martin, T. R. (2000) *Ancient Greece: From Prehistoric to Hellenistic Times.* New Haven, CT

Marvin, M. (1993) 'Copying in Roman sculpture: the replica series', in E. D'Ambra (ed.), *Roman Art in Context: An Anthology.* Upper Saddle River, NJ, 161–88

Mattusch, C. C. (1988) *Greek Bronze Statuary.* Ithaca, NY

Maurizio, L. (1993) 'Delphic Narratives: Recontextualizing the Pythia and her Prophecies'. (PhD dissertation). Ann Arbor, MI

(1998) 'The panathenaic procession: Athens' participatory democracy on display?', in D. Boedeker and K. Raaflaub (eds.), *Democracy, Empire, and the Arts in Fifth-Century Athens.* Cambridge, MA, 297–317

Mauss, M. (1972) *A General Theory of Magic.* London

Mazarakis Ainian, A. (1985) 'Contribution à l'étude de l'architecture religieuse grecque des âges obscures', *AC* 54, 5–48

(1988) 'Early Greek temples: their origin and function', in R. Hägg, N. Marinatos and G. C. Nordquist (eds.), *Early Greek Cult Practice: Proceedings of the Fifth International Symposium at the Swedish Institute at Athens, 26–29 June 1986.* Stockholm, 105–19

(1997) *From Rulers' Dwellings to Temples: Architecture, Religion and Society in Early Iron Age Greece (1100–700 BC).* Jonsered

McInerney, J. (1999) *The Folds of Parnassos: Land and Ethnicity in Ancient Phokis.* Austin, TX

McLelland, J. C. (1976) *God the Anonymous: A Study in Alexandrian Philosophical Theology.* Cambridge, MA

Meiggs, R. and Lewis, D. (eds.) (1988) *A Selection of Greek Historical Inscriptions to the End of the Fifth Century BC*, rev. edn. Oxford

Mendels, D. (1998) *Identity, Religion and Historiography: Studies in Hellenistic History.* Sheffield

Meyer, E. (1924) 'Apollonios von Tyana und die Biographie des Philostratos', in E. Meyer, *Kleine Schriften*, vol. II. Halle, 131–91 (first published in *Hermes* 52 (1917), 371–434)

Meyer, M. and Mirecki, P. (ed.) (1995) *Ancient Magic and Ritual Power.* Leiden

(2002) *Magic and Ritual in the Ancient World.* Leiden

Mikalson, J. (1983) *Athenian Popular Religion.* Chapel Hill, NC

(1991) *Honor Thy Gods: Popular Religion in Greek Tragedy.* Chapel Hill, NC

(1998) *Religion in Hellenistic Athens*. Berkeley, CA

(2005) *Ancient Greek Religion*. London

Millar, F. G. B. (1981) 'The world of the *Golden Ass*', *JRS* 71, 63–75

Miller, M. C. (1992) 'The parasol: an oriental status-symbol in late Archaic and Classical Athens', *JHS* 112, 91–105

Miller, S. G. (2004) *Ancient Greek Athletics*. New Haven, CT

Minchin, E. (2001) *Homer and the Resources of Memory: Some Applications of Cognitive Theory to the Iliad and the Odyssey*. Oxford

Mitchell, L. (2007) *Panhellenism and the Barbarian in Archaic and Classical Greece*. Swansea

Mitchell, W. J. T. (1986) *Iconology: Image, Text, Ideology*. Chicago, IL

Mondésert, C. (1944) *Clément d'Alexandrie: introduction à l'étude de sa pensée religieuse à partir de l'écriture*. Paris

Moreau, A. and Turpin, J.-C. (eds.) (2000) *La Magie du monde babylonien au monde hellénistique*, vol. 1. Montpellier

Morgan, C. (1990) *Athletes and Oracles: The Transformation of Olympia and Delphi in the Eighth Century BC*. Cambridge

(1994) 'The evolution of a sacral "landscape": Isthmia, Perachova and the early Corinthian state', in Alcock and Osborne, 105–42

(1995) 'The origins of pan-Hellenism', in Marinatos and Hägg, 18–44

(2003) *Early Greek States Beyond the Polis*. London

Morgan, J. (1977) 'Religion and culture as meaning systems: a dialogue between Geertz and Tillich', *JR* 57, 363–75

Morgan, K. A. (ed.) (2003) *Popular Tyranny: Sovereignty and its Discontents in Ancient Greece*. Austin, TX

Morris, I. (1987) *Burial and Ancient Society: The Rise of the Greek City-State*. Cambridge

(1992) *Death-Ritual and Social Structure in Classical Antiquity*. Cambridge

(1993) 'Poetics of power: the interpretation of ritual action in archaic Greece', in C. Dougherty and L. Kurke (eds.), *Cultural Poetics in Archaic Greece*. Cambridge, 15–45

(1994) *Classical Greece: Ancient Histories and Modern Archaeologies*. Cambridge

(2000) *Archaeology as Cultural History: Words and Things in Iron Age Greece*. Malden, MA

Mortley, R. (1973) *Connaissance religieuse et herméneutique chez Clément d'Alexandrie*. Leiden

Motte, A. (1987) 'Pèlerinages de la Grèce antique', in J. Chelini and H. Branhomme (eds.), *Histoire des pèlerinages non chrétiens: entre magique et sacré*. Paris, 94–135

(2000) 'À propos de la magie chez Platon: l'antithèse sophiste-philosophe vue sous l'angle de la pharmacie et de la sorcellerie', in Moreau and Turpin, 267–92

Moustaka, A. (1993) *Grossplastik aus Ton in Olympia* (Olympische Forschungen XXII). Berlin

Muckle, J. T. (1951) 'Clement of Alexandria on philosophy as a divine testament for the Greeks', *Phoenix* 5, 79–86

Munson, H. (1986) 'Geertz on religion: the theory and the practice', *Religion* 16, 19–32

Murphy, M. G. (1941) *Nature Allusions in the Works of Clement of Alexandria.* Washington, DC

Murray, G. (1912) *Four Stages of Greek Religion.* New York
  (1925) *Five Stages of Greek Religion.* Oxford

Murray, O. (1997) 'Rationality and the Greek city: the evidence from Kamarina', in M. H. Hansen (ed.), *The Polis as an Urban Centre and as a Political Community: Symposium 29–31 August 1996*, Acts of the Copenhagen Polis Centre 4. Copenhagen, 493–504

Murray, O. and Price, S. (eds.) (1990) *The Greek City from Homer to Alexander.* Oxford

Mylonopoulos, J. (ed.) (2010) *Divine Images and Human Imaginations in Ancient Greece and Rome.* Leiden

Nagy, G. (1979) *The Best of the Achaeans: Concepts of the Hero in Archaic Greek Poetry.* Baltimore, MD

Neer, R. (2007) 'Delphi, Olympia, and the art of politics', in A. Shapiro (ed.), *The Cambridge Companion to Archaic Greece.* Cambridge, 225–64
  (2010) *The Emergence of the Classical Style in Greek Sculpture.* Chicago, IL

Neils, J. (ed.) (1992) *Goddess and Polis: The Panathenaic Festival in Classical Athens.* Princeton, NJ
  (1996a) 'Pride, pomp, and circumstance: the iconography of procession', in Neils, 177–97
  (1996b) *Worshipping Athena: Panathenaia and Parthenon.* London

Neumer-Pfau, W. (1982) *Studien zur Ikonographie und Gesellschaftsfunktion hellenistischer Aphrodite Statuen.* Bonn

Newby, Z. (2005) *Greek Athletics in the Roman World: Victory and Virtue.* Oxford

Nicholson, N. J. (2005) *Aristocracy and Athletics in Archaic and Classical Greece.* Cambridge

Nielsen, T. H. (2007) *Olympia and the Classical Hellenic City-State Culture.* Copenhagen

Nightingale, A.W. (2004) *Spectacles of Truth in Classical Greek Philosophy: Theoria in its Cultural Context.* Cambridge

van Nijf, O. (2001) 'Local heroes: athletics, festivals and elite self-fashioning in the Roman East', in Goldhill (ed.), 306–34

Nilsson, M. P. (1951) Die Prozessionstypen im griechischen Kult: mit einem Anhang über die Dionysischen Prozessionen in Athen', *Opuscula Selecta*, vol. I. Lund, 166–214 (first published in *JDAI* 31 (1916), 309–39)
  (1952) 'Early orphism and kindred religious movements', in *Opuscula Selecta*, vol. II. Lund, 628–83 (first published in *HThR* 28 (1935), 181–230)

Nock, A. D. (1972a) 'Notes on the ruler cult I–IV', in Stewart, 134–59 (first published in *JHS* 48(1928), 21–43)
  (1972b) 'Paul and the magus', in Stewart, 308–30 (first published in F. J. Foakes-Jackson and K. Lake (eds.), *The Beginnings of Christianity*, vol. V. London, 1933, 164–88)

Norman, L. and Roberts, G. (eds.) (2000) *Witchcraft in Early Modern Scotland*. Exeter

Ober, J. (1989) *Mass and Elite in Democratic Athens: Rhetoric, Ideology, and Power of the People*. Princeton, NJ

(2005) *Athenian Legacies: Essays on the Politics of Going on Together*. Princeton, NJ

Oehler, K. (1984) 'Democrit über Zeichen und Bezeichnung aus der Sicht der modernen Semiotik', in L. Benakis (ed.), *Proceedings of the First International Conference on Democritus*. Xanthi, 177–87

Ogden, D. (1999) 'Binding spells: curse tablets and voodoo dolls in the Greek and Roman worlds', in Ankarloo and Clark, 1–90

(2001) *Greek and Roman Necromancy*. Princeton, NJ

(2002) *Magic, Witchcraft, and Ghosts in the Greek and Roman Worlds: A Sourcebook*. Oxford

(2008) *Night's Black Agents: Witches, Wizards and the Dead in the Ancient World*. London

Ortner, S. B. (1997) 'Thick resistance: death and the cultural construction of agency in Himalayan mountaineering', *Representations* 59, 135–62

Osborn, E. F. (1957) *The Philosophy of Clement of Alexandria*. Cambridge

Osborne, R. (1988) 'Death revisited, death revised: the death of the artist in archaic and classical Greece', *Art History* 11, 1–15

(1994) 'Looking on – Greek style: does the sculptured girl speak to women too?', in Morris, 81–96

(1998) *Archaic and Classical Greek Art*. Oxford

(2004) 'Hoards, votives, offerings: the archaeology of the dedicated object', *World Archaeology* 36, 1–10

(2010) 'The ecstasy and the tragedy: varieties of religious experience in art, drama, and society', in R. Osborne, *Athens and Athenian Democracy*. Oxford, 368–404 (first printed in C. Pelling (ed.) *Greek Tragedy and the Historian*. Oxford (1997), 187–220)

(2011) *The History Written on the Classical Body*. Cambridge

O'Sullivan, P. (2002) 'Victor statue, victory song: Pindar's agonistic poetics and its legacy', in D. J. Phillips and D. Pritchard (eds.), *Sport and Festival in the Ancient Greek World*. Swansea, 75–100

Pakkanen, P. (1996) *Interpreting Early Hellenistic Religion: A Study Based on the Mystery Cult of Demeter and the Cult of Isis*. Helsinki

Pals, D. (1996) *Seven Theories of Religion*. New York

Papalexandrou, N. (2005) *The Visual Poetics of Power: Warriors, Youths, and Tripods in Early Greece*. Lanham, MD

Parke, H. W. (1967) *The Oracles of Zeus: Dodona, Olympia, Ammon*. Oxford

Parker, Richard (1985) 'From symbolism to interpretation: reflections on the work of Clifford Geertz', *Anthropology and Humanism Quarterly* 10, 62–7

Parker, Robert (1983) *Miasma: Pollution and Purification in Early Greek Religion*. Oxford

(1995) 'Early orphism', in A. Powell (ed.), *The Greek World*. London, 483–510

(1996) *Athenian Religion: A History*. Oxford

(1997) 'Gods cruel and kind: tragic and civic theology', in C. Pelling (ed.), *Greek Tragedy and the Historian*. Oxford, 143–60

(1998a) *Cleomenes on the Acropolis: An Inaugural Lecture Delivered before the University of Oxford on 12 May 1997*. Oxford

(1998b) 'Pleasing thighs: reciprocity in Greek religion', in C. Gill, N. Postlethwaite and R. Seaford (eds.), *Reciprocity in Ancient Greece*. Oxford, 105–25

(2005) *Polytheism and Society at Athens*. Oxford

(2011) *On Greek Religion*. Ithaca, NY

Parry, H. (1992) *Thelxis: Magic and Imagination in Greek Myth and Poetry*. Lanham, MD

Parsons, T. (1937) *The Structure of Social Action: A Study in Social Theory with Special Reference to a group of Recent European Writers*, vol. 1. New York

Paton, W. R. (ed.) (1918) *The Greek Anthology*, vol. v. Cambridge, MA

Patterson, L. G. (1997) 'The divine became human: Irenaean themes in Clement of Alexandria', *Studia Patristica* 31, 497–516

Pearson, B. A. (1986) 'Christians and Jews in first-century Alexandria', *HThR* 79, 206–16

Pedley, J. (2002) *Greek Art and Archaeology*, 3rd edn. London

(2005) *Sanctuary and the Sacred in the Ancient Greek World*. Cambridge

Peek, W. (1941) *Kerameikos: Ergebnisse der Ausgrabungen III: Inschriften, Ostraka, Fluchtafeln*. Berlin

Peim, O. (2000) 'Die Siegerstatuen von Schwerathleten in Olympia und ihre Zusammenstellung durch Pausanias', *Nikephoros* 13, 95–109

Perniola, M. (2004) *The Sex Appeal of the Inorganic: Philosophies of Desire in the Modern Word*, transl. M. Verdicchio. New York (Italian orig. 2000)

Pfanner, M. (1989) 'Über das Herstellen von Porträts: ein Beitrag zu Rationalisierungsmaßnahmen und Produktionsmechanismen von Massenwahre im späten Hellenismus und in der römischen Kaiserzeit', *JDAI* 104, 157–257

Pfister, F. (1938) 'Albrecht Dieterichs Wirken in der Religionswissenschaft: zu seinem 30. Todestag', *Archiv für Religionswissenschaft* 35, 180–5

Philipp, H. (1981) *Bronzeschmuck aus Olympia* (Olympische Forschungen XIII). Berlin

Phillips, C. R. (1991) 'Nullum crimen sine lege: socio-religious sanctions on magic', in Faraone and Obbink, 220–76

Pirenne-Delforge, V. (2008) *Retour à la source: Pausanias et la religion grecque*. Liège

Platt, V. (2002) 'Viewing, desiring, believing: confronting the divine in a Pompeian house', *Art History* 25, 87–112

(2009) 'Virtual visions: *phantasia* and the perception of the divine in *The Life of Apollonius* of Tyana', in Bowie and Elsner, 131–54

(2011) *Facing the Gods: Epiphany and Representation in Graeco-Roman Art, Literature and Religion*. Cambridge

Plescia, J. (1970) *The Oath and Perjury in Ancient Greece*. Tallahassee, FL

de Polignac, F. (1995a) *Cults, Territory and the Origin of the Greek City State*, 2nd edn., transl. J. Lloyd. Chicago, IL (French orig. 1984)

(1995b) 'Repenser la "cité"? Rituels et société en Grèce archaïque', in Hansen and Raaflaub, 7–19

(1996) 'Offrandes, mémoire et compétition ritualisée dans les sanctuaires grecs à l'époque géometrique', in Alroth and Hellström, 59–66

(2009) 'Sanctuaries and festivals', in H. van Wees and K. Raaflaub (eds.), *Blackwell Companion to Archaic Greece*. Oxford, 427–43

van der Poll, C. (2001) 'Homer and homeric interpretation in the *Protrepticus* of Clement of Alexandria', in F. Budelmann and P. Michelakis (eds.), *Homer, Tragedy and Beyond: Studies in Honour of P. E. Easterling*. London, 179–99

Preisendanz, K. (1972) 'Fluchtafeln (Defixion)', *RAC* 8, 1–29

Preisendanz, K. and Henrichs, A. (eds.) (1973/1974) *Papyri Graecae Magicae: die griechischen Zauberpapyri*, 2nd edn. (2 vols.). Stuttgart

Price, S. R. F. (1980) 'Between man and god: sacrifice in the imperial cult', *JRS* 70, 28–43

(1984a) *Rituals and Power: The Roman Imperial Cult in Asia Minor*. Cambridge

(1984b) 'Gods and emperors: the Greek language of the Roman imperial cult', *JHS* 104, 79–95

(1999) *Religions of the Ancient Greeks*. Cambridge

Price, S. R. F. and Kearns, E. (eds.) (2003) *Oxford Dictionary of Classical Myth and Religion*. Oxford

Pritchett, W. K. (1953) 'The Attic stelai, part I', *Hesperia* 22, 225–99

von Prittwitz und Gaffron, H.-H. (1988) *Der Wandel der Aphrodite: archäologische Studien zu weiblichen halbbekleideten Statuetten des späten Hellenismus*. Bonn

Pulleyn, S. (1997) *Prayer in Greek Religion*. Oxford

Rabehl, W. (1906) 'De sermone defixionum atticarum' (PhD dissertation). Berlin

Rabinowitz, N. (1987) 'Female speech and female sexuality: Euripides' *Hippolytos* as model', in M. Skinner (ed.), *Rescuing Creusa: New Methodological Approaches to Women in Antiquity*. Lubbock, TX 127–40

Raschke, W. J. (ed.) (1988) *The Archaeology of the Olympics: The Olympics and Other Festivals in Antiquity*. London

Ratkowitsch, C. (ed.) (2006) *Die poetische Ekphrasis von Kunstwerken: eine literarische Tradition der Grossdichtung in Antike, Mittelalter und früher Neuzeit*. Vienna

Raubitschek, A. E. (1941) 'Phryne', *RE* xx.1, 893–907

Rausa, F. (1994) *L'immagine del vincitore: l'athleta nella statuaria greca dall'età arcaica all'ellenismo*. Rome

Raynor, D. H. (1984) 'Moeragenes and Philostratus: two views of Apollonius of Tyana', *CQ* 34, 222–6

Redfield, J. M. (1991) 'Classics and anthropology', *Arion* 5–23

Reitzenstein, R. (1904) *Poimandres: Studien zur griechisch-ägyptischen und früh-christlichen Literatur*. Leipzig

Renfrew, C. (1985) *The Archaeology of Cult: The Sanctuary at Phylakopi*. Oxford

(1994) 'The archaeology of religion', in C. Renfrew and E. B. W. Zubrow (eds.), *The Ancient Mind: Elements of Cognitive Archaeology*. Cambridge, 47–54

Renfrew, C. and Cherry, J. (eds.) (1986) *Peer Polity Interaction and Sociopolitical Change*. Cambridge

Reynolds, P. L. (1993) 'The essence, power and presence of God: fragments of the history of an idea, from Neopythagoreanism to Peter Abelard', in H. Westra (ed.), *From Athens to Chartres: Neoplatonism and Medieval Thought: Studies in Honour of Édouard Jeauneau*. Leiden, 351–80

Richter, G. M. A. (1950) *Sculpture and Sculptors of the Greeks*. New Haven, CT

Ridgway, B. S. (1971) 'The setting of Greek sculpture', *Hesperia* 40, 336–56

(1977) *The Archaic Style in Greek Sculpture*. Princeton, NJ

(1981) *Fifth-Century Styles in Greek Sculpture*. Princeton, NJ

(1997) *Fourth-Century Styles in Greek Sculpture*. Madison, WI

(2001) *Hellenistic Sculpture*. Madison, WI

Rigsby, K. G. (1976) 'Teiresias as magus in *Oedipus Rex*', *GRBS* 17, 109–14

Rives, J. (2002) 'Magic in the XII tables revisited', *CQ* 52, 270–90

(2003) 'Magic in Roman law: the reconstruction of a crime', *ClAnt* 22, 313–39

(2006) 'Magic, religion, and law: the case of the Lex Cornelia de sicariis et veneficiis', in C. Ando and J. Rüpke (eds.), *Religion and Law in Classical and Christian Rome*. Stuttgart, 47–67

(2007) *Religion in the Roman Empire*. London

Robbers, H. (1965) 'Christian philosophy in Clement of Alexandria', in *Philosophy and Christianity: Philosophical Essays Dedicated to Professor Dr. Herman Dooyeweerd*. Kampen, 203–11

Robertson, M. (1985) 'Greek art and religion', in Easterling and Muir, 155–90

Robertson, N. (1992) *Festivals and Legends: The Formation of Greek Cities in the Light of Public Ritual*. Toronto

Robinson, J. M. and Koester, H. (1971) *Trajectories through Early Christianity*. Philadelphia, PA

Rodenwaldt, G. (1944) *Theoi rheia zōontes* (Abhandlungen der Preußischen Akademie der Wissenschaften, philosophisch-historische Klasse 13). Berlin

Rohde, E. (1972) *Psyche: The Cult of Souls and Belief in Immortality among the Gods*, transl. W. B. Hills. New York (German orig. 1890/1894).

Roloff, D. (1970) *Gottähnlichkeit, Vergöttlichung und Erhöhung zu seligem Leben*. Berlin

Romano, I. B. (1980) 'Early Greek Cult Images' (PhD dissertation). Pennsylvania, PA

De Romilly, J. (1975) *Magic and Rhetoric in Ancient Greece*. Cambridge

Romm, J. (1990) 'Wax, stone, and Promethean clay: Lucian as plastic artist', *ClAnt* 9, 74–98

Roseberry, W. (1989) 'Balinese cockfights and the seduction of anthropology', in W. Roseberry, *Anthropologies and Histories: Essays in Culture, History, and Political Economy*. New Brunswick, 17–29 (first published in *Social Research* 49 (1982), 1013–28)

Rosenberger, V. (1999) 'Die Ökonomie der Pythia oder: wirtschaftliche Aspekte griechischer Orakel', *Laverna* 10, 153–64

(2001a) *Griechische Orakel: eine Kulturgeschichte.* Palermo

(2001b) 'Orakelsprüche und Weihgeschenke: Delphi als Kristallisationspunkt griechischer Identitäten', in R. von den Hoff and S. Schmidt (eds.), *Konstruktionen von Wirklichkeit: Bilder im Griechenland des 5. und 4. Jahrhunderts v. Chr.* Stuttgart, 107–19

Rouse, W. H. D. (1902) *Greek Votive Offerings: An Essay in the History of Greek Religion.* Cambridge

Rowe, W. L. (ed.) (2001) *God and the Problem of Evil.* Malden, MA

Rudhardt, J. and Reverdin, O. (eds.) (1981) *Le Sacrifice dans l'antiquité.* Geneva

Rüpke, J. (2004) 'Kult jenseits der Polisreligion: Polemiken und Perspektiven', *JbAC* 47, 5–15

(2010) 'Radikale im öffentlichen Dienst: Status und Individualisierung unter römischen Priestern republikanischer Zeit', in P. Barceló (ed.), *Religiöser Fundamentalismus in der römischen Kaiserzeit.* Stuttgart, 11–21

Russell, J. (1980) *A History of Witchcraft, Sorcerers, Heretics and Pagans.* London

Rutherford, I. (1995) 'Theoric crisis: the dangers of pilgrimage in Greek religion and society', *SMSR* 61, 276–92

(2000) 'Theoria and darsan: pilgrimage and vision in Greece and India', *CQ* 50, 133–46

(2001) 'Tourism and the sacred: Pausanias and the traditions of Greek pilgrimage', in Alcock et al., 40–52

(2004) 'The Keian theoria to Delphi: neglected data from the accounts of the Delphic naopoioi (CID 2.1–28)', *ZPE* 147, 107–14

Sabbatucci, D. (1965) *Saggio sul misticismo greco.* Rome

Saler, B. (1993) *Conceptualizing Religion: Immanent Anthropologists, Transcendent Natives, and Unbounded Categories.* Leiden

(1997) 'Conceptualizing religion: the matter of boundaries', in H.-J. Klimkeit (ed.), *Vergleichen und Verstehen in der Religionswissenschaft.* Wiesbaden, 27–35

Salomon, N. (1997) 'Making a world of difference: gender, asymmetry, and the Greek nude', in Koloski-Ostrow and Lyons (eds.), 154–73

Sansone, D. (1988) *Greek Athletics and the Genesis of Sport.* Berkeley, CA

(1991) 'Cleobis and Biton at Delphi', *Nikephoros* 4, 121–32

Sauer, E. W. (2004) *Archaeology and Ancient History: Breaking down the Boundaries.* London

Saunders, T. J. (1991) *Plato's Penal Code: Tradition, Controversy, and Reform in Greek Penology.* Oxford

Scanlon, T. F. (1984) 'The footrace of the Heraia at Olympia', *AncW* 9, 77–90

(2002) *Eros and Greek Athletics.* Oxford

Schachter, A. (1981) *The Cults of Boeotia*, vol. I. London

(ed.) (1992) *Le sanctuaire grec.* Geneva

Schäfer, P. and Kippenberg, H. G. (eds.) (1997) *Envisioning Magic: A Princeton Seminar and Symposium.* Leiden

Scheer, T. (2000) *Die Gottheit und ihr Bild: Untersuchungen zur Funktion griechischer Kultbilder in Religion und Politik.* Munich

Schefold, K. (1937) 'Statuen auf Vasenbildern', *JDAI* 52, 30–75

Scheid, J. (2005) *Quand faire c'est croire: les rites sacrificiels des Romains.* Paris

Schmitt Pantel, P. (1992) *La Cité au banquet: histoire des repas publics dans les cités grecques.* Rome

Scholten, C. (1995) 'Die alexandrinische Katechetenschule', *JbAC* 38, 16–37

Scobie, A. and Taylor, A. J. W. (1975) 'Perversions ancient and modern: agalmatophilia, the Statue Syndrome', *Journal of the History of Behavioral Sciences* 11, 49–54

Scott, M. (2010) *Delphi and Olympia: The Spatial Politics of Panhellenism in the Archaic and Classical Periods.* Cambridge

Scullion, S. (2005) '"Pilgrimage" and Greek religion: sacred and secular in the pagan polis', in Elsner and Rutherford, 111–30

Segal, A. F. (1981) 'Hellenistic magic: some questions of definition', in R. van den Broek and M. J. Vermaseren (eds.), *Studies in Gnosticism and Hellenistic Religion.* Leiden, 349–75

Serwint, N. (1993) 'The female athletic costume at the Heraia and the prenuptial initiation rites', *AJA* 97, 403–22

Sewell, W. (1997) 'Geertz, cultural systems, and history: from synchrony to transformation', *Representations* 59, 35–55

   (1999) 'The concept(s) of culture', in V. Bonnell and L. Hunt (eds.), *Beyond the Cultural Turn: New Directions in the Study of Society and Culture.* Berkeley, CA, 35–61

Shackleton Bailey, D. R. (ed.) (2000) *Valerius Maximus: Memorable Doings and Sayings.* Cambridge, MA

Shankman, P. (1984) 'The thick and the thin: on the interpretative program of Clifford Geertz', *Current Anthropology* 25, 261–79

Sharrock, A. B. (1991) 'Womanufacture', *JRS* 81, 36–49

Shear, J. L. (2011) *Polis and Revolution: Responding to Oligarchy in Classical Athens.* Cambridge

Shear, T. L. (1981) 'Athens: from city-state to provincial town', *Hesperia* 50, 356–77

Shipley, G. (1997) '"The other Lacedaimonians:" the dependent perioikic poleis of Laconia and Messenia', in M. H. Hansen (ed.), *The Polis as an Urban Centre and as a Political Community.* Copenhagen, 189–281

Shweder, R. A. and Good, B. (eds.) (2005) *Clifford Geertz by his Colleagues.* Chicago, IL

Sidebottom, H. (1999) 'Review of Flinterman 1995', *CR* 49, 34–5

   (2002) 'Pausanias: past, present and closure', *CQ* 52, 494–9

   (2009) 'Philostratus and the symbolic roles of the sophist and philosopher', in Bowie and Elsner, 69–99

Siewert, P. (1992) 'Zum Ursprung der Olympischen Spiele', *Nikephoros* 5, 7–8

   (1992) 'The Olympic rules', in W. Coulson and H. Kyrieleis (eds.), *Proceedings of an International Symposium on the Olympic Games 1988.* Athens, 113–17

(2006) 'Kultische und politische Organisationsformen im frühen Olympia und in seiner Umgebung', in Freitag et al., 43–54

Sinn, U. (1989) 'Die Votivgabe eines Athleten in Olympia', in H.-U. Cain, H. Gabelmann and D. Salzmann (eds.), *Festschrift für Nikolaus Himmelmann*. Mainz, 65–70

(1991) 'Die Stellung der Wettkämpfe im Kult des Zeus Olympios', *Nikephoros* 4, 31–54

(2000a) *Olympia: Cult, Sport, and Ancient Festival*. Princeton, NJ

(2000b) 'Greek sanctuaries as places of refuge', in Buxton, 155–79 (first published in Marinatos and Hägg, 88–109)

Smith, J. Z. (1978a) *Map is not Territory: Studies in the History of Religions*. Chicago, IL

(1978b) 'Towards interpreting demonic powers in Hellenistic and Roman antiquity', *ANRW* II, 16.1, 425–39

(1988) *Imagining Religion: From Babylon to Jonestown*. Chicago, IL

(1990) *Drudgery Divine: On Comparison of Early Christianities and the Religions of Late Antiquity*. Chicago, IL

(1995) 'Trading places', in M. Meyer and P. Mirecki (eds.), *Ancient Magic and Ritual Power*. Boston, 13–27

Smith, R. (2007) 'Pindar, Athens, and the early Greek statue habit', in S. Hornblower and C. Morgan (eds.), *Pindar's Poetry, Patrons, and Festivals*. Oxford, 83–139

Snodgrass, A. (1980) *Archaic Greece: The Age of Experiment*. Berkeley, CA

Sommerstein, A. H. and Fletcher, J. (eds.) (2007) *Horkos: The Oath in Greek Society*. Exeter

Sorabji, R. (1994) *Animal Minds and Human Morals: The Origins of the Western Debate*. London

Sørensen, J. P. (ed.) (1989) *Rethinking Religion: Studies in the Hellenistic Process*. Copenhagen

Sourvinou-Inwood, C. (1978) 'Persephone and Aphrodite at Locri: a model for personality definitions in Greek religion', *JHS* 98, 101–21

(1991) *'Reading' Greek Culture: Text and Images, Rituals and Myths*. Oxford

(1995) *'Reading' Greek Death: To the End of the Classical Period*. Oxford

(2000a) 'What is polis religion?', in Buxton, 13–37 (first published in Murray and Price, 295–322)

(2000b) 'Further aspects of polis religion', in Buxton, 38–55 (first published in *AION(archeol)* 10 (1988), 259–74)

(2003) *Tragedy and Athenian Religion*. Lanham, MD

Spiro, M. (1966) 'Religion: problems of definition and explanation', in M. Banton (ed.), *Anthropological Approaches to the Study of Religion*. London, 85–126

Spivey, N. (1996) *Understanding Greek Sculpture: Ancient Meanings, Modern Readings*. London

(1997) *Greek Art*. London

Stählin, O. (1905) *Clemens Alexandrinus*, vol. I: *Protrepticus und Paedagogus*. Leipzig

(1985) *Clemens Alexandrinus*, vol. II: *Stromata Buch I–VI*, new edn. by L. Früchtel with additions by U. Treu. Berlin

Steiner, D. (1995) 'Stoning and sight: a structural equivalent in Greek mythology', *ClAnt* 14, 193–211

(2001) *Images in Mind: Statues in Archaic and Classical Greek Literature and Thought*. Princeton, NJ

von Steuben, H. (1989) 'Belauschte oder unbelauschte Göttin? Zum Motif der knidischen Aphrodite', *Istanbuler Mitteilungen* 39, 535–46

Stewart, A. (1990) *Greek Sculpture: An Exploration* (2 vols.). New Haven, CT

(1997) *Art, Desire, and the Body in Ancient Greece*. Cambridge

(2008) *Classical Greece and the Birth of Western Art*. Cambridge

Stewart, P. (1999) 'The destruction of statues in late antiquity', in R. Miles (ed.), *Constructing Identities in Late Antiquity*. London, 159–89

(2003) *Statues in Roman Society: Representation and Response*. Oxford

(2009) 'Review: visuality and eroticism in ancient Rome (Elsner/Vout)', *Art History* 32, 417–20

Stewart, Z. (1972) *Essays on Religion and the Ancient World*, vol. I. Oxford

Stieber, M. (2004) *The Poetics of Appearance in the Attic Korai*. Austin, TX

van Straten, F. T. (1981) 'Gifts for the gods', in H. S. Versnel (ed.), *Faith, Hope and Worship: Aspects of Religious Mentality in the Ancient World*. Leiden, 65–151

(1992) 'Votives and votaries in Greek sanctuaries', in Schachter, 257–84

(1995) *Hiera Kala: Images of Animal Sacrifice in Archaic and Classical Greece*. Leiden

Stroud, R. (1973) 'Curses from Corinth', *AJA* 77, 228

Struck, P. T. (2002) 'The poet as conjurer: magic and literary theory in late antiquity', in Ciraolo and Seidel, 119–31

Sundermeier, T. (2002) 'Sacrifice in African traditional religion', in A. Baumgarten (ed.), *Sacrifice in Religious Experience*. Leiden, 3–12

Sutton, R. F. (1992) 'Pornography and persuasion on Attic pottery', in A. Richlin (ed.), *Pornography and Representation in Greece and Rome*. Oxford, 3–35

Swaddling, J. (2008) *The Ancient Olympic Games*, 2nd edn., rev. and updated. Austin, TX

Swain, S. (1996) *Hellenism and Empire: Language, Classicism, and Power in the Greek World, AD 50–250*. Oxford

(2009) 'Culture and nature in Philostratus', in Bowie and Elsner, 33–46

Tambiah, S. (1990) *Magic, Science, Religion and the Scope of Rationality*. Cambridge

Tandy, D. (1997) *Warriors into Traders: The Power of the Market in Early Greece*. Berkeley, CA

Tausend, K. (1992) *Amphiktyonie und Symmachie: Formen zwischenstaatlicher Beziehungen im Archaischen Griechenland*. Stuttgart

Thomas, C. (1981) 'The Greek polis', in R. Griffeth and C. G. Thomas (eds.), *The City-State in Five Cultures*. Santa Barbara, CA, 31–69

Thomas, K. (1971) *Religion and the Decline of Magic*. New York

Thomas, R. (1981) *Athletenstatuetten der Spätarchaik und des strengen Stils*. Rome

Thomassen, E. (1999) 'Is magic a subclass of ritual?', in Jordan et al., 55–66

Thompson, H. and Wycherley, R. (1972) *The Athenian Agora*, vol. xiv: *The Agora of Athens*. Princeton, NJ

Thompson, W. E. (1965) 'The date of the Athenian gold coinage', *AJPh* 86, 159–74

Tillich, P. (1963) *Christianity and the Encounter of the World Religions*. New York

Todorov, T. (1975) *The Fantastic: A Structural Approach to a Literary Genre*, transl. R. Howard. Ithaca, NY (French orig. 1970)

du Toit, D. S. (1997) *Theios Anthropos: zur Verwendung von θεῖος ἄνθρωπος und sinnverwandten Ausdrücken in der Literatur der Kaiserzeit*. Tübingen

　　(1999) 'Die Vorstellung eines Begleitdämons in Philostrats *Vita Apollonii*', *W&D* 25, 149–66

Tomlin, R. S. O. (1988) 'The curse tablets', in B. Cunliffe (ed.) *The Temple of Sulis Minerva at Bath*, vol. ii: *The Finds from the Sacred Spring*. Oxford, 59–277

Tremlin, T. (2006) *Minds and Gods: The Cognitive Foundations of Religion*. Oxford

Treu, G. (1894/1897) *Die Bildwerke von Olympia in Stein und Thon* (2 vols.). Berlin

Triantaphyllopoulos, J. (1974) 'Epigraphica', in *Mélanges hélléniques offerts à Georges Daux*. Paris, 331–8

Tripolitis, A. (2002) *Religions of the Hellenistic-Roman Age*. Grand Rapids, MI

Turner, V. (1967) *The Forest of Symbols: Aspects of Ndembu Ritual*. Ithaca, NY

Tylor, E. (1871/1873) *Primitive Culture: Researches into the Development of Mythology, Philosophy, Religion, Art, and Custom* (2 vols.). London

Underwood, P. (1972) *Into the Occult*. London

Valavanis, P. (2004) *Games and Sanctuaries in Ancient Greece: Olympia, Delphi, Isthmia, Nemea, Athens*, transl. D. Hardy. Los Angeles, CA (Greek orig. 2004)

Vallois, R. (1929) 'Topographie délienne II', *BCH* 53, 185–315

Verity, A. (2007) *Pindar: The Complete Odes*. Oxford

Vernant, J.-P. (1980) *Myth and Society in Ancient Greece*, transl. J. Lloyd. New York (French orig. 1974)

　　(1981) 'The myth of Prometheus in Hesiod', in Gordon, 43–56

　　(1991) *Mortals and Immortals: Collected Essays* (ed. F. I. Zeitlin). Princeton, NJ

Vernant, J.-P. and Vidal-Naquet, P. (1988) *Myth and Tragedy in Ancient Greece*, transl. J. Lloyd. New York (French orig. 1972)

Versnel, H. S. (1985) '"May he not be able to sacrifice . . .": concerning a curious formula in Greek and Latin curses', *ZPE* 58, 247–69

　　(1987) 'What did ancient man see when he saw a god? Some reflections on Graeco-Roman epiphany', in D. van der Plas (ed.), *Effigies Dei*. Leiden, 42–55

　　(1990) *Inconsistencies in Greek and Roman Religion*, vol. ii: *Ter unus: Isis, Dionysos, Hermes: Three Studies in Henotheism*). Leiden

　　(1991a) 'Some reflections on the relationship magic-religion', *Numen* 38, 177–97

　　(1991b) 'Beyond cursing: the appeal to justice in the judicial prayers', in Faraone and Obbink, 60–107

　　(1993) *Inconsistencies in Greek and Roman Religion*, vol. ii: *Transition and Reversal in Myth and Ritual*. Leiden

(1998) 'An essay on anatomical curses', in F. Graf (ed.), *Ansichten griechischer Rituale: Geburtstags-Symposium für Walter Burkert*. Stuttgart, 217–67

(2002a) 'The poetics of the magical charm: an essay in the power of words', in Meyer and Mirecki, 105–58

(2002b) 'Writing mortals and reading gods: appeal to the gods as a dual strategy in social control', in D. Cohen (ed.), *Demokratie, Recht und soziale Kontrolle im klassischen Athen*. Munich, 37–76

Veyne, P. (1988) *Did the Greeks Believe in their Myths?* transl. P. Wissing. Chicago, IL (French orig. 1983)

Vlassopoulos, K. (2007) *Unthinking the Greek Polis: Ancient Greek History Beyond Eurocentrism*. Cambridge

Vout, C. (2007) *Power and Eroticism in Imperial Rome*. Cambridge

Vrijhof, P. H. and Waardenburg, J. (eds.) (1979) *Official and Popular Religion: Analysis of a Theme for Religious Studies*. The Hague

Walbank, M. B. (1982) 'The confiscation and sale by the poletai in 402/1 BC of the property of the thirty tyrants', *Hesperia* 51, 74–98

Walker, W. H. and Lucero, L. J. (2000) 'The depositional history of ritual and power', M.-A. in Dobres and J. E. Robb (eds.), *Agency in Archaeology*. London, 130–47

Webb, R. (2009) *Ekphrasis, Imagination and Persuasion in Ancient Rhetorical Theory and Practice*. Aldershot

Webster, J. (2009) 'Introduction: systematic theology', in J. Webster, K. Tanner and I. Torrance (eds.), *The Oxford Handbook of Systematic Theology*. Oxford, 1–15

Weinreich, O. (1909) *Antike Heilungswunder: Untersuchungen zum Wunderglauben der Griechen und Römer*. Gießen

West, M. (1983) *The Orphic Poems*. Oxford

White, M. J. (1978) 'The statue syndrome: perversion? fantasy? anecdote?', *Journal of Sex Research* 14, 246–9

Whitehouse, H. and Laidlaw, J. (eds.) (2007) *Religion, Anthropology, and Cognitive Science*. Durham

Whitley, J. (2001) *The Archaeology of Ancient Greece*. Cambridge

Whitmarsh, T. C. (2001) *Greek Literature and the Roman Empire: The Politics of Imitation*. Oxford

Wilhelm, A. (1904) 'Über das Alter einiger attischer Fluchtafeln', *JÖAI* 7, 105–26

Willemsen, F. (1957) *Dreifusskessel von Olympia: alte und neue Funde* (Olympische Forschungen III). Berlin

(1990) 'Die Fluchtafeln', in W. K. Kovacsovics (ed.), *Die Eckterrasse an der Gräberstrasse des Kerameikos*. Berlin, 142–51

Wilson, C. (1988) *Beyond the Occult*. London

Wilson, P. (2000) *The Athenian Institution of the Khoregia: The Chorus, the City, and the Stage*. Cambridge

(2011) 'The glue of democracy? Tragedy, democracy, structure and finance', in D. M. Carter (ed.), *Why Athens? A Reappraisal of Tragic Politics*. Oxford, 19–43

Winkler, J. (1990) *The Constraints of Desire: The Anthropology of Sex and Gender in Ancient Greece*. New York

Witt, R. E. (1931) 'The Hellenism of Clement of Alexandria', *CQ* 25, 195–204

Wolfson, H. A. (1951) 'Clement of Alexandria on the generation of the Logos', *Church History* 20, 72–80

Woolf, G. (1997) 'Polis-religion and its alternatives in the Roman provinces', in H. Cancik and J. Rüpke (eds.), *Römische Reichsreligion und Provinzialreligion*. Tübingen, 71–84

Wrede, H. (1981) *Consecratio in Formam Deorum: vergöttlichte Privatpersonen in der römischen Kaiserzeit*. Mainz

Wünsch, R. (1897) *Defixionum Tabellae Atticae* (*IG* 3.3, Appendix). Berlin
  (1900) 'Neue Fluchtafeln', *RhM* 55, 62–85, 232–71

Yalouris, A. and Yalouris, N. (1987) *Olympia: Guide to the Museum and the Sanctuary*. Athens

Zak, W. F. (1995) *The Polis and the Divine Order: The Oresteia, Sophocles, and the Defense of Democracy*. Lewisburg, PA

Zeitlin, F. (1985) 'The power of Aphrodite: eros and the boundaries of the self in the *Hippolytus*', in P. Burian (ed.), *Directions in Euripidean Criticism*. Durham, 52–111

Zelenak, M. X. (1998) *Gender and Politics in Greek Tragedy*. New York

Ziebarth, E. (1934) 'Neue Verfluchungstafeln aus Attika, Böotien und Euboia', *Sitzungsberichte der Preussischen Akademie der Wissenschaften, phil.-hist. Klasse*, 1022–50

Zuntz, G. (1971) *Persephone: Three Essays in Religion and Thought in Magna Graecia*. Oxford

Index